How To
DRY FOODS

P9-DEV-648

by Deanna DeLong

Cover Photography: Myron Beck Photography; Cover Food Stylist: Norman Stewart
Interior Photography: deGennaro Associates Studios: Interior Food Stylist: Mable Hoffman
Cover Photo: Fruit Leather, page 36, and Crunchy Granola, page 144.

© 1992, 1979 Price Stern Sloan

Published by HPBooks
a division of Price Stern Sloan, Inc.
11150 Olympic Boulevard
Los Angeles, California 90064
Printed in the U.S.A.
ISBN: 1-55788-050-6
Revised Edition

10 9 8 7 6 5 4

Foreword
by George K. York, Ph.D.

Drying is one of the oldest–perhaps the oldest–methods of food preservation. Techniques for drying have been passed from generation to generation on the basis of what worked and what did not. During the last 50 years, science and technology have been applied to dehydration of foods and intense studies were conducted during and after World War II. The information generated by these studies led to increased commercial drying of a wide variety of foods. Unfortunately, most of this information has not been readily available to the individual who wishes to dry foods on a small scale at home.

Mrs. DeLong's book on home food drying is technically accurate and scientifically sound. Moreover, it is logically organized and contains easy-to-follow instructions and easy-to-use techniques. She gives detailed directions and the rationale for the different steps necessary to dry fruits, vegetables and meats successfully. Of special value are the explanations of the various methods or preparation, pretreatment, drying, packaging and storage, because most of us want to know *why* we are doing something as well as how to do it. The well-written material reflects the author's enthusiasm. The illustrations are informative and useful. Mrs. DeLong has unraveled the technical complexities of dehydration and presented them in a lucid and practical manner. As the most complete text available on drying food at home, this book will inspire you to try it too.

Dr. York is an international expert in food preservation technology. He recently retired from the University of California, Davis. He pioneered food dehydration education for Extension Services throughout the United States, and has authored numerous publications on dehydration.

Deanna DeLong

Deanna DeLong received her BS in Home Economics at the University of New Mexico, her MS in Education at Portland State University and has taught in high schools, in community colleges and at Brigham Young University. As consumer food drying increased in popularity, Deanna began teaching drying classes at community colleges. Several years and several thousand students later, *How To Dry Foods* was written.

Deanna has traveled extensively in the U.S. and abroad teaching about food drying. She has taught small scale, industrial food dehydration throughout Central America as part of a USAID team. She has traveled to Eastern Europe, teaching food drying to agricultural specialists and food processors.

Deanna owns her own dehydration and business management consulting company. She is married to David Feinauer and lives in Beaverton, Oregon with three of the eight children in their joint family.

Try Drying

Preserving foods when they are in season is not a new idea. Many of us have preserved foods by canning or freezing. Now more people are turning to drying as a way of preserving food. Here's why:

DRIED FOODS ARE ECONOMICAL

Drying food is inexpensive. A commercial dehydrator can easily pay for itself in a summer or two. You don't need canning jars, and there is no energy cost for storage as there is in freezing.

NUTRITIOUS TOO

If you are watching your sugar consumption, you'll appreciate dried foods because you don't add sugar. As food dries, the natural sugar in it concentrates, making it sweet. Dried fruits, fruit leathers and jerky are especially good replacements for sugar-laden snacks.

Nutritionally, drying compares well with other methods of preservation. For most foods, the nutritional value retained is about the same as with freezing. Drying has a lower heat exposure than canning and therefore destroys fewer vitamins. In fact, the loss of nutritive value during most drying processes is small in comparison to the loss during cooking. Generally, the only vitamins lost during drying are vitamins A and C which are available in many fresh foods.

There is wide concern today about additives and preservatives used in commercially prepared foods. When you dry your own, you know what's in it.

SOMETHING FOR EVERYONE

In this book you'll find recipes for soup mixes, salad sprinkles, baby foods, seasoning mixes, vegetable or fruit flakes, and much more.

Because dried foods are lightweight and low in volume—they take up about one-tenth the space of canned foods—they are ideal for backpacking and camping.

History of Drying

Dried food has been used for survival from early nomadic man to modern times. Ancient Egyptians and Greeks are known to have dried food.

Early sea-going expeditions survived on dried fruit, grains and meats. Columbus probably would have never discovered America if he hadn't fed himself and his crew with dried foods!

Drying food was a necessity for the colonists and early settlers of the New World, or any place where homes had to be self-reliant during the winter. Fruits, especially apples, pears, peaches and apricots, and some vegetables were dried for winter use. Quantities of fish and meat were dried and heavily salted to reduce the chance of spoilage. They probably tasted terrible by today's standards!

The first dehydrator used to dry fruits and vegetables by artificial means was introduced in France in 1795. It had a controlled temperature of 105°F (40°C) and a continuous hot air flow. It was used to dry thinly sliced vegetables and fruits.

Drying on a large scale was not used until the beginning of World War I when tremendous quantities of food were needed to feed troops in the field. Considerable research on drying foods was conducted in countries involved in the war.

The Great Depression of the 1930s caused a surge in home drying in the United States. Canning equipment was expensive and often not available. Many homemakers began drying foods the way early settlers had.

During World War II over 160 vegetable dehydration plants went into operation in the United States alone and tons of dried food were used by armies and navies. Dried food had the advantages of being lightweight, compact and easy to transport, with a reasonably long shelf life.

DRYING TODAY

Almost every American housewife enjoys the convenience of prepared dried foods—from the morning breakfast juice powder to dehydrated soup, dinner or dessert mixes.

Apricots, raisins, figs, prunes and other fruits are sun dried, with artificial help when the weather doesn't cooperate, and transported all over the world. Dried fruit production is now a multi-million-dollar industry.

The Drying Process

It's very simple. Increasing the temperature of food makes its moisture evaporate. Air moving over food carries the moisture away, but the moisture carrying capacity of air is dependent on the temperature. Each 27°F (15°C) increase in temperature doubles the moisture-carrying capacity of the air.

Both *drying* and *dehydration* refer to the removal of water and are used interchangeably. *Rehydration* and *reconstitution* are interchangeable and refer to returning water to dried foods.

Controlling temperature and air circulation prevents food from spoiling while it is drying. If the temperature is too low or the humidity too high, the food will dry too slowly, allowing the growth of microorganisms. If the temperature is too high, the food will *case harden* or form a hard shell that traps moisture inside.

Certain microorganisms are present in all foods. When they encounter warm temperatures and the water which is naturally present in foods, they multiply and the food spoils. If sufficient water is removed from the food, these microorganisms cannot multiply and the food is preserved. Drying temperatures do not kill the microorganisms, so they begin to grow again when water is added.

Pretreatment—All fruits and vegetables contain *enzymes* or chemicals which cause them to ripen. Drying slows the effect of these enzymes, but some continue to work even after the food has been dried, particularly in vegetables. This can lead to poor rehydration and flavor. Some fruits tend to *oxidize*—to combine with oxygen from the air—during drying and storage. This may cause browning, loss of vitamins and flavor loss. The action of enzymes can be stopped and oxidation minimized by pretreating with heat or sulfur dioxide. *Pretreatment is a matter of personal choice, but generally improves the quality and shelf life of dehydrated foods.*

STORAGE LIFE

Home-dried food is frequently still edible after many years in storage, but is not necessarily nutritious or tasty. Storage life is dependent upon:

Residual Moisture—Most dried fruits retain 15 to 20 percent of their moisture. Dried vegetables usually retain 5 percent. If fruits contain too much moisture, they will mold, no matter how well they are packaged. Too little moisture makes them unpalatable and causes great loss in nutritional value.

Storage Temperature—The lower the storage temperature, the longer dried foods will remain in prime condition. Temperatures below 60°F (16°C) will maintain most foods in good condition for at least a year. When stored at temperatures of 80° to 90°F (27° to 32°C), foods will begin to deteriorate after several months.

Exposure—Exposure to humidity, light and air during storage adversely affects the storage life of dried foods.

Packaging—All packaging materials should be airtight, moisture-proof and made of material which will keep out insects and rodents. Heat-sealed boilable plastic bags or freezer bags should have as much air removed as possible. Vacuum packing, page 13, is an excellent method.

Storage Time—I recommend a maximum storage time of one year for the best appearance, sensory quality and nutritional value. Vacuum packing greatly extends shelf life. Refrigeration or freezing will double or triple shelf life as long as the food remains properly packaged. Rotate and use dried foods just as you do other preserved foods. Commercially dehydrated foods packed in nitrogen are available for long-term storage.

Fresh Weight to Dried Weight

25 pounds of fresh-picked fruit such as apples, apricots, peaches or pears will yield 4 to 8 pounds of dried fruit, depending on the fruit and the weight loss from peelings, pits, seeds or cores.

25 pounds of fresh-picked vegetables such as beans, carrots, onions or peppers will yield 3 to 6 pounds of dried vegetables, depending on the vegetable and the weight loss from peelings and discarded stems or leaves.

Equipment

The proper drying equipment and utensils make the whole process of dehydration easier. Here are some items that are especially helpful.

Top row, left to right: A food processor and blender prepare foods for drying and puree fruit for fruit leathers. This commercial food dryer has fruit leather trays to simplify making fruit roll-ups.

Second row: Vacuum sealers are used for packaging, reducing exposure to oxygen and thus tripling the shelf life of dried foods. Packing can be done in bags, canning jars or special canisters.

Third row, left to right: A colander is handy for washing food before drying. This cherry pitter, from Back to Basics®*, simplifies pitting. Their suction apple peeler/corer/slicer attaches to any smooth surface and will peel, core and slice an apple in 5 seconds.

Bottom row, left to right: A pear corer minimizes waste in coring. This apple corer will also remove cores from pineapples. A stainless steel knife doesn't cause browning. Kitchen scissors are useful for cutting dried fruits and leathers. This handy apple corer is good for coring apples that are to be dried unpeeled.

*Back to Basics®
1 (800) 688-1989

Methods of Drying

Food drying can be done by a number of methods—each has advantages and disadvantages, and each gives different results. The method you use depends largely upon the quality you want in the food you're drying, and the time, effort and money you're willing to invest. Methods range from totally natural methods, such as sun drying or room drying, to more controlled methods, such as oven drying, or using a commercial or home-built drying cabinet. The following discussion of each method should help you choose the best method for your purposes.

Sun Drying

The majority of commercially dried fruits are sun dried. If you live in an area that has many consecutive days with temperatures ranging in the 90s, relatively low humidity and low air pollution levels, sun drying may be a good choice for you.

Sun drying has several advantages: The cost is low, the only investment is in drying trays and protective netting, and large quantities of food can be dried at one time. The sun's ultraviolet rays have a sterilizing effect which slows the growth of some microorganisms. Sun-dried fruit, particularly sulfured fruit, has an attractive sun-ripened color.

There are several disadvantages to sun drying: Sun drying requires considerable time and effort. Food that would be dried in 6 to 8 hours in a dryer may take up to 4 or 5 days in the sun. Not all foods can be sun-dried. They must have a fairly high sugar and acid content to prevent spoilage during the drying process because drying in the sun takes so long. You are entirely at the mercy of the weather. If it suddenly begins to rain, your hours of labor and the cost of the fruit may be lost. Sun-dried foods tend to have lower quality and nutritional value than foods dried under controlled conditions. Foods dried in the sun are dried under less sanitary conditions than those dried in a food dryer or oven.

WHAT CAN YOU SUN DRY?

The high sugar and acid content of most fruits allow reasonably good sun drying. Fruits chosen for drying should be the highest texture and ready-to-eat. *CAUTION:* Sun drying, because of the high temperatures and the length of drying time, can take as much as 50% of the nutrients out of the food.

Fruits recommended for sun drying:	
Apples	Grapes
Apricots	Nectarines
Cherries	Peaches
Citrus peels	Pears
Coconut, shredded	Pineapple
Currants	Plums
Dates	Prune plums
Figs	
Fruits not recommended for sun drying:	
Avocados	Papaya
Bananas	Persimmons
Berries	Rhubarb
Cranberries	Strawberries
Melons	

Fruit leather can be sun dried successfully in one day if the sun is hot and the humidity low.

Vegetables must be dried to a 5 percent or lower moisture content to store well. This is difficult to do with the sun because exposure to sunlight for more than one or two days may produce sunburn and scorching.

Red chili peppers may be sun dried when fully mature. Wash the peppers and string them with a sharp needle and thread through the stems, alternating the peppers so they hang in opposite directions. Hang them in a hot sunny place to dry and protect them from dust.

Vegetables recommended for sun drying:	
Chili peppers	Shell beans
Lentils	Soybeans
Peas	

Sun drying is not recommended for herbs and spices because of the high loss in aroma, flavoring oils and color.

When pioneers sun dried meat or fish, they used extremely high concentrations of salt as a preservative. We would find this high salt concentration unpalatable. The low acidity of meats and fish combined with low temperatures and long drying time presents a high risk of bacterial contamination and spoilage. Therefore, I don't recommend sun drying meats and fish.

EQUIPMENT

Drying Trays—You may buy them or build them at home. The section on Drying Trays, page 11, provides some guidelines.

Netting—To cover trays during drying and protect the food from contamination by insects.

Sulfuring Equipment—See page 20.

TECHNIQUE

The area used for sun drying should be conveniently located because you must turn the fruit 2 or 3 times a day. It should be free from dust and exhaust fumes and there should be adequate protection against insects and rodents and other animals. Cover the food with protective screening, nylon netting or cheesecloth. Sulfuring fruit also helps deter insects.

You will need direct sun for the first couple of days and shade for the rest of the drying time. Good air circulation is nearly as important as sun.

Solar Drying

Using a solar dryer is a slightly better method than sun drying. It collects the sun's rays and elevates the temperature 20° to 30°F (11° to 17°C) higher than the unaided sun. Higher temperature usually shortens the drying time. Depending on the dryer and its design, sanitation may be considerably better than with sun drying. The air outlets and intakes should be screened to prevent insects from sampling the drying food.

Solar dryers have a number of disadvantages. As with sun drying, you are at the mercy of the weather. There is usually no effective way to control temperature, which means lower quality dried food. You must invest time and money in construction and the results are not guaranteed.

Some solar dryers have a fan, which greatly increases efficiency and lessens drying time. Others operate by convection, which takes longer. The food must be turned and rotated to promote even and thorough drying.

More information on solar dehydrators is on page 12. Plans and resources for solar dryers are on page 156.

Room Drying

Room drying is a natural method which was employed by the pioneers with a reasonable amount of success. The relatively low temperatures of modern thermostatically controlled cooling and heating systems usually make room drying impossible. However, if the right conditions exist in your home, you may want to give it a try. Room drying is low cost because there is no investment in equipment, but there is a limit to the types of foods you can room dry.

WHAT CAN YOU ROOM DRY?

To be on the safe side, confine your room drying to herbs, nuts in the shell, or partially dried high-acid and high-sugar fruits such as apple rings. Strings of red chili peppers which have been partially dried by another method may also be room dried. Be sure the place where you dry your food is sufficiently warm and has enough air circulation to prevent molding before the food dried completely.

EQUIPMENT

Drying Trays—You may buy them or build them at home. The section on Drying Trays, page 11, provides some guidelines.
Blocks or Bricks—Use them for stacking trays.
A Fan—Keep the air moving over the drying food by placing a fan nearby.

TECHNIQUE

You will need a room with a temperature of 80°F (25°C) or above, preferably exposed to the sun for part of the day, and with relatively low humidity. A sunny kitchen window or a dust-free attic or basement are good places to dry. A furnace room can be used if there is no dust or soot from the furnace. Sometimes it is possible to dry in a car rear window or camper on a warm sunny day if the windows are opened slightly so the moisture can escape. Even the space above a gas clothes dryer or water heater can be used if the pilot light remains on and the ventilation is good. Partially sun dried fruits may be finished in a warm room with good air circulation.

Foods are usually room dried on trays. The trays are stacked with 5 to 6 inches of space between them to allow good air circulation. Use a fan to keep the air moving over the food. Rotate food regularly. Cover the trays to protect the food from insects.

Herbs may be hung root-end up inside a brown paper bag with holes for ventilation as discussed in the section on bag drying, page 66.

Stove-Top Drying

Stove-top dryers can be bought at a reasonable cost. During America's pioneer days, these were extremely popular and were in use continuously on top of wood-burning stoves during the harvest season. Today's models can be adapted to gas, electric or wood stoves and give the same advantages as a solar dryer: They speed the drying process by raising the temperature and the drying fruit can be kept cleaner than in sun drying. Some models are suspended from the wall behind the stove, others may sit directly on top of the stove. All use the leftover heat from cooking or the constant heat of a heating element set at a minimum temperature.

Depending on the model, air circulation may be good or poor. The temperature is difficult to control, although a thermometer can monitor the warmth on the various shelves. Stove-top dryers require constant heat until the food is dried and may tie up the top of the stove when you need it for something else.

Oven Drying

Oven drying is a good choice if you want to dry a small amount of produce at one time. There is little or no investment in equipment; you don't have to depend on the weather; and most foods can be dried in an oven.

One of the disadvantages of drying in an oven is the cost of the energy used. Oven drying takes 2 or 3 times longer than drying in a dehydrator and time is required to tend and rotate the food. Food dried in an oven is usually darker, more brittle and less flavorful than food dried in a dehydrator. *CAUTION:* The longer the drying time and the higher the temperature, the more nutrient loss in the food. Oven drying can potentially destroy large amounts of nutrients.

WHAT CAN YOU OVEN DRY?

Most unsulfured fruits, fruit leathers, vegetables, meats, fish and cereals can be oven dried. Sulfured fruits should not be oven dried because sulfur dioxide fumes may be irritating.

It is extremely difficult to oven dry foods with excessively high moisture content—over 90 percent—such as rhubarb or tomatoes, or foods such as prunes that dry slowly because their skins prevent evaporation.

Preparation and Pretreatment—Prepare the food for oven drying according to directions for the specific food with methods other than sulfuring.

EQUIPMENT

A Gas or Electric Oven—Test your oven with a thermometer for at least an hour before using it to dry food. Prop open the oven door as you will when actually drying food. The oven should maintain a temperature of 140° to 150°F (60° to 65°C). If it cannot be adjusted to this temperature, it is probably unsuitable for drying fruits and vegetables. Meats can be dried as high as 160°F (70°C).

In gas ovens manufactured before the mid 1960s, it is nearly impossible to dry foods with the oven turned on. The lowest temperature is usually around 200°F (95°C) which will cook the food before it dries. If you have an older oven, try drying with the heat of the pilot light. In the newer gas ovens, it is easier to maintain a constant low temperature with the oven on. Prop the door open 4 to 6 inches to let moisture escape.

In electric ovens, check to see that only the bottom element goes on. Disconnect the broiling element if necessary. Prop the door open 2 to 4 inches to let moisture escape.

Thermometer—Check the oven temperature with a thermometer which is accurate and easy to read. Place it on the top tray toward the back of the oven for a representative temperature. Also check the temperature on the bottom tray. Try to maintain a temperature of 120° to 140°F (50° to 60°C) while the food is drying.

Drying Trays—Their size will be determined by the size of your oven. Allow 3/4 inch clearance between all edges of the trays and the inside of the oven. Use a rack or blocks or spools to stack the trays. Leave 2 to 3 inches between trays for air circulation. Allow 3 inches clearance between the trays and the top and bottom of the oven.

For more information on drying trays see page 11.

Oven Racks—These may be used instead of drying trays if they are covered with four thicknesses of tightly stretched nylon net. You can sew the netting together like a pillowcase to fit over the racks. You can also use two layers of cheesecloth tightly stretched and pinned to the oven racks, but cheesecloth tends to sag more than nylon net. Extra oven racks are available in stores selling used appliances.

Baking Sheets—These give poor results because they do not allow air circulation. Those with non-stick surfaces are excellent for fruit leather, but uncoated metal baking sheets may give the fruit leather a metallic flavor.

Fan—Air circulaton is as important for efficiency in oven drying as in other methods. Some newer electric

---

CAUTION: MILK PRODUCTS

Milk and eggs are not recommended for home drying because of the high risk of food poisoning. Commercially dried milk and egg products are processed rapidly at temperatures high enough to prevent bacterial contamination. Home dryers cannot duplicate this process and the safety of home dried milk and eggs cannot be guaranteed. However, cheese and yogurt, because they are on the opposite end of the PH scale from milk and eggs, can be dried easily at home and are not included in this caution.

ovens have an exhaust system which circulates air through a venting system. This reduces heat loss and increases drying efficiency. A fan with enclosed blades may be positioned outside the

oven so air will circulate freely over the food, but extreme caution must be taken to avoid knocking it over.

Drying & Freezing

There are two techniques for preserving food which combine drying and freezing. Dehydro-freezing can be done at home, while freeze-drying is a commercial process.

Dehydrofreezing

Dehydrofreezing removes some moisture, then products are frozen for long-term storage.

This is an increasingly popular method for pre-serving apricots and prunes because they can remain as moist as commercially dried fruits without adding commercial preservatives.

To dehydrofreeze, dry the fruit or vegetable to about 30 percent moisture content (soft and pliable, with no pockets of water). Condition 1 day; see page 25. Package the food in airtight containers and store in the freezer until used.

Freeze-drying

Freeze-drying is a commercial process combining freezing and drying which causes a phenomenon known as sublimation to take place. Food is flash frozen, then placed in a vacuum chamber at low air pressure. Ice crystals go directly to a vapor, bypass-ing the liquid state. The vapor is removed and the dried product is packaged and stored without refrig-eration. Freeze-drying equipment is very expensive and freeze-dried products must be packaged careful-ly because they crush easily and must be protected from light and moisture.

Freeze-dried foods reconstitute quickly and have a better taste, appearance, texture and nutritive value than food dried by evaporation. Cell structure is maintained and foods after drying have the same volume as before.

Equipment for Dehydrating
Dehydrators, Convection Ovens, Solar Drying Equipment, Microwaves & Home-Built Dryers

A good-quality factory-made *dehydrator* is worth the investment. A food dehydrator will yield a better quality, more nutritious dried product than any other method of drying. Foods can be dried 24 hours a day without worrying about weather, unsanitary conditions or constant watching. Minimal time is needed for turn-ing or rotating the food. Operating costs are reasonable.

Three desirable features are provided by some but not all manufacturers: adjustable thermostat, fan or blower and an efficient heat source. An adjustable ther-mostat allows varied temperatures for different prod-ucts. A fan or blower removes moisture as it evaporates from the food, resulting in shorter drying time and thus a higher quality product. The heating element should be large enough for the drying area and is more cost-efficient if cycled by a thermostat.

Cleaning is simple on all units and they are safe for household use. Some dryers require occasional rotation of the food to ensure even drying.

Some manufacturers have a variety of accessories for making fruit leather, jerky or yogurt, as well as mesh screens for drying small foods or growing sprouts.

Several brands of *convection ovens* can also be used as food dryers. They dry as efficiently as dehydrators. Some manufacturers offer accessory drying racks,

either included with the oven or available separately.

Homemade dryers made of wood have numerous dis-advantages over commercial dehydrators. All wood dry-ers are a potential fire hazard because of the nature of the appliance—heat and wood. No matter how well the dehydrator is constructed, there is always some danger. Wood can also be a source of harmful microorganisms, because it is difficult to clean. Inefficient designs fre-quently require constant tending to keep food drying evenly and are costly to operate. If the challenge of building your own still appeals to you, contact your local County Extension Service for plans.

Solar drying equipment can be built inexpensively, does not present a fire hazard, and can be operated with minimal cost. Solar drying is best in areas with low humidity, but still can be used in more humid regions, although length of drying time increases.

A solar dryer should offer good protection from dust and insects and can be hybridized with a heat source to elevate drying temperatures during the night. A fan will improve air circulation and decrease drying time.

Microwave ovens will dry small quantities of herbs, but only models which also use convection, are suit-able for drying other foods. Check with the manufac-turer for dehydration instructions.

Dehydrators

AMERICAN HARVEST
Model: Gardenmaster® Dehydrator FD-1000
Drying area: 1 sq. ft. per tray, 4 circular trays (total 4 sq. ft.), expandable to 30 trays
Air circulation: Circulating fan
Air flow: Horizontal, across each tray; partially recirculating
Dimensions: Diameter: 15'' H: 9''
Weight: 10 lbs.
Wattage: 1000 watts
Temperature: Adjustable from 100°F (40°C) to 155°F (70°C)
Accessories: Fruit roll-up trays, clean-a-screens, yogurt factory, snack factory, jerky factory, jerky spices, 32 pg. recipe and instruction booklet
Other features: Patented Converga-Flow™: fan forces heated air up through the pressurized outer ring and core (not through the trays). The air is forced horizontally across each tray, converging on the core, for fast and even drying. No need to rotate trays. Opaque construction.
Warranty: Full 1-year warranty
Available from: American Harvest
Alternative Pioneering Systems, Inc.
4064 Peavey Road
Chaska, MN 55318-9908
(800) 288-4545 FAX (612) 448-3864

AMERICAN HARVEST
Model: Snackmaster® Dehydrator 2400 FD-50 (and 2-tray Snackmaster® Dehydrator 2200 FD-30)
Drying area: 0.86 sq. ft. per tray, 4 circular trays (total 3.44 sq. ft./2-tray: 1.72 sq. ft.), expandable to 12 trays (total 10.32 sq. ft.)
Air circulation: Circulating fan
Air flow: Horizontal, across each tray; partially recirculating
Dimensions: Diameter: 13'' H: 8''/2-tray: 4.5''
Weight: 6 lbs./2-tray: 5 lbs.
Wattage: 550 watts
Temperature: Adjustable from 95°F (35°C) to 145°F (65°C)
Accessories: Same as FD-1000
Other features: Same as FD-1000
Warranty: Full 1-year warranty
Available from: American Harvest

EXCALIBUR
Model: ED 700
Drying area: 1 sq. ft. per tray, 4 trays (total 4 sq. ft.)
Air circulation: Circulating 4-inch 5-blade fan (3600 rpm)
Air flow: Back to front
Dimensions: H: 6-1/8'' L: 16-1/4'' W: 13''
Weight: 7 lbs.
Wattage: 220 watts
Temperature: Adjustable from 85°F (30°C) to 145°F (65°C)
Accessories: Fruit roll-up sheets
Other features: Made of high impact ABS (cleans easily, durable, resists breakage). Door easily removed. Every other or all trays can be removed, allowing larger items to be dried. Drying trays made of space age polymers (same material as bullet proof windows). Horizontal air flow allows for even drying.
Warranty: Full 1-year warranty
Available from: Excalibur
6083 Power Inn Road
Sacramento, CA 95824
(916) 381-4254 FAX (916) 381-4256

Model: ED 600
Drying area: 1.62 sq. ft. per tray, 5 trays (total 8.1 sq. ft.)
Air circulation: Circulating 5-inch 9-blade fan (3600 rpm)
Air flow: Back to front
Dimensions: H: 8-1/2'' L: 19'' W: 17''
Weight: 13 lbs.
Wattage: 400 watts
Temperature: Adjustable from 85°F (30°C) to 145°F (65°C)
Accessories: Fruit roll-up sheets
Other features: Same as model ED700.
Warranty: Full 1-year warranty
Available from: Excalibur

MAGIC AIRE II™
Model: 300
Drying area: 0.78 sq. ft. per tray, 6 oblong trays (total 4.68 sq. ft.), expandable to 10 trays (total 12 sq. ft.)
Air circulation: Circulating fan
Air flow: Bottom to top
Dimensions: H: 14.875'' L: 17.125'' W: 11''
Weight: 12.3 lbs.
Wattage: 550 watts
Temperature: Preset to 135°F (55°C)
Accessories: Fruit roll-up trays, fine screened tray inserts
Other features: 100% solid state circuitry keeps drying chamber temperature constant. Auto adjusts 60 times/second.
Warranty: 5-year warranty
Available from: Magic Mill
1515 South 400 West
Salt Lake City, UT 84115
(801) 467-0707 (800) 888-8587 FAX (801) 486-0953

PRESSAIREIZER
Model: PressAIREizer
Drying area: 1 sq. ft. per tray, 6 circular trays (total 6 sq. ft.), expandable to 35 trays (total 35 sq. ft.)
Air circulation: Circulating fan
Air flow: Horizontal across each tray
Dimensions: Diameter: 15'' H: 13'' (6 tray)
Weight: 20 lbs.
Wattage: 1000 watts
Temperature: Adjustable from 100°F (40°C) to 170°F (75°C)
Accessories: Fruit roll-up trays, mesh screens, yogurt accessory, jerky press, jerky spices, 32 pg. recipe and instruction booklet
Other features: Pressurized air flow rises up outside ring and moves horizontally across each individual tray, resulting in even drying from top to bottom. Opaque construction.
Warranty: Full 1-year warranty
Available from: Professional Marketing Group, Inc.
P.O. Box 22490
Seattle, WA 98122
(206) 322-7303 (800) 227-3769 FAX (206) 322-4351

RONCO
Model: 187-04
Drying area: 0.75 sq. ft. per tray, 5 circular trays (total 3.75 sq. ft.), expandable to 7 trays (total 5.25 sq. ft.)
Air circulation: Convection
Air flow: Bottom to top
Dimensions: Diameter: 12.75'' H: 12''
Weight: 5 lbs. (5 trays) 7 lbs. (7 trays)
Wattage: 115 watts
Temperature: Preset to 125°F (50°C)
Accessories: Fruit roll-up trays, herb screen, extra trays, slicing machine, 24 pg. recipe and instruction booklet
Other Features: No noise, lid semi-transparent; no moving parts
Warranty: Limited 1-year warranty
Available from: Ronco Innovation, Inc.
5310 Derry Avenue
Agoura Hills, CA 91301
(818) 706-1806 FAX (313) 706-1829

Model: ED 900
Drying area: 1.62 sq. ft. per tray, 9 trays (total 14.58 sq. ft.)
Air circulation: Circulating 7-inch 5-blade fan (3600 rpm)
Air flow: Back to front
Dimensions: H: 12-1/2'' L: 19'' W: 17''
Weight: 16 lbs.
Wattage: 600 watts
Temperature: Adjustable from 85°F (30°C) to 145°F (65°C)
Accessories: Fruit roll-up sheets
Other features: Same as model ED700
Warranty: Full 1-year warranty
Available from: Excalibur

VITA MIX
Model: Harvest Savor Big-1
Drying area: 0.75 sq. ft. per tray, 10 circular trays (total 7.5 sq. ft.), expandable to 20 trays (total 15 sq. ft.)
Air circulation: Circulating fan
Air flow: Bottom to top
Dimensions: Diameter: 12'', H: 30'' (10 trays)
Weight: 6 lbs. (10 trays)
Wattage: 260 watts
Temperature: Preset to maintain 20°F over ambient room temperature
Accessories: Fruit roll-up sheets; 17 pg. instruction and recipe book
Other features: Continuous air flow from bottom to top which allows for addition of fresh foods during the drying process. Can also be used for incubating yogurt and proofing bread. Trays can be used for sprouting.
Warranty: Limited 1-year warranty
Available from: Vita Mix
8615 Usher Rd. Dept. HDR
Cleveland, OH 44138-2199
(800) 848-2649 FAX (216) 235-3726

WARING
Model: DF415-1
Drying area: 1.47 sq. ft. per tray, 5 circular trays (total 3.4 sq. ft.)
Air circulation: Circulating fan
Air flow: Bottom to top
Dimensions: Diameter: 16'' H: 13''
Weight: 9.7 lbs.
Wattage: 260 watts
Temperature: Preset at 140°F (60°C)
Accessories: Fruit roll-up trays and 22 pg. instruction/recipe book
Other features: Cake-cover-type top allows for even air flow, accessibility, and easy viewing as food dries. Stainless steel base cover is easy to clean.
Warranty: Full 1-year warranty
Available from: Waring
283 Main Street
New Hartford, CT 06057
(203) 379-0731 FAX (203) 738-0249

Convection Ovens

FARBERWARE CONVECTION/BROIL OVEN
Model: 461
Drying area: 1.17 sq. ft. per tray 3 rectangular trays (total 3.5 sq. ft.)
Air circulation: Circulating fan
Air flow: Circular
Dimensions: H: 13.3'' W: 13.5'' L: 21.4''
Weight: 24.4 lbs.
Wattage: 1320 watts
Temperature: Adjustable from 130°F (55°C) to 450°F (230°C)
Accessories: 3 stainless steel screen drying trays; 19 pg. recipe and instruction booklet; 6 pg. dehydration booklet
Other features: Three-chamber design with cooking chamber, cooling chamber and insulating chamber. Design allows for very even drying of food. 2-hour timer.
Warranty: 2-year limited warranty
Available from: Farberware
1500 Bassett Avenue
Bronx, New York 10461
(212) 863-8000 FAX (212) 409-0354

MAXIM CONVECTION OVEN

Model: Max 3
Drying area: 0.78 sq. ft. per tray 5 rectangular trays (total 3.9 sq. ft.)
Air circulation: Circulating fan
Air flow: Back to front
Dimensions: H: 13'' W: 17'' L: 14''
Weight: 23 lbs.
Wattage: 1600 watts
Temperature: Adjustable from 125°F (50°C) to 450°F (230°C)
Accessories: 5 stainless steel drying trays. 16 pg. dehydrating guide with basic information, recipes and tips accompanies stainless steel drying trays.
Other features: Door latch for venting moisture: built-in open-dehydrate door position allows 1 inch at top to vent moisture. 4-hour timer with automatic shut-off.
Warranty: 1-year warranty
Available from: Salton/Maxim Housewares, Inc.
550 Business Center Drive
Mt. Prospect, IL 60056
(800) 233-9054 FAX (708) 803-1186

TOASTMASTER "PROFESSIONAL" CONVECTION OVEN

Model: 7093 (7091 also available with similar features)
Drying area: 0.95 sq. ft. per tray 2 rectangular trays (total 1.9 sq. ft.)
Air circulation: Circulating fan
Air flow: Circular
Dimensions: H: 13.3'' W: 13.5'' L: 21.4''
Weight: 24.4 lbs.
Wattage: 1320 watts
Temperature: Adjustable from 130°F (55°C) to 450°F (230°C)
Accessories: 2 chrome-plated drying trays; 19 pg. recipe and instruction booklet; 6 pg. dehydration booklet.
Other features: Double-wall construction for cooler exterior surfaces. Interior light. Five separate systems in one: convection baking, regular baking, broiling, slow cooking and dehydrating.
Warranty: 2-year limited warranty
Available from: Toastmaster Inc.
1801 N. Stadium Boulevard, Columbia, MO 65202

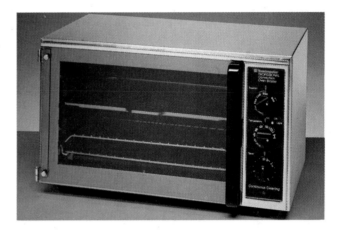

JENN-AIR CONVECTION OVEN

Models: D156, S176, SU146, W156, W256, W276
Drying area: 2.135 sq. ft. per rack 3 rectangular racks (total 6.4 sq. ft.) (can add up to 7 racks)
Air circulation: Circulating fan which produces 20 to 25 cubic feet per minute
Air flow: Circular throughout oven
Dimensions: Varies depending on model: range or built-in
Weight: Varies depending on model
Wattage: Varies depending on model
Temperature: Adjustable from 140°F (60°C) to 450°F (230°C)
Accessories: Oven racks must be covered with mesh covering to dry. 47 pg. Use and Care Manual; separate cookbook available with dehydrator instructions.
Other features: Electronic controls designed for ease of programming; timer; even drying; five separate systems in one: convection baking, regular baking, broiling, slow cooking and dehydrating
Warranty: 1st year full warranty parts and labor; 2nd year limited warranty parts only
Available from: Jenn-Air Company
3035 Shadeland
Indianapolis, IN 46226-0901
(317) 545-2271 FAX (317) 549-2503

Vacuum Packaging

Air is necessary for life. However, the oxygen in air robs stored foods of freshness and nutritional value through oxidation.

Up until now, our familiarity with the term "vacuum" was limited to a clinical scientific vacuum, the vacuum "cleaner" or "vacuum packaged" foods from the supermarket. Now with home vacuum technology, you can extend the shelf life of foods just like the commercial processors.

All kinds of dried foods benefit from vacuum packaging. Dried fruits and fruit leathers remain flavorful and pliable when vacuum packed. Dried vegetables, cereal products, pasta, flour, nuts, trail mix, etc. have a much longer shelf life with vacuum packaging.

Storage times, pages 26 and 56, are increased three to four times when foods containing oil are vacuum packaged and stored at low temperatures. Even at room temperature, vacuum packaging increases shelf life three to four times.

VACUUM PACKERS

Vacuum packers for home use vacuum seal foods in flexible plastic bags or tempered glass jars. All are countertop appliances that are convenient to operate, both with bags and jars.

Bags are ideal for dry products that will not crush or puncture the bag. For fragile or brittle items, package in jars. Use tempered canning jars to avoid the danger of jar breakage from the pressure created by the vacuum.

The products included in this section vary in their ability to pull a commercial quality vacuum (24 to 28 inches mercury). Any removal of air will be beneficial in the storage time of dried foods, but the better the vacuum, the better the keeping quality.

FOODSAVER® COMPACT HOME VACUUM PACKING SYSTEM
Model: Compact
Housing construction: Heavy-duty shock resistant ABS
Pump construction: Nylon piston pump (noncorrosive)
Dimensions: H: 3.5'' L: 15'' W: 5.5''
Weight: 6 lbs.
Power: 115 volts, 50 to 60 Hz, 5 amp
Vacuum: 25 inches mercury
Accessories:
Bags; Patented multilayer laminate polyethylene/nylon bags are boilable, reusable, dishwasher safe, USDA-approved for food storage and totally prevent freezer burn. Available in rolls or precut sizes.
Jar Sealers; Regular or wide-mouth jar sealer
Canisters; Foodsaver Canisters are ideal for vacuum packing large quantities of food, as well as liquids and delicate or crushable items. See-through heavy-duty polycarbonate canisters are dishwasher safe. Available in 2, 3, 5, 6 and 8 quart sizes.
Other features: Accompanied by "How-To" video
Warranty: 1-year full warranty
Available from: Nationwide Marketing, Inc.
340 Townsend Street
San Francisco, CA 94107
(415) 243-9890 (800) 777-5452 FAX (415) 777-2634

FOODSAVER® PROFESSIONAL
HOME VACUUM PACKING SYSTEM
Model: Professional
Housing construction: Heavy-duty shock resistant ABS
Pump construction: Nylon piston pump (non-corrosive)
Dimensions: H: 4'' L: 19.5'' W: 6.25''
Weight: 9 lbs.
Power: 115 volts, 50-60 Hz, 3.8 amp
Vacuum: 26 inches mercury
Accessories: Same as Compact model
Other features: Accompanied by "How-To" video
Warranty: 1-year full warranty
Available from: Nationwide Marketing, Inc.

PROLOCK PUMP ACTION VACUUM SEALING SYSTEM
Model: Prolock (Pak-N-Save and Doubleseal models only pull a partial vacuum)
Housing construction: Heavy-duty shock resistant ABS
Pump construction: Reciprocal-type pump, air nozzle operated
Dimensions: H: 3.75'' L: 14.5'' W: 6.5''
Weight: 7 lbs.
Power: 120 volts, 60 Hz, 3.8 amp, 160 watts
Vacuum: 26 inches mercury
Accessories:
Bags; High-density polyethylene bags are boilable, reusable, dishwasher safe, USDA-approved for food storage and totally prevent freezer burn. Available in 33-foot rolls
Jar Sealers; Wide-mouth jar sealer
Warranty: 2-year full warranty
Available from: Decosonic, Inc.
2159 South Tamiami Trail
Venice, FL 34293
(813) 493-6443 FAX (813) 497-5093
or
Decosonic, Inc.
1515 Pitfield Blvd.
St. Laurent, Quebec H4S 1G3, Canada
(514) 745-3710 FAX (514) 745-3698

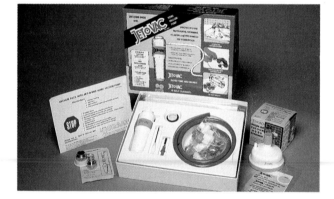

JET-O-VAC VACUUM SYSTEM
Model: Jet-O-Vac
Housing construction: Heavy-duty shock resistant ABS
Dimensions: Fittings adapt to kitchen sink
Weight: 2 lbs.
Vacuum: Variable with water pressure (with a water pressure of 35 psi, commercial quality vacuum is achieved)
Accessories:
Bags; High-density polyethylene bags are boilable, reusable, USDA-approved for food storage and eliminate freezer burn.
Seal Kaddy; Stock No. 0370: a simple heat sealing device that uses a regular clothes iron to seal vacuum pouches as well as all heat-sealable plastic film material.
Narrow-mouth Jar Sealer; Included with Jet-O-Vac
Warranty: Lifetime warranty, providing pump or components are not willfully damaged
Available from: Sandhof Corporation
37-21 60th Street
Woodside, NY 11377
(718) 898-4518

Fruits

Fruits are generally grouped according to the climate in which they grow. *Tropical fruits,* such as bananas and pineapples, must have warm humid climates to flourish. *Subtropical fruits* need a warm constant climate with moderate moisture. These include citrus fruits, figs, dates and olives. *Temperature-zone fruits* include apples, apricots, berries, cherries, peaches, pears and plums. With a few exceptions, fruits from all three groups may be dried. Because of availability, most fruits used in home drying in the United States are from the temperate-zone group.

Fruits contain B complex vitamins, vitamin C, carbohydrates and mineral salts such as iron, phosphorus and calcium. Some vitamin C may be lost through the drying process, but other nutrients are relatively unaffected. The amount of vitamins retained by dried fruits depends largely on how they are processed, dried and stored. In particular, the longer the drying time and the higher the temperatures, the more nutrient loss in the food. With a fast, low temperature dehydrator, there is little nutrient loss during the drying process itself. Also, all vitamins, minerals and fiber in fruits are concentrated by drying, leaving a higher density of nutrients by weight. Thus dried fruits are a good source of nutrition for snacking and as an outdoor food, and of roughage, which helps our digestion.

YOU NEED TO KNOW

Most fruits are covered with a skin which keeps the fruit fresh and holds in the seed, juicy flesh and, incidentally, the flavor. For fruits to dry quickly enough to prevent spoilage or fermentation, that skin has to be perforated in some way to allow moisture to escape. There are various ways to do this, depending on the type of fruit and the drying method being used.

Halving—Fruits such as apricots and small peaches or pears may be cut in half. When the pits are removed, the fruit halves are dried skin-side down and the moisture gradually evaporates. The bottom portion of the skin prevents the juices from dripping out and helps keep in the flavor during drying.

Slicing—To speed the drying process in larger fruits, they should be peeled and cut into slices 1/4 to 1/2 inch thick. The entire surface area of the fruit will dry in less time than in fruits left whole or halved. Also, uniform slices will dry in the same amount of time. With some fruits, such as pears or peaches, slicing *lengthwise* will give you fewer, larger pieces than slicing crosswise. A very sharp, high quality stainless steel knife should be used to minimize browning on the cut surface.

Checking—Small fruits such as prunes, cherries or grapes, have a *waxy bloom* or thin natural waxlike coating which keeps moisture in. This waxlike coating may be cracked or *checked* before drying so the moisture can escape. This will decrease the drying time. Checking is perforating the waxy bloom by chemical, heat or mechanical means.

Commercially, fruits such as prunes are checked by dipping the whole fruit in a lye solution. *This is not recommended for home drying because of the danger of handling lye and the possible retention of lye in the fruit.*

You can speed the drying process in whole small fruits by dipping them in boiling water just long enough to crack the skins. This will hasten evaporation and shorten drying time. Fruits which have been dipped in boiling water are less flavorful than those that have not.

Pitting—Fruits with a pit or stone, such as cherries, should be pitted before drying. This will shorten drying time and produce a better tasting dried fruit. Larger fruits, such as prunes, can be halved to remove the pits. You can also shorten the drying time of prunes or apricots by flattening them. Use your thumbs to press the rounded side in. This process, called *popping the backs,* exposes more drying surface to the air.

MOISTNESS

The moisture content of home dried fruits should be about 15 to 20 percent. Because dried fruits are usually eaten withou rehydration, some moisture is necessary for a chewy texture. Fruits that are overdried to a moisture level of 5 to 10 percent lose color, flavor and nutrients and have a less palatable texture. The dryness test for home dried fruits is simply touching and tasting. The fruit should be chewy and leather-like with no moisture pockets.

Fruit leather makes a delicious snack anytime, and you can dry your own. Directions are on pages 36 to 41.

Home-dried fruits are considerably drier than commercially dried fruits. The dehydration industry uses chemical agents that inhibit the growth of mold and other microorganisms and slow browning during storage. With these additives, commercially dried fruits may contain as much as 30 to 35 percent moisture without spoiling, although they will still brown somewhat during storage. See Dehydrofreezing, page 9.

APPEARANCE & FLAVOR

Some fruits lend themselves to the drying process better than others, page 26. The flavor and texture of some fruits change when the fruit is dehydrated. The end result may be quite different from the fresh flavor. Personal preference will be your guide. With fruits such as oranges, cantaloupe and watermelon, be prepared for a new flavor and texture, more like candy slices than fresh fruit, because of the concentration of sweetness and flavor.

Variety—Some varieties of the same fruit have a stronger flavor and a higher sugar content or firmer texture. All these qualities produce a better product when dried. Although some varieties are listed in the instructions on how to dry specific fruits, pages 27 to 35, you'll need to compare the varieties available in your area to select those best suited for drying.

The methods used for drying may alter the appearance and flavor of some fruits. The drying method you choose will depend on the climatic conditions where you live and the fruits you choose to dry. But remember, sun drying is a costly way to dry in terms of nutrition; the extreme heat can take as much as half of the nutrients out of the food. Fruits dried under controlled conditions, as in a dehydrator, differ in appearance from those dried in the sun. The sun's ultraviolet rays and the increased drying time affect the color and wrinkling in some fruits. The color in sulfured cut fruit tends to be much more pronounced when sun dried. Dark fruits, such as prunes or raisins, get much darker and more wrinkled when sun dried. Apricots dried in a dehydrator are a nice bright orange. However, when sulfured apricots are exposed to bright sunlight for even 4 to 6 hours during drying, that bright orange color changes to a very deep orange. Fruits to be dried in the sun need a considerably higher sulfur-dioxide content because they will lose so much sulfur-dioxide in the lengthy sun-drying process.

Maturity—The maturity of a fruit when it is harvested and processed has a great deal to do with its quality when dried. If under-ripe fruit is dried, it will have less sweetness, flavor and color. Overripe fruit will have a slightly fermented flavor, poor texture and may darken excessively. Some fruits, such as pears, prunes or bananas, may be picked when still green and ripened under controlled conditions in commercial storage or at home. Other fruits must be picked when they are at their peak ripeness becaue they will not continue to ripen satisfactorily during storage. Peaches and apricots, if picked green, will never develop the same full sweet flavor as peaches or apricots allowed to ripen on the tree. Many industrial food processors forego the added sweetness and flavor and pick the perishable fruit slightly underripe so it won't be damaged during transportation, handling or processing. You will find that maturity and natural sugar content are much more important in drying than in canning, because sugar is not added to dried fruits.

Hold the cut fruit in an ascorbic acid or a sodium bisulfite solution to prevent browning while you finish cutting.

Drying Fruits— How to Begin

Sort and select the highest quality ripe, ready-to-eat fresh fruit. Fully ripe fruit should be firm and heavy for its size. If it's perfect for eating, it's perfect for drying! Handle fruits gently and process them quickly because when they are at the right stage for drying, they are also the most fragile.

Washing—Gently wash all fruits to remove dirt, bacteria and insect larvae. Cold water will preserve freshness. Wash just before processing. Don't let fruit remain in water for long periods, because some of the nutrients will be dissolved and lost. Fruits with skins such as cherries or prunes, must be washed particularly well. Insect larvae cannot be seen on fresh fruit, but may hatch after the fruit has been dried and stored unless they are washed off before drying or killed during *pasteurizing,* page 25.

Preparation—To prepare fruit for pretreatment and drying, remove stems and peels. Core or pit fruit and cut it into halves, quarters or slices. Peels may be left on some fruit, but they tend to be tough and occasionally bitter. Trim away any bruised or soft spots. One soft spot can spoil an entire batch!

Prepare only as much fruit as you can pretreat and dry at one time.

Browning—Oxidation and the continuous reaction of enzymes cause some fruits, such as apples, pears, peaches and apricots, to turn brown when cut and exposed to air. Unless fruits are treated to slow oxidation and enzyme reaction, browning will continue during processing and storage. Much flavor and vitamins A and C will then be lost.

Holding Solutions—Place cut fruits that tend to brown in an *ascorbic acid* or *sodium bisulfite* holding solution as soon as you cut them. This will reduce browning during preparation. *Do not keep cut fruit in a holding solution for more than 1 hour.* Longer holding increases moisture content and extends drying time. **See caution regarding use of sodium bisulfite, page 23.**

Ascorbic acid is an effective anti-oxidant used in canning and freezing to prevent discoloration. Small quantities of ascorbic acid or lemon juice, which is high in ascorbic acid, may be added to fruit-leather puree to maintain color and increase the vitamin C content. Sodium bisulfite mixed with water, slows oxidation and browning. Use 1/4 teaspoon sodium bisulfite for each quart of water. Sodium bisulfite can also be used as a pretreatment method called *sulfiting* or *sulfite soaking* when drying fruits. See pages 22 and 23.

Pretreatment—NOTE: No pretreatment is NECESSARY with any fruit.

Pretreating some fruits before drying will reduce vitamin loss, flavor loss, browning and deterioration during storage. When not pretreating, storage in the refrigerator or the freezer will also dramatically reduce deterioration. Sulfuring, sulfiting, syrup blanching and steaming are all methods of pretreatment to keep fruits in prime condition for drying or storage. *Do not hold cut fresh fruit in salted water. This gives an undesirable flavor and a gray color to the fruit.* Ascorbic acid or lemon juice (used very successfully in canning and freezing to retard oxidation) may be used as an anti-oxidant pretreatment for drying fruits, although the dehydration process tends to reduce its effectiveness.

Sulfur-dioxide treatments are the most effective for retarding oxidation and spoilage. Fruit flavor and storage life are also improved. Sulfur dioxide is a combination of sulfur and oxygen. Sulfur is a solid nonmetallic element found in eggs and many strong smelling vegetables, such as cabbage, horseradish and onions. The small quantity of sulfur dioxide remaining in dried fruits is not harmful when consumed. Treating fruit with sulfur dioxide may be accomplished in two ways. **Sulfuring** exposes the fruit to sulfur-dioxide fumes by burning *flowers of sulfur* in a closed container with fruit. The fumes penetrate the surface area of the fruit about 1 to 2 millimeters deep. **Sulfuring must be done in the open because the fumes are harmful to people and animals.**

Sulfiting, page 22, is soaking fruit for a specified time in a solution of water and *sodium bisulfite.* This releases sulfur dioxide and has the same general effect as sulfuring, but it is not as effective. Sulfiting may be done in your kitchen. Drying time is longer than with sulfuring because of the water absorbed during soaking.

Sulfuring

1/Place fruit on drying trays with pit cavities or cut surfaces up. If the fruit is sliced thinly, do not overlap the slices.

The sulfuring process is simple and relatively inexpensive. Fruits are first prepared for drying. The pieces are placed on trays and covered with an adjustable vented chamber, a cardboard or wooden box, and exposed to sulfur dioxide (SO_2) fumes created by burning sulfur.

Sulfuring requires *framed trays* to hold the fruit during sulfuring. Screens allow the SO_2 to penetrate all sides of the fruit evenly. The screening should be teflon-coated fiberglass, stainless steel or plastic. Do not use aluminum or galvanized metal screening material because SO_2 will corrode it. Plastic or fiberglass screens should be placed far enough away from the burning sulfur to keep them from melting. Metal frames may be used and wiped thoroughly after sulfuring, although they will corrode with continued use. Wooden slatted trays are likely to harbor bacteria, are difficult to clean and do not allow the SO_2 to penetrate as evenly.

You can either stack the trays using bricks as shown in the photos, or you can make a wooden rack to fit your trays. A rack is very convenient, will save you time, and is less likely to overturn than bricks. Allow at least 10 inches clearance above the ground, and 1-1/2 to 2-1/2 inches between trays.

A *box* is needed to cover the fruit. It should be made of either wood or heavy cardboard and have no cracks or openings other than the desired vents. Television boxes are fine. If you use a cardboard box, seal any cracks with heavy tape and cut two vents in the box as shown in the picture. One vent should be cut in the bottom near where the sulfur will be placed, and the other at the upper edge of the opposite side. If the box is constructed of wood, these vents may be hinged and a glass window may be inserted in the top of the box to allow you to see the fruit. The more airtight the box is, the less sulfur is needed and the more effective the sulfuring treatment will be.

Use only *sublimed sulfur*, U.S.P. standard, for burning. It is also called *flowers of sulfur*. It is free of impurities, burns readily and may be purchased at most pharmacies. You can also buy it in large quantities at a reasonable price from chemical supply companies. It can be stored indefinitely or you can share the purchase with neighbors or friends. Garden-dusting sulfur has more impurities and is not recommended.

HOW TO SULFUR

Spread fruit in a single layer on trays with the pit cavity or cut surface up. Be careful not to overlap fruit.

Select a good location outside for sulfuring. It should be away from people or pets and open windows. A slight breeze is helpful. Place the box with *the lower vent facing into the breeze* so air will flow through the box. Set the first tray on the rack or on bricks so it is at least 10 inches above the ground. The fruit cut first should be closest to the burning sulfur. Use wooden blocks or spools to stack the remaining trays 1-1/2 inches apart. Measure the sulfur and place it in a clean shallow *metal container,* such as a pie tin.

The amount of sulfur varies with the length of time the fruit is to be sulfured, the weight of the fruit and the dimensions of the box. When using a cardboard box like the one in the photo, *use 1 tablespoon of sulfur per pound of fresh prepared fruit. If the box is made of wood and is more air-*

2/Arrange the sulfuring equipment outdoors. Stack the drying trays and measure the sulfur. Place the sulfur in a metal container in front of the stacked trays. Sulfur should face the breeze.

3/Place the prepared box with the vents open over the trays. Openings have been cut in this box to illustrate how to position the box and trays. The lower vent of the box should face the breeze so air will flow through the box.

tight, use 1-1/2 teaspoons of sulfur per pound of fresh prepared fruit. Place the container of sulfur *in front of the trays,* not underneath them. The bottom tray should be 10 inches or more from the burning sulfur.

Cover the trays with the box, leaving the vents open. If you are using a cardboard box, seal the bottom edges of the box with dirt.

CAUTION

During the sulfuring process, sulfur dioxide fumes *must not be inhaled*. They can cause damage to the delicate membranes of the lung. Sulfur fruit outside where there is a good flow of fresh air. Do not breathe the fumes and be certain that animals or children are not close by.

Natural food advocates maintain that sulfured fruit is harmful and that sulfuring is done mainly for cosmetic reasons. There is currently no evidence to substantiate this claim. It has been proven that sulfuring retards spoilage and darkening of fruits, lessens the contamination by insects during sun drying, and reduces the loss of vitamins A and C.

If sulfured fruit is dried in the oven there is also danger of inhaling the fumes. Dry sulfured fruit in the sun or in a dehydrator.

Light the sulfur. Do not leave burned matches in the container because this will retard burning. **BE CAREFUL NOT TO INHALE THE SULFUR DIOXIDE FUMES. THESE FUMES CAN BE HARMFUL TO YOUR LUNGS.**

Start timing. The burning time of sulfur will vary with the ventilation, the size of the container and the weather conditions. The sulfur dioxide fumes do the work, not the actual burning process. When about 2/3 of the sulfur is consumed, about 10 minutes, close the vents and leave the fruit in the box for the recommended time. Vents may be taped closed with heavy sealing tape.

Sulfuring times vary with the type of fruit being sulfured, the size of the pieces, the condition and maturity of the fruit, and the sulfuring equipment. Approximate times for sulfuring are given in the directions for drying specific fruits, pages 27 to 35. However, these are only approximate and the following variables should be considered.
- Freshly cut fruit absorbs SO_2 most rapidly.
- Immature fruit requires a higher concentration of SO_2 because it does not retain the SO_2 as long as fully ripe fruit does.
- Sun-dried fruit requires a higher SO_2 concentration than fruit dried in a dehydrator because much more of it is lost in exposure to sun and air.
- Fruit that is not in prime fresh condition may

1/Apricots at top left were pretreated by steaming. Apricots on the right were syrup blanched. The middle row shows apricots pretreated with ascorbic acid on the left and with sodium bisulfite on the right. On the bottom row, apricots on the left were dried without any pretreatment. Those on the right were sulfured.

2/Apples at top left were steamed before drying. Those on the right were syrup blanched. Middle row shows apples treated with ascorbic acid on the left and with sodium bisulfite on the right. Bottom row, apples on the left were not pretreated and those on the right were sulfured.

require more sulfuring to make it palatable.

● Larger pieces of fruit require more sulfuring.

● Fruit to be stored 6 months or longer, or at a temperature above 60°F (15°C), should have a higher SO_2 concentration.

Sulfuring is finished when fruit is bright and glistening and a small amount of juice appears in the pit cavity. The skin will peel off easily and the color will be even. Dry in the sun or in a dehydrator.

Do not dry sulfured fruit in the oven. When drying sulfured fruit in a dehydrator, place it outside or in a room vented to the outside for the first 4 to 6 hours.

Sulfiting

> **You Will Need:**
> **Sodium bisulfite**
> **Glass or stainless steel container**

Soaking fruits in a solution of *sodium bisulfite* has an effect similar to sulfuring. Sodium bisulfite, also identified as *sodium metabisulfite,* resembles table salt. When mixed with water and used as a soaking solution, it penetrates the surface, retarding browning and loss of vitamins.

Use only *food-grade sodium bisulfite.* It is available through winemaking supply stores, stores that carry dehydrating supplies, some pharmacies and—in large quantities—from chemical supply companies.

HOW TO SULFITE

If you are using a holding solution before sulfiting, slice the fruit into a colander submerged in the holding solution. When the colander is full, transfer it to the full-strength solution of sodium bisulfite. Set your timer. Soaking time varies with the type of fruit and its thickness. Sulfite should penetrate 1 to 2 millimeters to be effective during drying and storage.

The same variables apply to sulfite soaking as to sulfuring, page 21. Strength of the solution depends on those variables. As a general guideline, use 1 to 2 tablespoons sodium bisulfite per gallon of water. Soak sliced fruit 5 minutes and halved fruit 15 minutes.

After soaking, lightly rinse the fruit under cold tap water. Rinsing improves the flavor of dried fruit, but lowers the sulfite content slightly. Place the rinsed fruit on drying trays. Sulfited fruit generally takes 15 to 20 percent longer to dry than sulfured fruit because of the water absorbed during soaking.

Follow these precautions when using sodium bisulfite:
• Keep dry granules and holding and pretreatment solutions out of reach of children and pets.
• Discard holding and pretreatment solutions promptly after use.
• Dry pretreated fruits only in a well-ventilated area.
• If any adverse reation to preparing or eating pretreated fruit is noticed, discontinue use of the pretreatment.
• Persons on a salt-restricted diet should check with their doctors before using this pretreatment.

Syrup Blanching

> You Will Need:
> Large saucepan
> Sugar

Syrup-blanched fruits have good color. However, they are sweeter and have a softer texture than sulfured and sulfited fruits. They also contain less vitamins A and C.

HOW TO SYRUP BLANCH

Prepare the fruit as you would for sulfuring. Prepare a sugar syrup by mixing 1 cup sugar, 1 cup white corn syrup and 2 cups water. Bring to a boil; add 1-1/2 pounds prepared fruit. Simmer 5

minutes. Drain and rinse lightly with cold water. Dry on drying trays.

Steaming

> You Will Need:
> Steamer

Steaming destroys the natural flavor and texture of fruit and much of the vitamins A and C. Steamed fruit doesn't have the full flavor of sulfured fruit nor the sweetness of syrup-blanched fruit. It is the least-effective way to pretreat fruits for drying, but is used by people who prefer not to use sulfur dioxide or a sweetened syrup.

HOW TO STEAM

As you prepare the fruit, place it in an ascorbic-acid or a weak sodium-bisulfite solution. Drain and place the fruit in the perforated section of a steamer without letting the fruit touch the water. Cover tightly and steam until heated through. To test for heat penetration, bite into a piece or break it and touch the center. Place the fruit on drying trays.

Sulfuring-Steaming Combination

> You Will Need:
> See Sulfuring, page 20
> See Sulfiting, opposite
> Steamer

A combination of sulfuring and steaming gives a more tender, translucent fruit than sulfuring alone. It produces a better flavor than fruit pretreated by steaming alone, without the added sugar of syrup blanching.

HOW TO SULFUR-STEAM

Prepare the fruit as you would for sulfuring or sulfiting. Sulfur or sulfite fruits that turn brown. Dry treated fruit on drying trays until 50 percent of the moisture is removed. The fruit should feel leathery but still have pockets of moisure.

Remove from the drying trays; steam until heated through. Dry again until leathery with no pockets of moisture.

How to Dry Fruits

Preheat the dryer to get the drying process under way immediately. Arrange prepared and pretreated fruit on drying trays, leaving small spaces between slices or pieces for air circulation. Different fruits may be dried together because they do not have the strong flavor or odor of some vegetables. Dry fruit halves or slices of similar size on the same tray to save sorting near the end of the drying process. Smaller fruits, such as cherries, should be stirred occasionally to promote even drying.

Try to interrupt the drying process as little as possible. Sun drying is slowed at night because the temperature drops or the fruit is brought inside. Prolonging drying at low temperatures or interrupting the drying of fruits may result in fermentation or spoilage.

Do not add fresh moist pieces to a dryer filled with partially dried fruit. The increased humidity will greatly increase the drying time of the partly dried fruit.

Check the suggested drying temperatures for each fruit, pages 27 to 35. Some fruits contain considerably more water than others and the initial drying temperature can be as high as 160°F (70°C) to remove surface moisture quickly. Other fruits should not exceed 140 or 150°F (60 to 65°C) in the initial stages because higher temperatures will destroy heat-sensitive nutrients. If you dry two fruits which have different suggested drying temperatures at the same time, make a compromise between the two. If it is impossible to vary the temperatures, the fruit will still dry, but the quality will suffer.

Sun dried fruit should be placed in direct sunlight for the first 2 or 3 days of drying. After that, the fruit can be placed in the shade for the remainder of drying time. This will give you fruit with better flavor and less loss of color and nutrients. This is sometimes called *sun-shade drying.*

TESTING FOR DRYNESS

Watch fruits carefully near the end of the drying process. Test frequently to avoid overdrying. Let a piece of fruit cool to room temperature. Touch and taste it. It should feel pliable and leather-like,

How Do You Know They're Dry?

Most people will rely on the taste and touch test; see the Dryness Test for each fruit on pages 27 to 35. If you taste and touch and are still not sure, comparing the weight of the fruit before and after drying will help you.

After peeling the fruit and removing the pits, seeds or cores, weigh it. Write down the weight and begin the drying process.

To calculate the desired weight after drying, first look up the water content of the fruit you are drying. This figure is given for each fruit on pages 27 to 35.

For example, if you are drying apricots, weigh them after removing the pits. Suppose you have 25 pounds. On page 28, the water content of apricots is given at 85% or 0.85. The percent of water most fruits must lose in the drying process is 80% to 85%. We can use 0.80, the decimal equivalent of 80%.

1. Find the total weight of water in the fruit:

Weight of edible fresh fruit times the percent of water content equals the total weight of water.

For your apricots:

25 x 0.85 = 21.25 pounds of water

2. To find the weight of water which must be removed, multiply the total weight of water by the percent of water to be removed:

Total weight of water times the percent of water to be removed equals the weight of water to be removed.

For your apricots:

21.25 x 0.80 = 17 pounds to be removed

3. To find out how much the apricots should weigh after they are dried, subtract the weight of water to be removed from the weight of the fresh apricots:

Weight of fresh fruit minus the weight of water to be removed equals the weight of dried fruit.

For your apricots:

25 - 17 = 8 pounds of dried fruit

When you think the apricots are sufficiently dried, weigh them. They should weigh about 8 pounds. If they weigh 9 pounds or more, they need to be dried longer.

As soon as the dried fruit is cool, place it in a container, cover it tightly and leave it in a cool place for up to 1 week.

If dried food has been exposed to insects, it needs to be processed so there will be no further insect growth. One way to thwart insect larvae is to place the fruit in the freezer for 48 hours after it is packaged. Another method of pasteurization is to place the unwrapped dried fruit in a roasting pan in the oven.

and have no pockets of moisture. Most fruits should contain between 15 and 20 percent moisture when properly dried.

CONDITIONING

When drying is completed, some pieces will be more moist than others because of the size of the pieces or their location in the dryer. *Conditioning* is a process used to distribute the residual moisture evenly in the fruit. It reduces the chance of spoilage, particularly from mold.

After the dried fruit has cooled, loosely pack it in plastic or glass containers to about 2/3 full. Metal containers may give an unpleasant flavor to the fruit. Cover the containers tightly and let them stand for 2 to 4 days. The excess moisture in some pieces will be absorbed by the drier pieces. Shake the containers daily to separate the pieces and check for signs of condensation on the lids. If condensation occurs, the fruit should be returned to the drying trays for more drying.

PASTEURIZING

Washing fruit does not always remove insect larvae, so fruits which have been exposed to insects before or during the drying process must be *pasteurized* to prevent spoiling during storage.

Two methods of pasteurizing may be used.

Freezer Method—After the fruit has been dried and conditioned, seal it in heavy plastic bags. Place them in a freezer set below 0°F (-20°C) for at least 48 hours or up to 2 weeks before storing.

Oven Method—A second method of pasteurizing fruit is done after conditioning but before the fruit is packaged. Vitamin loss is high with this method. Layer the fruit loosely, not more than 2 inches deep, in a roasting pan. Place the pan in an oven preheated to 175°F (80°C) for 15 minutes or 160°F (70°C) for 30 minutes. Remove and cool the fruit and package it for storage.

PACKAGING

Dried fruit should be cooled and conditioned before packaging, then vacuum packaged in bags or jars (if possible) or packed in plastic freezer bags with excess air removed. See Vacuum Packaging, page 14. Package fruit in amounts that can be used within several days after opening. Every time dried fruit is exposed to air, there will be a slight deterioration in the quality. Seal freezer bags with a heat sealer or heavy rubber band and store smaller bags inside large plastic or metal containers.

STORAGE

Storage life of dried fruits is dependent upon the moisture in the fruits, their sulfur dioxide content and storage conditions (light and temperature).

Moisture Content—The desired moisture content in most dried fruits is 15 to 20%. Store fruits with 20 to 30% moisture in the freezer to prevent mold.

Sulfur Dioxide Loss—Warm temperatures and exposure to air result in the loss of sulfur dioxide, causing darkening and flavor loss.

Storage Temperature—The chart below shows fruits stored at refrigerator or freezer temperatures so that you can compare storage times with frozen food or canned food. Dried foods take from one-tenth to one-twentieth of the stored volume of frozen or canned. Dried fruit should be stored in the very coolest place available, preferably below 60°F (15°C) or frozen to keep the highest quality and nutritional value. For every 18°F (10°C) drop in temperature, the shelf life of dried fruits increases 3 to 4 times. For example, if a fruit will remain in good condition for 4 months at 70°F (20°C), storing it at 0°F (-20°C) will keep it in prime condition for 5 to 8 years!

Light—Dried fruit colors tend to fade when exposed to light. Light also destroys vitamins A and C.

Fruits at a Glance

FRUIT	SUITABILITY	SUITABILITY FOR LEATHER	STORAGE TIME FOR BEST QUALITY 34°F (0°C)	0°F (-20°C)
Apples	Excellent	Excellent	18 to 24 months	5 to 8 years
Apricots	Excellent	Excellent	24 to 30 months	8 to 10 years
Avocados	Not Recommended	Not recommended		
Bananas	Good	Fair to good	8 to 16 months	30 to 60 months
Berries (seeds)	Not recommended	Excellent	18 to 24 months	5 to 8 years
Blueberries	Good	Only in combination	18 to 24 months	5 to 8 years
Cherries	Excellent	Excellent	30 to 48 months	10 to 16 years
Citrus fruits	Fair to good	Only in combination	18 to 24 months	5 to 8 years
Citrus peel	Excellent	Only in combination	18 to 24 months	5 to 8 years
Coconuts	Excellent	Only in combination	2 to 4 months	8 to 16 months
Crab Apples	Not recommended	Only in combination		
Cranberries	Fair	Only in combination	18 to 24 months	5 to 8 years
Currants	Good	Not recommended	24 to 30 months	8 to 10 years
Dates	Excellent	Only in combination	30 to 48 months	10 to 16 years
Figs	Excellent	Only in combination	18 to 24 months	5 to 8 years
Grapes	Excellent	Fair to good	18 to 24 months	5 to 8 years
Guavas	Not recommended	Only in combination		
Kiwi fruit	Excellent	Excellent	18 to 24 months	5 to 8 years
Melons	Fair to good	Not recommended	4 to 8 months	12 to 30 months
Nectarines	Excellent	Excellent	18 to 24 months	5 to 8 years
Olives	Not recommended	Not recommended		
Papayas	Good	Better in combination	18 to 24 months	5 to 8 years
Peaches	Excellent	Excellent	18 to 24 months	5 to 8 years
Pears (all)	Excellent	Excellent	18 to 24 months	5 to 8 years
Persimmons	Fair	Not recommended	8 to 16 months	30 to 60 months
Pineapples	Excellent	Excellent	24 to 30 months	8 to 10 years
Plums	Good	Good	24 to 30 months	8 to 10 years
Pomegranates	Not recommended	Not recommended		
Prune plums	Excellent	Excellent	30 to 48 months	10 to 16 years
Quince	Not recommended	Not recommended		
Rhubarb	Good	Fair	8 to 16 months	30 to 60 months
Strawberries	Excellent	Excellent	18 to 24 months	5 to 8 years

*Shelf life is increased drastically with cooler storage and/or vacuum packaging. See Storage Temperatures, above, and Vacuum Packaging, pages 14 and 15. Fruits can be stored at higher temperatures than those above without spoiling as long as they are properly packaged. However, there will be a gradual deterioration in sensory quality and nutritive value.

How to Use Dried Fruit

REHYDRATION

Most dried fruit is eaten or used in recipes as it is. However, you may wish to *plump* or soften the fruit slightly to make it more chewable. You can use one of three methods.

- Cover the dried fruit with boiling water or fruit juice. Let it stand 5 to 10 minutes, then drain.
- Place the dried fruit in the top of a steamer over boiling water and steam 3 to 5 minutes until the fruit is plump.
- Sprinkle the dried fruit with fruit juice or water and let it stand several minutes.

Once moisture has been returned to dried fruits, they are quite perishable and should be used soon or refrigerated.

COOKING

Dried fruit may be cooked in hot water or juice until it is tender. Soaking first, then simmering, gives a more tender fruit. Sugar and spices should be added near the end of the cooking time.

Delicious recipes for using dried fruit start on page 92.

HOW TO CHOP DRIED FRUIT

With **kitchen scissors** or a **knife**:
- Run the scissors or knife through hot water occasionally to prevent stickiness, or
- Coat the scissors or knife with vegetable oil, or
- Toss the fruit lightly with vegetable oil, or
- Toss the fruit lightly with flour from the recipe you are using.

In a **blender** or **food processor**:
- Freeze the dried fruit first. Then chop with the appropriate blade and speed.

In a **food grinder**:
- Freeze the dried fruit first.
- If the grinder gets gummy or sticky, put a few small pieces of dry bread through it.

Fruits: A to Z

Apples

Apple peelers, corers and slicers greatly reduce preparation time. Keep in mind that peelings tend to be tougher when dried. Vary the flavor of dried apples by sprinkling them with flavored gelatin powder or cinnamon and sugar before drying.

Quality When Dried—Excellent.

Varieties Best For Drying—Gravenstein, Granny Smith, Jonathan, Newton, Rome Beauty and other firm-textured, tart varieties are usually preferred.

Selection—Apples should be mature but very firm and free from bruises or soft spots. They should have a good color for their variety. Store at refrigerator temperature, 35° to 40°F, (1° to 3°C), to maintain the highest quality.

Water Content Before Drying—84%.

Preparation—Wash, peel if desired, core and slice into 1/4-inch slices or cut in quarters. Hold in solution of 1 teaspoon ascorbic acid per quart of water or 1/4 teaspoon sodium bisulfite per quart of water until ready to pretreat.

Pretreatment—Sulfur 1/4-inch slices 45 minutes to 1 hour. Sulfur quarters 1 to 2 hours. Or slices or quarters may be soaked for 10 to 15 minutes in a solution of 1 to 2 tablespoons sodium bisulfite per gallon of water and rinsed in clear water. The least effective pretreatment is to steam blanch for 3 to 5 minutes.

Drying Temperature—150°F (65°C) for 2 to 3 hours, 130°F (55°C) until dry.

Dryness Test—Pliable to crisp. Apples store best when they are slightly crisp. They should contain about 10% moisture.

How To Use—Rehydrate dried apples and use in applesauce, granola crisps, cobblers and pies. They may be cooked in apple dumplings or fritters or fried with ham and eggs. They are a delicious dried snack.

Apricots

Because apricots are especially high in vitamin A, careful pretreatment and drying are important so vitamin loss will be minimal.

Quality When Dried—Excellent.

Varieties Best For Drying—Blenheim/Royal is used most frequently for drying, although Tilton may also be used.

Selection—Apricots should be picked at their peak ripeness to have the best flavor when dried. They should be plump, well-formed and fairly firm with a deep yellow or yellow-orange color. If they are yellow-green, they are not fully ripe. Although unripened apricots will soften and change color during storage, their flavor will not be as pronounced and they will tend to be tough and more shriveled.

Water Content Before Drying—85%.

Preparation—Apricots should be washed, halved, pits removed and held in a solution of 1 teaspoon ascorbic acid per quart of water or a solution of 1/4 teaspoon sodium bisulfite per quart of water until ready to pretreat.

Pretreatment—The most effective pretreatment for apricots is sulfuring. If you choose not to sulfur, the best alternative is syrup blanching. Sulfur halves skin-side down for 2 to 3 hours. If using a dehydrator, expose apricots to the sun for at least 4 to 6 hours after sulfuring to deepen the color and improve the flavor. Another alternative is for dehydrator drying only: steam the apricots 2 to 4 minutes, sulfur 1 hour, then dry them.

Drying Temperature—160°F (70°C) for 2 to 3 hours, 130°F (55°C) until dry.

Dryness Test—Pliable with no pockets of moisture.

How To Use—Apricots are one of the most versatile of all dried fruits and may be used dried or rehydrated in meat dishes, salads, desserts, glazes, candies or granola.

Additional information and recipes may be obtained by sending a business-size, self-addressed, stamped envelope to the California Apricot Advisory Board, 1280 Boulevard Way, Suite 107, Walnut Creek, CA 94595. (510) 937-3660 FAX (510) 937-0118

Avocados

The avocado is extremely soft-textured, very perishable and contains an oil content of about 16 percent. It is not recommended for drying.

Bananas

Vary the flavor of dried bananas before drying them by sprinkling them with flavored gelatin powder or dipping them in lemon juice or a lemon juice and honey mixture. After dipping, they may be rolled in chopped nuts, sesame seeds or shredded coconut. Bananas do not sun dry well. They ferment before they have dried sufficiently.

Quality When Dried—Good.

Varieties Best For Drying—Large yellow, smooth-skinned varieties such as Cavendish, Gros Michel or Martinique dry best. A smaller, red-skinned variety such as the Red Jamaica or Baracoa may also be dried. Plantains are unsuitable for drying as a fruit because they are hard and starchy. They may be dried like potatoes, see page 63.

Selection—Bananas should be solid yellow or slightly brown flecked with no green on the peel. Avoid bruised or over-ripe bananas. Bananas which are slightly brown flecked will have the sweetest, most pronounced flavor when dried. Solid yellow bananas will not be quite as sweet or as strong-flavored. They ripen rapidly at room temperature. Once ripe, they may be held 3 to 4 days in the refrigerator.

Water Content Before Drying—65%.

Preparation—Peel and slice bananas 1/4 to 3/8 inch thick crosswise or lengthwise.

Pretreatment—Bananas are best dried with no pretreatment. Because of their soft texture, bananas are not sulfited, steamed or syrup blanched and are leathery when dried. Store-bought banana chips are flavored with sugar and banana flavoring, then deep-fried.

Drying Temperature—150°F (65°C) for 1 to 2 hours, 130°F (55°C) until dry.

Dryness Test—Pliable to crisp.

How To Use—Dried bananas are delicious snacks. They may also be used in dry or cooked cereals, granola or baby foods. Bananas may be rehydrated for use in banana breads, cakes and cookies.

Berries

Blackberries, boysenberries, huckleberries and raspberries are not recommended for drying because of their high seed content and slow drying rate. However, berries make excellent fruit leather.

Blackberries

See Berries, above.

Blueberries

Quality When Dried—Good.

Selection—Select large firm, fully ripe berries that have a deep blue color all over.

Water Content Before Drying—83%.

Preparation—Wash berries and remove stems.

Pretreatment—Berries may be dried with no pretreatment. Dipping in boiling water in a colander or sieve removes the waxy covering and shortens the drying time. When it is dried with no pretreatment, the dried blueberry has a puffy appearance and texture rather than a raisin-like quality.

Drying Temperature—150°F (65°C) for 2 to 3 hours, 130°F (55°C) until dry.

Dryness Test—Leathery and pliable with no pockets of moisture.

How to Use—Dried blueberries are delicious eaten alone as a snack.

If you want to know the amount of moisture lost from fruits during drying, use the information and calculations on page 24.

Boysenberries

See Berries, page 28.

Cherries

Look in your local cookware or gourmet shop for a German-made cherry pitter which pits a large quantity of cherries in a short time with little loss of juice or pulp.
Quantity When Dried—Excellent.
Varieties Best For Drying—Sweet varieties such as Lambert, Royal Ann, Napoleon, Van or Bing are excellent as a dried snack or used in cooking instead of raisins. The tart or sour varieties such as Early Richmond or Large Montmorency dry well but are better used in cooking than as a snack.
Selection—Select large, plump and firm, fully ripe cherries with fresh-looking stems. Avoid small under-ripe fruit or cherries with dark stems, dull color or soft appearance. Store cherries at refrigerator temperature, 35° to 40°F (1° to 3°C), to maintain highest quality.
Water Content Before Drying—sour, 84%; sweet, 80%.
Preparation—Wash cherries and remove stems. Slice in half and remove pit or pit and dry whole.
Pretreatment—Cherries may be dried with no pretreatment but the color will be very dark and the flavor more raisin-like. Sulfured cherries hold their color and flavor better, especially for longer storage. Sulfur halves for 30 minutes; sulfur whole pitted cherries for 1 hour.
Drying Temperature—160°F (70°C) for 2 to 3 hours, 130°F (55°C) until dry.
Dryness Test—Pliable and leathery with no pockets of moisture.
How To Use—Dried cherries are excellent snacks. They may be substituted for or combined with raisins in cooking. Sour cherries may be reconstituted and used in pies or cobblers.

Citrus Fruits and Peels

Quality When Dried—Fair to Good.
Varieties Best For Drying—The peels of citron, grapefruit, kumquat, lemon, lime, orange, tangelo or tangerine may be dried. Thick-skinned navel orange peel is better for drying than thin-skinned Valencia peel. Try to dry only the sweetest oranges and grapefruits. Otherwise, they will be bitter when dried.
Selection—Select firm, juicy thick-skinned fruit with no signs of mold or decay. Do not dry the peel of fruit marked *color added*. Store citrus fruits, except limes, at refrigerator temperature, 35° to 40°F (1° to 3°C), to maintain the highest quality. Store limes at 40°F (5°C) or above.
Water Content Before Drying—86%

Preparation—Wash well and remove dirt and any trace of fungicide. Peels: Thinly peel the outer 1/16 to 1/8 inch of the peel. Avoid the white bitter pith just under the peel. The outer part of the peel contains the flavoring oils. To candy (glacé) citrus peel, see the directions on pages 44 and 45. Whole fruit: Slice 1/8 to 1/4 inch thick.
Pretreatment—None.
Drying Temperature—To avoid loss of delicate flavoring oils, dry at 135°F (55°C) for 1 to 2 hours, 120°F (50°C) until dry.
Dryness Test—Crisp. Snap when broken.
How to Use—Peels: Store in strips until ready to use. Then chop the strips in a blender and substitute for grated lemon or orange peel. Dried peel has about twice the strength of fresh, so adjust the amount accordingly. Citrus peels may also be candied, then dried and used in cakes, puddings or candies. Sliced fruit: Break off rind and eat as snack. Float in summer punch or hot tea. Hang on Christmas tree as brightly colored, transparent ornaments. Powder and use in yogurt, breads, cereals, etc.

Coconuts

To sweeten coconut, sprinkle it with sifted powdered sugar before drying. Dried coconut has a high oil content and keeps best in an airtight container in the refrigerator or freezer.
Quality When Dried—Excellent.
Selection—Select coconuts that appear fresh, are heavy for their size and full of coconut milk. Shake the coconuts to hear the milk slosh. Keep coconuts refrigerated until ready to dry. Coconuts with moldy or wet *eyes* are not fresh.
Water Content Before Drying—51%.
Preparation—Pierce the end of the coconut with an ice pick and drain the milk for drinking or to blend with other fruit juices. Crack around the middle of the hard outer shell with a hammer and steam 30 seconds to 1 minute to loosen the coconut meat or pry it out with a sturdy knife. Trim the dark outer skin. Grate or slice in chunks for drying.
Pretreatment—None.
Drying Temperature—110°F (45°C) until dry.
Dryness Test—Leathery to crisp.
How to Use—Dried coconut may be used in cakes, cookies, desserts, granola, appetizers, candies or pies. It is a delicious garnish for fruit leathers and fresh fruit salad.

Crab Apples

Because of their small size and tartness, crab apples are not recommended for drying. However, the pleasant tart varieties may be combined with other fruits in fruit leather. Avoid bitter varieties.

Cranberries

Cranberries are best combined with other fruits in fruit leather.

Quality When Dried—Fair.

Selection—Either the large bright red variety or the smaller sweeter dark cranberry may be dried. Select fresh, firm glossy berries. Before processing, cranberries should be stored at refrigerator temperature, 35° to 40°F (1° to 5°C), to maintain the highest quality.

Water Content Before Drying—88%.

Preparation—Wash to remove any traces or dirt or fungicide.

Pretreatment—Dipping in boiling water to crack the skins is optional, but if cranberries are dried without any pretreatment, they remain puffy, very lightweight and take forever to dry!

Drying Temperature—140°F (60°C) until dry.

Dryness Test—Shriveled, light in weight with no sign of moisture, although the dried berries tend to be sticky. The moisture content in dried cranberries should be only about 5%.

How To Use—Dried cranberries may be used in cranberry sauce but are not very satisfactory. Crumbled and added to desserts, they will give a tangy flavor.

Currants

Do not attempt to dry red currants. Dry only black currants which are a variety of grape.

Quality When Dried—Good.

Selection—Firm, ripe, seedless black varieties such as the Black Corinth, may be dried, resulting in a dark raisin with a tart, tangy flavor.

Water Content Before Drying—81%.

Preparation—Do not remove stems. Wash well to remove dirt or bacteria. Or they may be dried first and then lightly washed, stems removed and redried for a few minutes to remove surface moisture.

Pretreatment—None.

Drying Temperature—140°F (60°C) for 2 to 3 hours, 130°F (55°C) until dry.

Dryness Test—Leathery.

How To Use—Substitute for raisins in cookies and breads. Dried currants are traditionally used in Hot Cross Buns.

Dates

Store-bought dates are usually sun dried.

Quality When Dried—Excellent.

Varieties Best For Drying—Fresh dates are classified as dry, semi-dry or soft. Dry varieties contain sucrose, not inverted sugar, and only a small amount of moisture when ripe. They are non-perishable. Most soft or semi-dry varieties are perishable because of the moisture content. Deglet Noor is the most popular dried date.

Selection—Fresh dates should be plump with a rich red or golden color. Allow to ripen on the tree.

Water Content Before Drying—23%.

Preparation—Wash Well.

Pretreatment—None.

Drying Temperature—130°F (55°C) until dry.

Dryness Test—Leathery with a deep russet or brown color.

How To Use—Dates may be eaten as a snack or added to cookies, cakes, granola, breads and desserts. Or use to sweeten fruit leathers or yogurt.

Figs

Figs are the only dried fruit high in calcium and phosphorus, minerals which are necessary for bone building and body maintenance. They have an extremely low sodium content. Three pounds of fresh figs make 1 pound dried. Figs are naturally sweet and 55 percent of the weight of dried figs is natural sugar. For sun drying, stack trays of partly dried figs. Overexposure to the sun toughens their skin and reduces their flavor.

Quality When Dried—Excellent.

Varieties Best For Drying—The Black Mission variety has rather small seeds and a pleasant flavor when dried. White Adriatics are medium-size, have a high sugar content and an attractive dried appearance. The all-purpose Kadota is relatively small, almost seedless, and a beautiful creamy amber color when ripe. The Calimyrna fig is very large, has a rich yellow color and large seeds.

Selection—Figs mature slowly compared with most fruits and the sugar concentration also increases slowly while they mature. They are not picked from the tree, but allowed to fall. Ripeness or maturity cannot be judged by size. They should be quickly harvested when they fall from the tree, as they are already partly dried and usually free from mold or decay.

Water Content Before Drying—78%.

Preparation—Wash carefully to remove dirt. Remove stems. Large figs may be halved or quartered to shorten the drying time. Dry them skin-side down.

Pretreatment—Figs to be sun dried may be sulfured for 1 hour to discourage insects. Figs dried in a dehydrator need no pretreatment.

Drying Temperature—160°F (70°C) for 1 to 2 hours, 130°F (55°C) until dry.

Dryness Test—Leathery. No pockets of moisture.

How To Use—Dried figs may be stewed or added to fruit compotes and garnished with yogurt or whipping cream. Chopped stewed figs may be sweetened with honey, combined with nuts and served as an unusual sandwich spread or used as a filling for a thin dessert omelet. Use them in fruit salads, cakes, puddings, breads and cookies. Additional information and recipes may be obtained from the California Fig Advisory Board, Dept. DD, 3425 North First, Suite 109, Fresno, CA 93726. (209) 445-5626 FAX (209) 224-3449. Include a business-size, self-addressed, stamped envelope.

Grapes

About 4-1/2 pounds of grapes yield 1 pound of raisins. Raisins are high in iron and contain about 70 percent natural sugar. Stored at 40° to 50°F (5° to 10°C), raisins will retain their color, flavor and nutritional value up to 15 months.

Quality When Dried—Excellent.

Varieties Best For Drying—The Thompson Seedless is best for drying. Sultanas may also be dried. The Muscat is dried commercially and its seeds are removed mechanically during processing. The seeded varieties may be home dried, but the seeds must be removed by hand.

Selection—Select fully ripe sweet grapes which are still firmly attached to the stems. They should be smooth and plump and well-colored. Store grapes at refrigerator temperature, 35° to 40°F (1° to 3°C), to maintain the highest quality. If grapes are harvested during rainy periods or following slight freezes, store for a very short time.

Water Content Before Drying—81%.

Preparation—For golden raisins, sulfur the Thompson variety 1 hour before drying. It is possible to steam them until the skin cracks, which decreases drying time, retains light color, but lessens flavor.

Drying Temperature—160°F (70°C) for 1 to 2 hours, 130°F (55°C) until dry.

Dryness Test—Leathery. No pockets of moisture.

How To Use—Raisins are a treat alone or combined with other dried fruits and nuts. They add texture and flavor to baked goods, pancakes or muffins, and can be sprinkled on cold or hot cereals.

Additional information and recipes are available free of charge from the California Raisin Advisory Board, P.O. Box 5335, Fresno, CA 93755. (209) 224-7010 FAX (209) 224-7016

Huckleberries

See Berries, page 28.

Kiwi Fruit

Originally called the *Chinese gooseberry,* the kiwifruit was introduced to the U.S. from New Zealand. Sparkling green flesh is hidden underneath the fuzzy brown exterior of this 2-inch oval fruit. With a flavor and edible seeds similar to strawberries, this fruit dries very well.

Quality When Dried—Excellent.

Varieties Best For Drying—Hayward variety is the only one presently available.

Selection—Kiwi fruit should be soft as a ripe peach, free from decay, internal injury or broken skin. Ideal storage conditions are 32°F (0°C) with 90 to 95% humidity. Ripe kiwi fruit can be stored for about 4 weeks under these conditions. Shelf life is about 2 weeks for moderately ripe fruit.

Water Content Before Drying—82%.

Preparation—Wash and remove outer skin. Slice 1/2 inch thick, either crosswise or oblong.

Drying Temperature—140°F (60°C).

Dryness Test—Leathery and pliable with no pockets of moisture.

How to Use—Eat as a candylike snack.

Additional information and recipes may be obtained free of charge from the California Kiwi fruit Commission, 1540 River Park Dr., Suite #110, Sacramento, CA 95815. (916) 929-5314 FAX (916) 929-3740

Melons

Dried muskmelons have a distinct musklike flavor. Dried melon tastes like saltwater taffy! Choose the ripest melons for the sweetest dried flavors.

Quality When Dried—Fair to Good.

Varieties Best for Drying—Muskmelon, such as cantaloupe and honeydew, and watermelon.

Selection—Melons should be picked when they are mature, firm and heavy for their size.

Water Content Before Drying—81%.

Preparation—Wash and remove outer skin, any fibrous tissue and seeds. Slice 1/2 inch thick.

Pretreatment—None.

Drying Temperature—160°F (70°C) for 2 to 3 hours, 130°F (55°C) until dry.

Dryness Test—Leathery and pliable with no pockets of moisture; taffy-like.

How to Use—Eat as a candylike snack. The strong, distinctive flavor will prohibit mixing with other fruits.

Nectarines

Nectarines have smooth skins. Although the skin is tough when dried, most people prefer to leave it intact. Nectarines may be used interchangeably with peaches.

Quality When Dried—Excellent.

Selection—Pick mature nectarines for flavor and sweetness. They do not increase in sugar after harvesting. They should be fully colored, firm and plump with a slight softening along the seam. Store at refrigerator temperature, between 35° and 40°F (1° to 3°C), for short periods before processing to maintain highest quality.

Water Content Before Drying—82%.

Preparation—Wash and halve fruit; remove pit. Either cut into 3/8- to 1/2-inch slices or cut into quarters and dry skin-side down.

Pretreatment—Sulfur slices for 45 minutes to 1 hour; sulfur halves or quarters for 1-1/2 to 3 hours. *Or* soak for 10 to 15 minutes in a solution of 1 to 2 tablespoons sodium bisulfite per gallon of water. Rinse in clear water.

Drying Temperature—160°F (70°C) for 2 to 3 hours, 130°F (55°C) until dry.

Dryness Test—Pliable or leathery with no pockets or moisture.

How To Use—Nectarines may be used dried or slightly plumped in breads, chutney, cobblers, cookies, dumplings, granola and pies.

Papayas

The drug *papain* is extracted from the papaya. Papain is used in treating digestive ailments and is the main ingredient in meat tenderizers.

Quality When Dried—Good.

Selection—Papayas are round to oblong, yellow to dark orange and as heavy as 10 to 12 pounds. Select mature, smooth-skinned fruit. May be ripened at room temperature.

Water Content Before Drying—89%.

Preparation—Wash outer skin well, cut in half and remove the black seeds attached to the walls of the inner cavity. Peel thinly and cut lengthwise into 3/8-inch slices.

Pretreatment—None.

Drying Temperature—160°F (70°C) for 1 hour, 130°F (55°C) until dry.

Dryness Test—Leathery and pliable with no pockets of moisture.

How To Use—Dried papaya may be eaten alone or combined with pineapple, orange and banana.

Peaches

Quality When Dried—Excellent.

Varieties Best For Drying—Both freestone and clingstone varieties may be dried. Freestone peaches usually have a softer texture than clingstone and do not dry as well, but their stones are easier to remove.

Selection—Peaches must ripen on the tree. Their flavor and sweetness will not develop during storage. Select firm ripe fruit that is heavy for its size, firm-textured rather than pithy, and with the most pronounced flavor. Green or underripe fruit will yield a grayish product with poor flavor and woody texture. If you must wait to process peaches, hold them at refrigerator temperature, 35° to 40°F (1° to 3°C) for best quality.

Water Content Before Drying—89%.

Preparation—Wash and scald to remove skins. When sun drying, halve or quarter washed, unpeeled peaches and remove pits. Sun dry with skins intact. Or cut peaches into 1/2-inch slices. Hold in a solution of 1 teaspoon ascorbic acid per quart water *or* a solution of 1/4 teaspoon sodium bisulfite per quart water until ready to pretreat.

Pretreatment—Sulfur 1/2-inch slices for 45 minutes to 1 hour. Sulfur halves or quarters for 2 to 3 hours. *Or* soak for 5 to 15 minutes, depending on the thickness, in a solution of 1 to 2 tablespoons sodium bisulfite per gallon water. Rinse in clear water.

Drying Temperature—150°F (65°C) for 2 to 3 hours, 130°F (55°C) until dry.

Dryness Test—Leathery and pliable with no pockets of moisture.

How To Use—Peaches may be used dried or slightly plumped in breads, chutney, cobblers, cookies, dumplings, granola and pies.

Pears

Pears do not readily absorb sulfur fumes, hence the longer sulfuring times.

Quality When Dried—Excellent.

Varieties Best For Drying—Bartlett or Summer pears are the best variety for drying, although other varieties may be dried.

Selection—Pears ripen to perfection only when they are removed from the tree. They should be picked while still green and stored at refrigerator temperature, 35° to 40°F (1° to 3°C), until ready to ripen. Ripen in a dark place between 65° and 75°F (20° to 25°C). When ready for drying, the pears should be fully ripe but not soft or mushy.

Water Content Before Drying—83%.

Preparation—The dried peel tends to be tough and grainy, so wash pears and peel thinly. Remove core with spoon or pear corer and cut lengthwise into 1/2-inch slices. Pears may also be halved or quartered; drying time will be considerably longer and the flavor slightly different. Hold in a solution of 1 teaspoon ascorbic acid per quart of water *or* a solution of 1/4 teaspoon sodium bisulfite per quart of water until ready to pretreat. Do not prepare large quantities at a time because the soft texture will begin to deteriorate.

Pretreatment—Sulfur 1/2-inch slices for 45 minutes to 1 hour. Sulfur halves or quarters for 3 to 6 hours. *Or* soak in solution of 1 to 2 tablespoons sodium bisulfite per gallon of water for 5 to 15 minutes, depending on thickness. Rinse in clear water.

Drying Temperature—160°F (70°C) for 2 to 3 hours, 130°F (55°C) until dry.

Dryness Test—Leathery and pliable with no pockets of moisture.

How To Use—Pears may be used dried or slightly plumped in breads, chutney, cobblers, cookies, fritters and granola.

Pears (Asian)

The Asian pear is juicy like a pear and crisp like an apple. It is a true pear (not a hybrid of apple/pear) and a relative newcomer to the American market.

Quality When Dried—Excellent.

Varieties Best For Drying—There are about 10 different varieties, all suitable for drying.

Selection—Skin color is a fairly reliable guide to ripeness. They are usually sold ripe and ready to eat. Green-skinned varieties are at their best for eating when they turn yellow-green in color. They will store refrigerated, unwashed, in a plastic or paper bag for up to 3 months, at room temperature for about a week.

Water Content Before Drying—81%.

Preparation—Wash and remove outer skin. Core and slice crosswise 1/2 inch thick crosswise.

Drying Temperature—140°F (60°C).

Dryness Test—Leathery and pliable with no pockets of moisture.

How to Use—Eat as a candylike snack or use in recipes as you would dried pears.

Persimmons

Quality When Dried—Fair.

Varieties Best For Drying—Fuyu or Hachiya may both be dried.

Selection—Persimmons are round or egg-shaped and are usually less than 2 inches in diameter. They are usually yellowish or orange but may be streaked with red. For a sweeter fruit flavor, select fully ripe fruit that looks wrinkled and almost spoiled. Persimmons contain a strong mouth-puckering astringent. It is particularly strong in slightly under-ripe fruit.

Water Content Before Drying—79%.

Preparation—Wash carefully and remove the stem cap. Cut the fruit in half and then into 3/8- to 1/2-inch slices.

Pretreatment—None.

Drying Temperature—140°F (60°C) for 1 to 2 hours, 130°F (55°C) until dry.

Dryness Test—Dried persimmons are light to medium brown. They should be tender and pliable but not sticky.

How to Use—Dried persimmons may be eaten as a snack or used in sweet breads or cookies.

Pineapples

Because of the high acid content and the enzyme, bromelin, large quantities of fresh or dried pineapple eaten at one time may give some people canker sores. If you plan to dry more than 2 to 3 pineapples at one time, wear rubber gloves during preparation to protect your hands from the acid.

Quality When Dried—Excellent.

Selection—Dry only fully ripe pineapples with a yellowish-brown shell. Pineapples may be harvested when partly green and, although the color changes during transportation, pineapples will not actually ripen after they are picked. The natural sugar content does not increase after picking. Large pineapples are a better buy than small ones. Fresh, deep crown leaves indicate freshness. Smelling the bottom of the pineapple can sometimes tell you how sweet it is or if it is over-ripe and has begun to ferment. Over-ripe fruit may be slightly decayed at the base and the sides may have dark, soft, watery spots. Store pineapples at room temperature away from the sun until fully colored to lower the natural acid content, then refrigerate at 45°F (5°C) to prevent spoilage.

Water Content Before Drying—86%.

Preparation—Wash, peel and remove thorny eyes. Slice lengthwise and remove the small core. Cut crosswise into 1/2-inch slices.

Pretreatment—Pineapple may be dried without any pretreatment. For longer storage or to retain more vitamin C, sulfur 1/2-inch slices for 1 hour.

Drying Temperature—160°F (70°C) for 1 to 2 hours, 130°F (55°C) until dry.

Dryness Test—Leathery but not sticky.

How To Use—Dried pineapple has a high natural sugar content. Use it in cakes, cookies, candies, fritters or sauces. Do not use dried pineapple in gelatin because the enzyme will prevent the gelatin from setting.

Plums

All prunes are plums, but not all plums are prunes. Most varieties of plums will ferment if dried with pits in. Slice fruit from the pits and dry.

Quality When Dried—Good.

Varieties Best For Drying—There are over 150 important varieties of plums, most of which can be dried satisfactorily. They may be as small as a cherry or as large as a small peach and are red, blue, purple, green or yellow. Prune plums are specific varieties which are grown for drying and are listed separately, see below.

Selection—Select fully mature, fresh, sweet fruit, free from soft spots and blemishes. Before processing, store plums at refrigerator temperature, 35° to 40°F (1° to 3°C), to maintain highest quality.

Water Content Before Drying—Damon, 81%; Japanese and Hybrid, 87%.

Preparation—Wash and cut in half. Many plums must be cut free from the stone, others may have a freestone which is easily removed. Cut into 1/4- to 3/8-inch slices, leaving peel intact.

Drying Temperature—160°F (70°C) for 1 to 2 hours, 130°F (55°C) until dry.

Dryness Test—Pliable and leathery.

How To Use—Dried plums are excellent eaten as is, although the skins are slightly tough. Use them in cookies, muffins, breads, cakes, granola and puddings.

Prune Plums

About 2-1/2 to 3 pounds of fresh prunes with pits yield 1 pound of dried prunes. Prunes are an excellent source of iron and also contain potassium, calcium and phosphorus, vitamin A, thiamine, riboflavin and niacin. They supply the soft bulk necessary for good elimination, and are very high in natural sugar.

Quality When Dried—Excellent.

Varieties Best For Drying—High-quality prunes should have a good flavor, be medium to large in size, have a fine texture, high sugar content and smooth small pits. The D'Agen or California French Prune makes up 92 percent of the commercial production of California prunes. Other good varieties for drying include Imperials, Robe de Sergeant, Sugar, Burtons, Brooks and Italian.

Selection—Prunes should fully ripen on the tree before being picked to ensure the highest natural sugar content. Shake the tree and the ripe prunes will fall, or pick only those which come off very easily. They should be slightly soft but not mushy, very sweet, and have a lustrous color. Before processing, store prunes at refrigerator temperature, 35° to 40°F (1° to 3°C), to maintain the highest quality.

Water Content Before Drying—79%.

Preparation—Wash well to remove dirt or insect larvae. Halve, remove stone and flatten by pushing in the cupped side with your thumbs. This will greatly reduce drying time by increasing drying surface. Dry skin-side down to prevent juice dripping. Prunes may be dried whole, but the drying time will be about 4 times as long. To dry whole, dip in boiling water to crack or *check* the skins. This hastens drying time by about 50 percent. Prunes dried whole tend to drip more during drying.

Pretreatment—None.

Drying Temperature—160°F (70°C) for 2 to 3 hours, 140°F (60°C) until dry.

Dryness Test—Leathery and pliable with no pockets of moisture. Because no preservatives are added to inhibit mold growth, the moisture content should be about 18% to store satisfactorily. If it is higher, the prunes will mold during storage.

How To Use—Dried prunes are excellent as a snack. To plump, steam 2 to 3 minutes or soak in fruit juice. To stew, simmer for a few minutes, season with all-spice, cloves, cinnamon, lemon, nutmeg, orange, sherry or vanilla. Prunes can be used in cookies, muffins, brownies, breads, coffeecakes, strudels and pies. They are delicious in candies, salads, puddings, stuffings, gelatin desserts and meat sauces.

Additional information and recipes are available from the California Prune Advisory Board, World Trade Center, San Francisco, CA 94111.

Rhubarb

Rhubarb is technically a vegetable, but it is usually served in desserts as a fruit. *The leaves of rhubarb contain poisonous oxalic acid salts and should not be eaten.*

Quality When Dried—Good.

Varieties Best For Drying—The bright red sweeter varieties such as Canada Red, Valentine, Ruby, MacDonald or Victoria dry best.

Selection—Rhubarb stalks should be pulled soon after they reach full size and should be firm, straight, crisp, glossy and brightly colored. To harvest, remove the larger outside stalks, pulling firmly from the base. Leave at least 1/3 of the inner plant stalk intact, as rhubarb is a perennial plant and will continue to produce for 5 to 8 years. Do not cut the stalks. Refrigerate them until ready to process. Rhubarb can be stored 2 to 3 weeks at refrigerator temperature, 35° to 40°F (1° to 3°C).

Water Content Before Drying—95%.

Preparation—Wash, trim and slice diagonally into 1-inch slices. *Discard leaves.*

Pretreatment—Steam for 1 to 2 minutes or until slightly tender but not soft.

Drying Temperature—150°F (65°C) for 2 to 3 hours, 130°F (55°C) until dry.

Dryness Test—Tough to crisp.

How To Use—Rhubarb may be combined with strawberries or apples in pies, or used as a filling for strudels, tarts or in other baked goods.

Strawberries

Quality When Dried—Excellent.

Varieties Best For Drying—Sweeter varieties which have a full red color and firm texture dry best.

Selection—Choose firm, ripe, red berries with a solid color. They should be picked when fully ripe. They will not develop natural sugar if picked when slightly green and will not continue to ripen off the vine.

Water Content Before Drying—90%.

Preparation—Gently wash strawberries about a quart at a time in plenty of cold water. Remove berries from the water with a slotted spoon and drain in a colander. Remove the cap and cut into 1/2-inch slices, or cut smaller berries in half. Dry skin-side down. Berries sliced too thin will stick to the drying surface.

Pretreatment—None is necessary. They may be dipped in a solution containing 1/2 teaspoon of ascorbic acid per cup of water to increase the vitamin C content.

Drying Temperature—150°F (65°C) for 1 to 2 hours, 130°F (55°C) until dry.

Dryness Test—Strawberries should be pliable and leathery with no pockets of moisture.

How To Use—Dried strawberries may be eaten as a snack, sprinkled on dry or cooked cereals, combined with granola or used in ice cream, milk shakes or yogurt. They are not good when rehydrated because they lose their firm texture.

Drying Canned Fruit

Fruit which has been canned in its own juice or sugar syrup may be removed from the can (or jar) and dehydrated. This is an ideal way to use canned or bottled fruit that is older than a year or that your family doesn't enjoy.

Simply drain, place in a colander and rinse lightly under cool water to remove the surface syrup and reduce stickiness when dry.

Dry fruits until they are leathery with no visible pockets of moisture. Dried canned fruits resemble glacéed or candied fruits, make great lunch box or hiking snacks and can be used for candied fruit in most fruitcake recipes.

How Much Does Your Dried Fruit Cost?

To figure your cost, multiply the cost in *cents* per kilowatt hours, which you can find from your electric bill, *times* the *hours* to dry and then *divide* by the finished weight of your food. Add the initial *cost* of the *fresh food divided by* the *weight* of the *dried food*.

$$\frac{\text{Cost per kwh X Hours to dry}}{\text{weight of dried foods}} + \frac{\text{initial cost of food}}{\text{weight of dried food}} = \frac{\text{cost per pound}}{\text{of dried food}}$$

For example, if you can load 10 pounds of apples (at \$.25 per pound) in your dryer and it takes 12 hours to get 2 pounds of dried apples, at \$.06 per Kwh (an average rate in the U.S.), the cost would be:

$$\frac{.06 \text{ X } 12}{2} + \frac{\$2.50}{2} = \$1.61 \text{ per pound of dried apples}$$

Commercially dried foods cost more because the price includes the cost of the fruit or vegetables, drying, packaging materials, distribution costs, advertising and retailer's markup.

Fruit Leather

Fruit leather is a chewy fruit product. It is made by pureeing fresh, canned or frozen fruit to a smooth thick liquid which is poured onto a flat surface. As the puree slowly dries, it takes on a leather-like appearance and texture. When dry, fruit leather can be pulled off the drying surface and still hold its shape.

A delicious snack, fruit leather is perfect for lunch boxes during the winter when fresh fruit is expensive or unavailable. It can be cut into small pieces or chips and added to cereals, puddings and desserts for a fresh fruit flavor.

No one knows where the idea for fruit leather originated. It has been made for several hundred years by the people of Hunza, a small state in the Himalayan mountains in northwest Pakistan. Apricots are one of the most important foods to the long-living Hunzakuts who use primitive methods to make them into leather. They first pound the apricot pulp until it is smooth and then spread it on smooth flat surfaces to dry in the sun.

Recently fruit leather has been made commercially. The next time you're in the supermarket, look in the produce or candy section for long thin cellophane-wrapped rolls called *fruit rolls* or something similar. You'll probably find them expensive and decide it's more economical to make fruit leather at home. It is fun to make and, if made from fresh fruit, has the advantage of being free of preservatives. Fruit leather can be made with or without added sweetenings.

WHAT FRUITS CAN YOU USE

The fruit combinations are limitless. You can vary them by adding spices, garnishes or fillings. Use the table on pages 42 and 43 as a guide to create your own delicious fruit leather blends.

Fresh Fruits—Use fresh fruits in season. Fruit leather is ideal for using the culls and slightly bruised or over-ripe fruit unsuitable for canning or drying. Cut away any bruised or spoiled portions, then puree. What about citrus fruits? Citrus fruits should only be used in combination with other fruits because they contain so much liquid and so little pulp.

If you are canning fruits, puree some of the fruit in the blender, cook if necessary, and freeze it in airtight containers. When you aren't pressed for time and your dryer isn't full, thaw the puree and dry as you would fresh puree.

Canned Fruits—You can make fruit leather from fruit which has been home or commercially canned. Drain the syrup and puree the fruit in the blender. For a fresher flavor, add 1 tablespoon fresh lemon juice per quart of puree or blend the pureed canned fruit with a puree of fresh fruit such as pineapple or apple.

Frozen Fruits—Thaw frozen fruit and follow the directions for making fruit leather.

Leftover Pulp—When canning juices or making homemade jelly, save the pulp. Press it through a food mill or colander to remove the seeds and peels. Add enough juice to flavor it and bring it to a pouring consistency. Then dry the pulp mixture as you would pureed fresh fruit.

HOW TO MAKE FRUIT LEATHER

> **You Will Need:**
> **Heavy plastic sheets**
> **Blender**

Line a drying tray with a fruit-leather sheet or use mylar or food-grade 4mil plastic. Kitchen plastic wrap may be used, but must be taped to all four sides with masking tape. This prevents the wrap from blowing over the leather as it dries. *Do not use wax paper or aluminum foil.* They tend to stick and you might have to eat them with the leather! You can also use non-stick baking sheets lightly coated with vegetable oil or with a non-stick vegetable spray.

Wash and prepare the fruit according to the directions on the fruit leather table, pages 42 and 43. Puree the fruit in the blender until it is very smooth. To make leather 18" x 14" x 1/4", you will need about 2-1/2 cups of puree. In some blenders, you may have to add a small amount of water or fruit juice to start the blending process.

1/Sort, wash and remove any stems, peels or cores. Blend the fruit to a smooth puree.

2/Pour the puree onto prepared drying trays. The puree should be about 1/4 inch thick.

Add as little water or juice as possible. Heat some fruit purees, page 42, to prevent darkening and cool them before combining with other purees or flavorings.

Combine fruits after they have been pureed. Then add sweetening, spices or flavorings. Fruit that is fully ripe produces the best flavored leather and usually needs no sweetening. If the puree is too tart, add 1 tablespoon of light corn syrup or honey for each quart of puree. Repeat until puree is sweet enough.

Pour the puree onto the prepared drying tray. Slightly tilt the tray to help the puree spread evenly. Leave at least a 1-inch border to allow for spreading during drying. You may also make 4- to 6-inch fruit leather pancakes by pouring smaller amounts. Garnish leather while it is still moist, then dry it until it feels leather-like and is pliable. There should be no sticky spots in the center.

Remove the leather from the tray *while it is still warm* and roll it up. Cooled fruit leather does not roll as easily.

Fruit leather dried in a dehydrator is usually done in 6 to 8 hours. Sun dried leather may take 1 to 2 days depending on the temperature, humidity and breeze. Oven drying may take up to 18 hours. And remember, sun and oven drying, because of the longer drying times, will remove more nutrients from the fruit.

SUN DRYING FRUIT LEATHER

Fruit leather can be sun dried successfully in one day if the sun is hot and the humidity low. The only problem is protecting the leather from insects. They usually find it as delicious as we do! Fruit leathers do not have the protection of sulfuring as fruits do to keep away the bugs. Secure cheesecloth or nylon netting over the leather to protect it without touching it. Be sure the screening is anchored. If it blows into the drying leather, you'll have a very sticky mess!

If not completely dry, some of the fruit particles will stick to the drying tray. Occasionally the top surface may be dry, yet the bottom is a little too moist. If this is the case, flip the leather over and dry the bottom until it is no longer sticky.

IF YOU WANT TO ADD SWEETENING

Most leathers need no added sweetening. If the fruit is a little under-ripe or not quite sweet enough, add mild honey or light corn syrup. The honey flavor

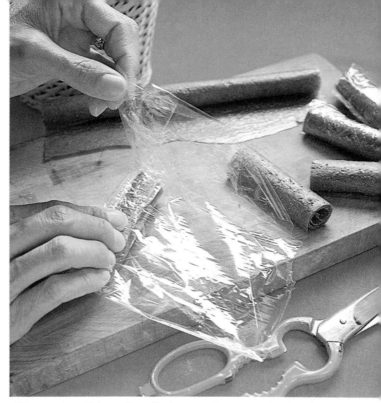

3/Dry the puree until it feels leather-like and pliable. Remove it from the trays while it's still warm and roll it.

4/Cut each roll into 4 to 6 pieces and wrap each piece in plastic wrap. Or wrap each whole roll in plastic wrap.

may be too strong for some fruits. You may prefer to use mild-flavored white corn syrup. Granulated sugar added to fruit leather may crystallize during storage making the leather brittle. Brown sugar doesn't crystallize as readily as granulated sugar, but it adds a different flavor. You may also use liquid brown sugar and artificial sweeteners:

The natural sweetness or any added sweetening will concentrate as the fruit leather dries. Remember this as you taste the puree and gauge the amount of sweetening you add accordingly.

IF YOU WANT TO ADD SPICES OR FLAVORINGS

Spices or flavorings will concentrate when dried so use them sparingly. Experiment with spice and fruit combinations. Add one spice or flavoring at a time in small amounts.

Start with just a pinch of spice or 1/4 teaspoon per quart of puree. Taste the puree before adding more. You should be able to tell that something has been added, but not what. If the flavor shouts at you, you have used too much.

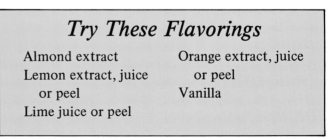

Try These Spices

Allspice	Mace
Cinnamon	Mint
Cloves	Nutmeg
Coriander	Pumpkin Pie Spice
Ginger	

Extracts and fresh juices are fine for flavoring leathers. Extracts are more concentrated than fresh juices, so begin with 1/4 to 1/2 teaspoon per quart of puree. To use fresh citrus juice, begin with 1 tablespoon per quart of puree.

If you want to use grated citrus peel, try 1 teaspoon per quart of puree.

Try These Flavorings

Almond extract	Orange extract, juice
Lemon extract, juice	or peel
or peel	Vanilla
Lime juice or peel	

HOW TO GARNISH

Sprinkle garnishes on fruit leather before drying or while the leather is still quite moist so the garnish will stick. Or mix some of the garnishes with the puree before pouring it out to dry. You can use a garnish alone or combine two or more for a special flavor blend.

Try These Garnishes	
Coconut, shredded	Nuts, chopped
Dates, chopped	Raisins, chopped
Dried fruit, chopped	Poppy seeds
Granola	Sesame seeds
Miniature marshmallows	Sunflower seeds

HOW TO STORE FRUIT LEATHER

Leave the rolls whole or cut them into 4- to 6-inch pieces, which are a good snack size. For 1- to 2-week short-term storage, cut fruit leather rolls into bite-size pieces and shake them in a container with powdered sugar or cornstarch, or both.

Wrap each piece in plastic wrap. Do not roll the plastic wrap inside with the fruit leather as some leathers will stick to the wrap. Place the wrapped pieces in a heavy plastic bag or airtight container. Label the bags or containers clearly with a magic marker or stick-on labels. Include both the date and the flavor. Store them in a cool, dry, dark place.

For longer storage, place the bags or containers in the refrigerator or freezer. Leathers containing nuts or coconut should be stored in the freezer. Do not store leathers with fillings.

To seal leathers for longer storage, place the cut unwrapped rolls of leather inside clean, dry, canning jars. Place a new lid on each jar and lightly screw on the rings. Place the jars in a 165°F (65°C) preheated oven for 25 minutes. Remove the hot jars from the oven and screw on the rings tightly. When the jars are cooled and sealed, a partial vacuum will be created which protects the leather from air and moisture. Label the jars with the date and flavor of fruit leather. Store in a cool, dry, dark place.

How to Garnish Fruit Leather

1/After you have poured the fruit puree onto the drying tray, sprinkle it with garnishes such as nuts and cinnamon. Garnishes will stick to partially dry leather if it is still moist.

2/When the fruit leather is dry, cut it into bite-size pieces. You may prefer to roll up the garnished fruit leather before cutting it.

1/Unroll the fruit leather and spread it with a filling such as cream cheese, leaving about a 1-inch margin.

2/Roll up the fruit leather jelly-roll fashion.

3/Cut the roll into bite-size pieces.

YOU CAN FILL THEM TOO

Filled leathers are festive treats and are much more nutritious than candy. Unroll leathers which have already been dried and spread them with fillings. Then roll again jelly-roll fashion and cut the rolls into bite-size pieces.

Try These Fillings

Chocolate, melted
Cream cheese, softened
Process Cheddar cheese spread
Fruit fillings, see recipes on pages 106 to 108
Fruit jam or preserves
Marmalade
Marshmallow cream
Peanut butter, smooth or crunchy

Secrets of Successful Fruit Leather

Problem	Cause	Prevention or Solution
Puree is too thin.	Very juicy fruits. Too much water added during blending.	Combine with thicker fruit puree. Slowly cook the puree over low heat to evaporate some of the water before drying.
Puree is too thick.	Type of fruit—apple or pumpkin. Using leftover pulp from making juices or jellies—apple, apricot, cherry, grape or plum.	Add fruit juice or water to thin to pouring consistency.
Insects are attracted to leather during sun drying.	Insects find fruit leather delicious!	Cover with cheesecloth or nylon net during drying, using blocks or spools to elevate. Be sure covering is secure and will not blow into the sticky leather.
Leather sticks to drying surface.	Drying surface is not suitable for drying leather. Wax paper or foil do not work. Puree is too thin. Fruits low in natural pectin stick more than fruits higher in pectin—blackberry, cranberry, loganberry, marionberry, raspberry.	Lightly coat surface with vegetable oil or non-stick vegetable spray. Pour puree 1/4 inch thick. Combine low-pectin fruits with fruits containing more pectin such as apple.
Leather is brittle around the edges and still sticky in the middle.	Puree was thicker in center. Uneven air flow in oven or dehydrator.	Tilt drying surface before drying to distribute puree evenly or pour puree a little thicker around the edges Rotate shelves more often. Sun dry if weather permits.
Leather becomes brittle during drying or storage.	Type of fruit—pear, pineapple or rhubarb. Insufficient air circulation as in oven drying. Too high heat, leather dried too quickly. Overdrying.	Combine with other fruits. Rotate trays or sun dry. Check temperature. It should not exceed 140°F (60°C). Watch carefully near end of drying. Use brittle leather chips as dessert toppings, in baked goods or reconstituted in baby food.
Leather is grainy.	Peelings were left on fruit when pureed—especially pears.	Peel fruit for leather. Combine pear with other fruit such as apples.
Leather is too seedy.	Failure to sieve out enough seeds.	Sieve puree through strainer to remove as many seeds as possible before drying.
Leather turns excessively dark.	Enzymatic browning occurs in some fruits—apple, apricot, peach and pear. Improperly wrapped for storage—light, air and moisture tend to darken fruit leather. Storage location is too warm—heat tends to darken.	Heat puree to almost boiling to retard browning. Wrap securely in plastic wrap, then store in moisture-proof containers in a dark place. Store in cool place or in freezer.
Leather molds during storage.	Leather is too moist when wrapped. Improperly packaged so moisture is absorbed by the leather.	Be sure leather has no moist or sticky areas. Wrap securely in plastic wrap, then store in moisture-proof container.

Fruit Leather at a Glance

Fruit	Preparation	Combine With Other Purees	Spices or Flavorings And Sweetening
Apples	Wash and core. Puree with or without skins in blender in a small amount of water or juice. Or apples may be cooked, then pureed.	All fruits	Allspice, cinnamon, cloves, coriander, lemon, mint, nutmeg, orange, vanilla, white corn syrup, honey
Apricots	Wash and pit. Puree with skins in blender. To retain light color, heat to almost boiling, or add 1/16 teaspoon sodium bisulfite to 1 quart uncooked puree.	Apple Pineapple Plum	Allspice, cinnamon, cloves, coriander, lemon, nutmeg, orange, white corn syrup, honey, brown sugar
Bananas	Peel. Puree in blender.	Apple-Berry Lemon-walnut Orange-pineapple	Cinnamon, cloves, coriander, lemon, nutmeg, orange, vanilla, white corn syrup, honey, brown sugar
Berries Blackberries Loganberries Marionberries	Wash. Puree in blender. Sieve to remove most of seeds.	Combine with apple to improve texture.	Cinnamon, lemon, white corn syrup
Blueberries	Wash. Puree in blender.	Too bland alone; combine with apple or peach.	Cinnamon, coriander, lemon, white corn syrup
Cherries	Wash and remove stones. Puree in blender. Heat to almost boiling. Cool.	Apple Apple-pineapple Banana Pineapple Raspberry Rhubarb	Almond extract, cinnamon lemon, orange, white corn syrup
Cranberries	Wash. Puree in blender.	Apple Apple-date Apple-orange Apple-pear	Cinnamon, cloves, ginger, lemon, orange, white corn syrup, honey
Grapes	Wash. Puree in blender. Sieve to remove seeds. Cook to thicken. If using leftover pulp from grape juice, put through food mill to remove seeds and skins; add juice for desired consistency.	Apple Raspberry	Lemon, white corn syrup
Peaches Nectarines	Boil 2 minutes to remove skins. Halve fruits; remove stones. Puree in blender. To retain light color, heat to almost boiling or add 1/16 teaspoon sodium bisulfite to 1 quart uncooked puree.	Apple Blueberry Pineapple Plum Raspberry	Cinnamon, cloves, ginger, almond, nutmeg, white corn syrup, honey
Pears	Peel and core. Puree in blender. To retain light color, heat to almost boiling or add 1/16 teaspoon sodium bisulfite to 1 quart uncooked puree. Puree tends to be watery when not mixed with another puree.	Improved when combined with Apple Apple-cranberry Pineapple Rhubarb	Cinnamon, cloves, coriander lemon, mace (dash only), nutmeg, orange, white corn syrup, honey
Pineapples	Remove outer skin, eyes and core. Puree in blender.	Apple-orange Apricot Cherry Rhubarb-strawberry	Lemon, orange, white corn syrup

Fruit Leather at a Glance (continued)

Fruit	Preparation	Combine With Other Purees	Spices or Flavorings And Sweetening
Plums	Wash and remove stones. Puree in blender.	Apple Apricot Peach Pear	Cinnamon, coriander, lemon orange, white corn syrup
Pumpkin	Cut into large pieces, peel and remove seeds. Steam until soft. Puree in blender.	Apple	Cinnamon, ginger, nutmeg, pumpkin pie spice, white or dark corn syrup, honey
Raspberries	Wash. Puree in blender. Sieve to remove seeds.	Apple	Lemon, mint, orange, white corn syrup
Rhubarb	Wash and steam until tender. Puree in blender.	Improved when combined with Cherry Raspberry Strawberry Strawberry-pineapple	Lemon, orange, white corn syrup
Strawberries	Wash. If desired, puree in blender. Sieve through fine strainer to remove seeds.	Apple Apple-rhubarb Peach Pineapple Rhubarb	Lemon, orange, white corn syrup

FRUIT LEATHER CHIPS

If it is dried too long, fruit leather may become brittle and crack when peeled off. If this happens, chip off the brittle pieces for snacking, or chop them in the blender to make *leather chips* for toppings on cereals and puddings.

Leather chips can be reconstituted by soaking in hot water for 10 to 15 minutes. Use 1/2 cup of hot water for each cup of chips. Stir the reconstituted chips in a blender for a smooth consistency.

Reconstituted fruit leather is a delicious and nutritious flavoring for yogurt, ice cream, milk shakes and baby cereal; see pages 72 and 73. Store dried chips in airtight glass or plastic containers.

Camping & Trail Foods

Dried foods are ideal for backpacking and camping because they keep well without refrigeration and are low in bulk and weight. Meat and fish jerky are satisfying snacks. Dried nuts and seeds are not only delicious but high in protein, fat and other nutrients, making them excellent sources of energy. Dried fruits and fruit leathers will appeal to a camper's sweet tooth and are quick energy foods.

If you start with supermarket convenience foods and dress them up with home dried foods, you will add flavor and nutritive value to outdoor meals. Try a ready-to-cook soup base with your own dried vegetables. Add dried meats and vegetables to packaged rice or potato dishes. For dessert, stir dried fruits into prepared puddings.

Dried foods will be easy to carry and use if you package them in individual plastic bags. Group the small bags in larger bags according to the meals they will be used for. Then label the large bags: *Breakfast, Lunch, Dinner* or *Trail Food* so the dried foods needed for each meal will be easily accessible in one bag.

Allow enough time to reconstitute dried foods. An hour or two before you plan to cook, add water to the fruits and vegetables in their own plastic bags. To prevent leaks, place the bags in a second plastic bag. Let the food rehydrate while you set up camp and start the fire.

Glacé Fruit

Glacé or candied fruit is made by removing 50 to 60 percent of the water in the fruit and replacing it with sugar. The fruit is then dried. The process must be done over a 4-day period. The result is candied fruit with a much higher sugar concentration than natural fruit.

Fruits that glacé well are apples, apricots, cherries, citrus peel, peaches, pears, pineapple and prunes. See the individual fruits, pages 27 to 35, for proper selection. When you prepare apples, apricots, peaches and pears, holding the cut pieces in a solution of 1 teaspoon ascorbic acid per quart of water until all the pieces are ready will preserve their fresh color and texture.

Preparing Fruit for Glacé

Fruit	Preparation
Apples	Wash, peel, core and slice apples 1/4 inch thick.
Apricots	Wash and cut in half. Remove pits.
Cherries	Wash cherries and remove stems and pits.
Citrus peel	To prevent bitterness, use the outer 3/16 inch of peel. Cover with water and boil 15 minutes. Drain before adding peel to syrup.
Peaches	Wash and scald peaches. Skin will peel off easily. Cut in 1/2-inch slices.
Pears	Wash, peel thinly and core. Cut lengthwise in 1/2-inch slices. Do not prepare large quantities of pears at a time as the soft texture will begin to deteriorate.
Pineapple	Wash and peel pineapple. Remove thorny eyes. Cut lengthwise and remove the core. Cut crosswise in 1/2-inch slices.
Prune Plums	Wash, cut in half and remove stone. Flatten by pushing in the cupped side with your thumbs.

How to Glacé Fruit

1/Assemble the ingredients and equipment. Prepare the sugar syrup and proceed with the recipe.

2/After the fruit and syrup have cooked, cooled and stood at room temperature, carefully remove the fruit from the syrup with a slotted spoon. Add sugar to the syrup and bring the mixture to a boil.

HOW TO GLACÉ

The following directions are for 1-1/2 pounds of prepared fruit. To glacé citrus peel, use 3/4 pound of peel and halve the remaining ingredients.

FIRST DAY

2 cups water   1/2 cup white corn syrup
2/3 cup sugar   1-1/2 lbs. prepared fruit

Combine all ingredients in a large saucepan. Bring to a boil. Add prepared fruit. Heat syrup-fruit mixture to 180°F (80°C) on a candy thermometer. Remove from heat. Cool. Cover and let stand at room temperature 18 to 24 hours.

SECOND DAY

1-1/4 cups sugar

Carefully remove fruit from syrup with a slotted spoon. Add 1-1/4 cups sugar to syrup in saucepan. Bring to a boil. Remove from heat. With a large metal spoon, skim foam from surface of syrup and discard. Add fruit to syrup and heat to 180°F (80°C) on a candy thermometer. Remove from heat. Cool. Cover and let stand at room temperature 18 to 24 hours.

THIRD DAY

2 cups sugar

Repeat process of the second day but add 2 cups of sugar to remaining syrup after removing fruit.

FOURTH DAY

1 cup sugar

Repeat process of the second day but add 1 cup sugar to remaining syrup after removing fruit. After final standing time, remove fruit from syrup. Place in a colander and rinse with cold water. Dry on drying trays at 120° to 140°F (50° to 60°C) until fruit is leathery and has no pockets of moisture. Drying time for glacé fruit will be one-fourth of the drying time for fresh fruit because so much moisture has been replaced by sugar.

FRUIT-FLAVORED PANCAKE SYRUP

The fruit-flavored syrup that is left is delicious on pancakes or waffles. Bring it to a boil, skim the foam from the surface of the syrup and pour the syrup into hot sterilized canning jars. Fill the jars to within 1/8 inch from the top and seal them with sterilized lids and screw bands.

3/Skim the foam from the syrup with a metal spoon before returning the fruit to the syrup. Proceed with the recipe.

4/Serve Glacé Fruit such as apricots and cherries as an elegant confection. Packaged in an attractive gift container, your own Glacé Fruit makes a thoughtful gift.

Vegetables

Vegetables are the edible parts of plants. They can be grouped by the part of the plant we eat. In one group of vegetables we eat the *fruit of the plant,* such as cucumbers, eggplant, melons, peppers, squashes and tomatoes. Another category consists mainly of *leaves* and *stems* of plants. These include asparagus, cabbage, lettuce, rhubarb, spinach and other leafy greens. Another group contains *root* or *tuber* vegetables, such as beets, carrots, onions, parsnips, potatoes, rutabagas and turnips. When we eat beans, sweet corn, peas and soybeans, we are eating the *seeds* of another class of vegetables. Some foods, such as tomatoes and cucumbers are really fruits, but are eaten as vegetables.

Generally, the fruit of the plant, the root or tuber portions and the seeds dry and rehydrate better than stems and leaves. Exceptions are described in the information on specific vegetables, pages 57 to 64.

Vegetables are excellent sources of vitamin A, thiamin, niacin and vitamin C, and also contain minerals, such as calcium, phosphorus and iron. Vegetables add bulk, which aids the digestive process. Peas and beans are good sources of protein.

The only nutrients affected by the drying process are vitamins A and C. Depending on how carefully the vegetables are dried and stored, their loss can be minimized.

YOU NEED TO KNOW

Drying vegetables at home requires a little extra effort for a good-quality product that will be stable in storage, rehydrate well and be tasty and tender when cooked. Some vegetables do not rehydrate satisfactorily and, if you choose to preserve them, are better canned or frozen. Frozen asparagus, cauliflower and broccoli are far superior to dried. Some vegetables, such as carrots and potatoes, are available fresh at reasonable prices all year. I don't recommend drying these unless you do it for convenience or for backpacking.

The fresher the vegetable when it is processed and dried, the better it will taste when rehydrated and cooked. Many dried vegetables that have been rehydrated and cooked are tougher than fresh or frozen ones. This can be caused by the quality of the fresh vegetable when it is processed, the pretreatment before drying, the method used to dry or the storage time.

Freshness—Tenderness may be influenced by *lack of freshness* of the vegetable when it was dried. Green beans, for example, may be kept in the refrigerator for one or two days after picking, then cooked and eaten. They will taste quite fresh. If those same beans are refrigerated two or three days before they are dried, they will be much less tender when rehydrated and cooked.

● Harvest only fresh and mature vegetables.

● Don't let vegetables stand at room temperature any longer than is absolutely necessary.

● If you cannot process vegetables immediately after picking, refrigerate them.

● Do not wash vegetables until just before you are ready to process them. Then dry them as soon as possible. Water speeds up deterioration and loss of nutrients.

Pretreatment—Another factor that influences tenderness of rehydrated vegetables is *pretreatment before drying.* Most vegetables are much more fibrous than fruits. Pretreating by steam or water blanching, softens the tissues. This lets water escape more readily during drying and lets it re-enter cells more easily during rehydration.

Drying Time and Temperature—Vegetables are much lower in sugar and acid than fruits, and so must be dried under more controlled conditions to prevent spoilage during the drying process. *Drying time and temperature* are crucial to the tenderness of dried vegetables. The longer the drying time, the less tender they will be. Use uniformly cut pieces. Drying time is proportional to the thickness squared. If a 1/4-inch dice dried in 2 hours, a 1/2-inch dice will take 8 hours, or 4 times as long.

Storage Time—Even when properly packaged, most vegetables will not keep in good condition as long as fruits, unless stored in the refrigerator or freezer where they will last for years; see page 56. Otherwise, use dried vegetables within 6 months. Properly packaged vegetables will not spoil, but will gradually deteriorate in flavor and nutrition.

Vegetable Chips; see page 73. From top right: Cucumber Chips, Carrot Chips, Zucchini Chips and Tomato Chips.

Drying Vegetables—How to Begin

Sort and select the highest quality fresh tender vegetables. Some vegetables such as green beans should be young and tender to dry best, others such as carrots should be more mature. If vegetables are immature, they tend to have weak or poor color and flavor. Overly mature vegetables are inclined to be tough, woody or fibrous. Drying characteristics of vegetables are indicated on pages 57 to 64.

WASHING

Water left on vegetables increases deterioration, so wash them quickly just before processing. Use cold water because it helps preserve freshness. Many vitamins and minerals dissolve in water and will be lost by soaking. Soil may contain illness-causing bacteria that are difficult to kill. If vegetables are covered with garden dirt, wash them under cool running water so the dirt doesn't resettle on the food. Wash carefully to avoid bruising.

PREPARATION

Most vegetables need to be peeled, trimmed, cored, cut, sliced or shredded. Peeling some vegetables is optional but be aware that peelings tend to be tougher when dried. Remove any fibrous or woody portion and core when necessary. Cut away decayed or spoiled spots as they may contain enough bacteria to contaminate an entire batch of dried vegetables!

Prepare only as many vegetables as you can dry at one time. Keep pieces a uniform size so they will dry at the same rate.

PRETREATMENT

> **You Will Need:**
> **Large pan with wire basket *or* steamer**

Pretreating most vegetables before drying will decrease the chances of spoilage and increase quality and storage life. Vegetables deteriorate much more rapidly than fruits during storage because of continued *enzyme action.* Enzymes are chemicals in all fruits and vegetables which cause them to ripen. The higher sugar content and acidity of fruits counteracts this enzyme action. In vegetables, enzymes will continue to react, resulting in toughness and loss of flavor and color.

Enzymes are destroyed by heat so almost all vegetables should be *blanched*—heated in boiling water or steam—before drying. Blanching is appropriate for vegetables because you will probably use the dried vegetable as a cooked vegetable. In *water blanching*, the vegetables are placed in a wire basket and submerged in boiling water. In *steam blanching* the vegetables are suspended above the boiling water in a colander or wire basket and heated only by the steam. *Steam blanching is preferred because less water-soluble vitamins and minerals are lost.* Blanching sets the color and shortens the drying and rehydration time by relaxing the tissue walls so moisture can escape or re-enter more rapidly. It also kills most organisms that cause spoilage. Blanched vegetables take less time to cook because they are already partially cooked.

WATER BLANCHING

Fill a pot 2/3 full of water and bring it to a rolling boil. Place the vegetables in a wire basket or colander and submerge them in the boiling water. After putting the vegetables in the water, bring it to a boil again before beginning timing. If it takes longer than a minute to come to the second boil, you probably have too many vegetables in the pot.

STEAM BLANCHING

You'll need a double-boiler arrangement with water in the bottom part, a perforated upper pan or container which lets the steam circulate freely without water touching the vegetables and a tight-fitting lid to prevent steam from escaping. Place 1 to 2 inches of water in the bottom part and bring it to a rolling boil. Layer the prepared vegetables in the upper perforated part no more than 2 to 2-1/2 inches deep. They should be loosely packed. Cover tightly with the lid and steam for the specified time. Begin timing from the moment the lid is replaced. Grated or small pieces of vegetables may need occasional stirring to expose all their surfaces to the steam.

1/After the beans are washed and the pod ends snipped off, cut them crosswise into 1-inch pieces, slanting the knife to make a diagonal cut. Green beans may also be cut lengthwise for a French cut.

2/The storage life of green beans will be longer if they are steam blanched over water containing sodium bisulfite for 4 to 6 minutes.

How to Dry Green Beans

3/Place the cut beans on a drying tray and freeze them until they are solid, 30 to 40 minutes. This will make the beans more tender. Other vegetables do not need to be frozen.

4/Dry the beans until they are brittle or crisp.

Blanching or steaming times vary with the altitude, the amount of vegetables and the thickness of the pieces. The times given on pages 57 to 64 should serve as guidelines but test the pieces frequently to prevent underblanching or overblanching. As a general rule, vegetables should feel and taste firm, yet tender. They should not be cooked as they would be for eating, yet should be heated all the way through. Some vegetable pieces will appear almost translucent to the center when cut. At higher altitudes, about 5,000 feet, increase water blanching time 1 minute and steam blanching time 2 minutes. Underblanching may cause deterioration in storage, poor rehydration or bad color. Overblanching results in loss of color, flavor, nutrition and poor texture when rehydrated.

Drain vegetables if necessary by pouring them directly onto the screened drying tray placed over the sink. If there is excess water on the tray, wipe the underside with a clean dish towel. Draining on a paper towel or cloth, then transferring to the drying tray results in unnecessary handling of tender vegetables.

You may or may not want to dip blanched or steamed vegetables in cold or ice water immediately to stop the action of the heat. If vegetables continue to cook after they have been blanched, they may be overblanched. However, dipping in ice water exposes blanched vegetables to more water, therefore more color and vitamin loss. You may compensate for this by slightly underblanching or understeaming the vegetables, realizing that they will cook a little longer in the dryer. If the vegetables are transferred directly from the steamer to the drying trays and placed immediately in a preheated dryer, the dryer process begins quickly because the vegetables are already warm. With this information plus a little experimenting, you can decide which method works best for you.

Some vegetables need other types of pretreatment to increase their storage life and nutritional value or to hold their color.

SULFITING DURING STEAM BLANCHING

Sulfiting is suggested for vegetables which tend to deteriorate rapidly during storage, such as green beans, corn or potatoes. Sulfiting increases shelf life, holds the color and lessens losses of vitamins A and C. I recommend it if you plan to store these vegetables longer than 3 months. Or, store dried vegetables in the refrigerator or freezer. Here they will last for years without any pretreatment and take up far less space than your frozen foods. See page 56.

To sulfite, add 1 teaspoon sodium bisulfite per cup of water to the steaming water. Sodium bisulfite may slightly affect flavor but it is not harmful. *Do not add sodium bisulfite when water blanching vegetables.* The vegetable will absorb the sulfur taste from the water.

OTHER PRETREATMENT METHODS

Some vegetables require specific pretreatment methods: Adding baking soda to the blanching water, which you can do with celery, page 59, or dipping blanched vegetables, such as carrots, page 59, in a cornstarch solution to lessen vitamin loss. Some vegetables require no pretreatment, such as tomatoes and onions.

How to Dry Vegetables

HOW TO DRY VEGETABLES

Preheat the dryer. Arrange the prepared vegetable pieces on drying trays, leaving a little space between for air circulation. Dry pieces of similar size on the same tray. Thinly layer grated or diced vegetables, or small vegetables, such as corn or peas, to allow good air circulation. Stir them occasionally.

All vegetables except garlic, onions and peppers may be dried together. Garlic, onions and peppers may be dried with each other, but tend to flavor milder vegetables. Do not dry extremely thin vegetables or herbs, such as parsley or greens, in a dryer heavily loaded with larger, more moist fruits or vegetables.

A controlled temperature must be maintained so that the internal temperature of the vegetable does not exceed 140°F (60°C) anytime during the drying process. When the dryer is fully loaded and the vegetables are very moist, the actual temperature of the vegetables may be as much as 20° to 30°F (10° to 15°C) cooler than the air temperature because of the cooling effect of moisture evaporation. This is why vegetables and most dried foods are usually dried at higher temperatures at the beginning. After much of the water has been removed, lower the temperature. If vegetables reach temperatures above 140°F (60°C), this will cause loss of nutrients and reduced tenderness. Too low temperature will encourage the growth of bacterial mold. The drying temperatures and drying times are given for each vegetable on pages 57 to 64.

Legumes such as shell beans, lentils and soybeans may be partially dried on the plant. When the pod turns light brown and the seeds are mature, they should be harvested. If not harvested soon enough, the pods may break, spilling their seeds on the ground.

Place the pods in a cloth sack and hang it in a warm place to finish drying, up to 2 weeks. When completely dry, shake or hit the sack to break the pods and release the seeds. Remove the pods and pour off the seeds.

Pasteurize the seeds; see page 53. Store them in an airtight moisture-proof container in a cool dark place.

TESTING FOR DRYNESS

Near the end of drying, check vegetables frequently and remove those that appear dried. Remove a piece, let it cool, feel and taste it. Most vegetables when dry are described as *tough, brittle, crisp or cracking hard.* Some would shatter if hit with a hammer.

Because vegetables are dried to such a waterless state, the conditioning process which is used in fruits is not necessary.

SPOILAGE

Unlike home-canned vegetables, there is no danger from botulism in dried vegetables. Once a vegetable is dried, spoilage will occur only if moisture is reabsorbed. Spoilage can be caused by the amount of moisture in the vegetables. The less moisture dried vegetables contain, the longer they will keep. Generally, they should have no more than 4 or 5 percent moisture when fully dried, compared to 15 to 20 percent in fruits. If the vegetables were not completely dry when removed from the dryer or were not packaged properly, mold and a spoiled smell will tell you they are unsafe to eat.

Long storage time, heat or exposure to air may cause some vegetables to develop a strong unpleasant taste. They are safe to eat but their nutritional value may be poor.

How Do You Know They're Dry?

The Dryness Test for individual fruits (pages 27 to 35) and vegetables (pages 57 to 64) is a taste-and-touch test. If you want to doublecheck for dryness, you will need to compare the weight of the fruit or vegetable *before* drying and *after* drying. This method is reassurance for those people who don't trust their judgement of texture or appearance to tell when food is dry enough.

With this method you must accurately weigh the prepared food just before you put it on the drying tray and you must not add fresh food to the dryer until one batch is dry and removed. (This is a general rule to avoid prolonging drying time and keep the best quality in your dried produce.)

One problem with this procedure is the assumption that all pieces are of equal size and have dried at the same rate. Since that is not always the case, there may be some pieces that are still too moist and some that are over-dry when the calculated weight is reached. While proper conditioning can equalize small differences in moisture content, **thorough visual inspection is necessary to avoid mold from under-drying.**

MULTIPLY:

weight of prepared food (minus peelings, stems, pits, etc.) times **% water** (See: Fruits, Vegetables A to Z—water content before drying) = **weight of water**

SUBTRACT:

weight of prepared food minus the **weight of water** = **weight of dry matter**

MULTIPLY:

weight of dry matter times **% of final moisture** = **weight of residual water**
(Fruits should have 15% residual water
Vegetables should have 5% residual water)

ADD:

weight of dry matter plus **weight of residual water** = **final desired weight**

Dry and weigh until you have the final desired weight.

Gourmet Dried Tomatoes

Gourmet shops, specialty food outlets and many supermarkets are featuring a new product—*sun dried tomatoes*. Quite expensive, they range from $10.00 to $20.00 per pound. You'll find them in a variety of forms: sliced, minced, powdered and halved or chopped. They may be packaged dry, or in a seasoned or unseasoned oil.

The Italians first introduced this delicacy to the American market and are still one of the primary sources of dried tomatoes found on U.S. supermarket shelves. Made from *paste* tomatoes, the majority are lightly salted and dried in the sun.

The prime variety used in drying are the *Roma* or plum-shaped tomatoes. They are most frequently used in making tomato paste because of their robust sweet flavor. Most varieties of round tomatoes only have about 6% solids and 94% water. The *Roma* varieties may contain as much as 15% solids, with 85% water. A higher solids content means that you have more tomato left after the water is removed!

Some common varieties of plum-shaped tomatoes good for drying are: *Red Pear, Roma VF, LaRoma, Del Oro, San Marzano, Hungarian Italian, Viva Italia and Super Italian Paste*. The *Super Italian Paste* is the meatiest of all, sweet, flavorful and frequently up to 6 inches long.

Not all tomatoes can be dried successfully. Tomatoes low in acid may develop black spots during the drying process. The black spots do not represent spoilage, but result in a slight change in flavor and are certainly not as appetizing as the fully red, robust dried tomato.

Be sure that plum tomatoes are fully ripe before drying. Tomatoes picked ripe are richly colored; those picked before ripening are lighter in color. Tomatoes picked early and commercially ripened may have a rich red color, but are not as flavorful as a vine-ripened tomato.

Wash carefully and halve them lengthwise. Set the halves on drying racks with the cut sides up, close together, but not overlapping. If desired, sprinkle lightly with salt. Paste tomatoes will take about 10 to 15 hours to dry in a dehydrator at 140°F (60°C). If you're drying round tomatoes, slice 1/2 to 3/4 inch thick. When dry, they will be paper thin. If you slice them thinner, they will be difficult to remove from the drying racks.

The amount that you can dry at once depends on the surface area of your dehydrator or convection oven. If you live in a very hot, arid climate, you can successfully sun dry them by lightly salting and protecting from insects.

Proper storage of dried tomatoes is critical if you want them to maintain a good quality. If left out at room temperature, or in a container that is not airtight, they will deteriorate rapidly and absorb moisture from the air.

Ideally, they should be vacuum packaged and stored in the freezer. If this isn't practical for you, package in freezer bags, and then inside of airtight glass jars. Store in a refrigerator or freezer until needed.

Do not chop or flake them until ready to use. When making tomato flakes or chunks, put the dried tomatoes in a food processor or blender and chop to the desired size. Chopping a few at a time results in a nicer quality. Too many at once will gum up the blades of the blender or food processor.

If you want to marinate them in a seasoned oil for use in Italian or other dishes, be sure to store them in the refrigerator.

PASTEURIZING

Pasteurize dried vegetables only if they have been exposed to insects while drying.

Freezer Method—Freezing packaged dried vegetables for 48 hours will kill any insect larvae.

Oven Method—Dried vegetables may be heated in the oven at 160°F (70°C) for 30 minutes before packaging, but more vitamin loss can occur than with the freezer method.

PACKAGING

Cool vegetables before packaging to prevent any remaining moisture from condensing in the package. Place only enough dried vegetables in one bag to be used within one week. Every time a container is opened and the food is exposed to air, humidity re-enters, causing deterioration.

Vacuum package in glass jars if possible. Vacuum packaging retards oxidation, one of the primary reasons for quality and nutritive loss.

Store in the coolest place possible, preferably the freezer or refrigerator. If space isn't available, store in the coolest darkest place in your home.

If vacuum packaging is not available, dried vegetables should be stored in freezer bags with as much air removed as possible. Then place bags inside of airtight glass, plastic or metal containers for long term storage. Since light fades vegetable colors and decreases their vitamins A and C content, they should also be protected from the light.

STORAGE

Storage temperatures are extremely important. For every 18°F (10°C) decrease in temperature, the shelf life of vegetables increases 2 or 3 times. For example, vegetables that last 6 months at 80°F (25°C) will keep 12 to 18 months if stored at 60°F (15°C). Store dried vegetables in the coolest place in your home—a basement or cellar is good, but a refrigerator or freezer is better.

How to Use Dried Vegetables

REHYDRATION OR RECONSTITUTION

Home-dried vegetables rehydrate slower than fruits because they have lost more water.

Dried vegetables are usually more tender if they have been soaked long enough to reabsorb most of their lost water. If they are placed directly into a boiling soup or stew and are cooked without given time to plump, they will be tough.

Use only as much water as necessary to cover the vegetables. Boiling water shortens rehydration time, but cold water may be used. Rehydration water contains some dissolved nutrients, so use it in soups, stew or sauces.

Rehydrating may take 15 minutes to 2 hours, depending on the vegetable, thickness of pieces and temperature of water used. Do not let vegetables stand in water more than 2 hours without refrigerating them. Holding them at room temperature gives bacteria a chance to grow—just as it would in fresh or thawed frozen vegetables.

Pour boiling water over the dried vegetables and let them soak until they are plump.

COOKING

After rehydration, vegetables are ready to be cooked. Simmered vegetables are more tender than those cooked over high heat. In a fully rehydrated vegetable, the cooking time is about the same or slightly longer than it would be for the same frozen vegetable. If the vegetable is used in a baked food such as Scrumptious Carrot Cake, page 143, it may be reconstituted, drained and used in the recipe without further cooking.

Because most dried vegetables do not have the same eye appeal or color as fresh or frozen, it helps to dress them up a bit. You can combine them with fresh or frozen vegetables, use them in soups, stews, casseroles, serve them in a sauce or give them extra flavor and color with seasonings. See the recipes beginning on page 129. Add salt or seasonings after rather than before or at the beginning of cooking.

After the vegetables have simmered until they are tender, add the desired seasonings.

Vegetable Flakes & Powders

Use your blender to chop dried vegetables into flakes or a fine powder and you will never again have to buy commercially prepared soup bases or seasonings for salads and other dishes.

HOW TO PREPARE THEM

The storage life and nutritional value of powdered or flaked vegetables is much less than that of sliced or whole dried vegetables, so do not chop or powder more dried vegetables than you will use within 1 month. Vegetables may be flaked or powdered separately or several vegetables may be blended together to make mixed flakes or powder.

Dried vegetables should be very dry and crisp before chopping. Be sure the blender is completely dry. If any moisture is present, the vegetables will clump instead of becoming powder or flakes.

Process about 1/2 to 1 cup of dried vegetable pieces at one time. Larger amounts will not powder or flake evenly. A blender mini-jar, which is available for some blenders, is convenient but not necessary. A standard 1/2-pint or 1-pint canning jar fits the cutting assembly of some blenders.

Put the dried vegetable pieces in the blender. Set the blender speed on chop for several seconds. Turn it off, scrape down the sides with a rubber spatula and chop again for several more seconds. Repeat until the vegetables are flaked or powdered.

Fresh vegetables may be pureed before drying, then dried as vegetable leather. See Vegetable Leathers, page 73. Vegetable leather can be powdered or flaked in the blender for use in soups, sauces or baby food. The nutrient and flavor loss is higher than with pieces of dried vegetables because of additional exposure to air during drying.

HOW TO STORE THEM

Store vegetable flakes and powders in airtight containers with as little air as possible. Select the size container which best corresponds to the amount of flakes or powder. Empty spice jars and baby food jars are a good size. Store them in a cool dry place and use them within 1 month.

Flakes and powders made from unblanched vegetables will not keep as long as those made from blanched vegetables. They may also develop an unpleasant flavor during storage.

HOW TO USE THEM

Creamed Soups and Sauces—Flavor a creamed soup or sauce base with reconstituted vegetable powder. Combine 1 tablespoon vegetable powder and 1/4 cup boiling water for each cup of soup or sauce. Let the mixture stand for 10 to 15 minutes before adding to the soup or sauce base.

Salad Sprinkles—Coarsely chopped vegetable flakes such as carrots, cucumbers, zucchini, onions, celery or tomatoes add flavor and texture to salads. They don't need to be reconstituted because they will absorb moisture from the salad and dressing.

Seasonings—Both vegetables and herbs can be powdered and flaked and used alone or combined with other seasonings. Because home dried vegetable seasonings and herbs have no anti-caking additives, make small quantities and store them in airtight containers. Make seasoning salts by mixing vegetable and herb powders with table salt. The addition of salt decreases the tendency of the powder to cake.

Baby Food—See How To Make Your Own Baby Food, pages 72 and 73.

Recipes—Substitute reconstituted vegetable powders and flakes for finely chopped fresh vegetables in recipes. If you don't reconstitute the powders or flakes before adding to the recipe ingredients, add a small amount of liquid to the recipe. Allow 1/4 cup liquid for each tablespoon of powder and each 1-1/2 tablespoons of flakes.

Tomatoes powder well but are extremely concentrated. One tablespoon of tomato powder is equivalent to 1 medium fresh tomato.

Equivalent Measurements for Most Vegetables

1 tablespoon vegetable powder or	4 tablespoons
1-1/2 tablespoons vegetable flakes =	chopped
or	fresh
2 tablespoons dried pieces	vegetables

How to Make Vegetable Flakes

1/Store dried vegetables in the form they were dried and keep them very dry and crisp. Before chopping them into flakes, be sure your blender is completely dry.

2/Vegetable flakes make excellent seasonings for soups and sauces. Or sprinkle them over salads to add texture and flavor. Use them in creamed soups and sauces or to make your own baby food.

Vegetables at a Glance

VEGETABLE	SUITABILITY	STORAGE TIME FOR BEST QUALITY	
		34°F (0°C)	0°F (−20°C)
Artichokes	Fair	4 to 8 months	12 to 30 months
Asparagus	Poor to fair	4 to 8 months	12 to 30 months
Beans, green	Fair to good	12 to 15 months	4 to 5 years
Beans, lima	Fair	12 to 15 months	4 to 5 years
Beets	Fair to good	12 to 15 months	4 to 5 years
Broccoli	Poor to fair	4 months	15 months
Brussels sprouts	Not recommended		
Cabbages	Fair	4 months	15 months
Carrots	Good	18 to 24 months	5 to 8 years
Cauliflower	Poor	4 months	15 months
Celery	Poor	4 to 8 months	12 to 30 months
Collard greens	Poor	4 to 8 months	12 to 30 months
Corn, sweet	Good	12 to 15 months	4 to 5 years
Cucumbers	Poor	4 to 8 months	12 to 30 months
Eggplant	Poor to fair	4 to 8 months	12 to 30 months
Garlic	Good	8 to 16 months	30 to 60 months
Horseradish	Good	8 to 16 months	30 to 60 months
Kale	Poor	4 to 8 months	12 to 30 months
Kohlrabi	Fair	4 to 8 months	12 to 30 months
Lettuce	Not recommended		
Mushrooms	Good	4 to 8 months	12 to 30 months
Mustard greens	Poor	4 to 8 months	12 to 30 months
Okra	Fair to good	8 to 16 months	30 to 60 months
Onions	Good to excellent	8 to 16 months	30 to 60 months
Parsley	Good	12 to 15 months	4 to 5 years
Parsnips	Good	1 to 2 years	5 to 8 years
Peas	Fair to good	12 to 15 months	4 to 5 years
Peppers, green or red	Good	24 to 30 months	8 to 10 years
Peppers, chili	Excellent	24 to 30 months	8 to 10 years
Popcorn	Good	18 to 24 months	5 to 8 years
Potatoes	Good	8 to 16 months	30 to 60 months
Pumpkins	Fair to good	4 months	15 months
Radishes	Not recommended		
Rutabagas	Fair to good	4 to 8 months	12 to 30 months
Spinach	Poor	4 to 8 months	12 to 30 months
Squash, summer	Poor to fair	4 months	15 months
Squash, winter	Not recommended		
Sweet potatoes	Fair	4 months	15 months
Swiss chard	Poor	4 to 8 months	12 to 30 months
Tomatoes	Good	8 to 12 months	30 to 48 months
Turnips	Fair to good	4 to 8 months	12 to 30 months
Turnip greens	Poor	4 to 8 months	12 to 30 months
Yams	Fair	4 months	15 months
Zucchini	Poor to fair	4 months	15 months

*Shelf life is increased drastically with cooler storage and/or vacuum packing. See Storage Temperatures, page 26, and Vacuum Packaging, page 13. Vegetables can be stored at higher temperatures than those mentioned above and will not spoil as long as they are properly packaged. However, there will be gradual deterioration in sensory quality and nutritive value.

Vegetables: A to Z

Artichokes

Quality When Dried—Fair.
Varieties Best For Drying—Globe.
Selection—Dry only the tender hearts of fresh young artichokes with few bruises. Before processing, store only briefly at refrigerator temperature, 35° to 40°F (1° to 3°C), to maintain highest quality.
Water Content Before Drying—87%.
Preparation—Wash artichokes and trim leaves. Save leaves to eat later. Remove and discard the fuzzy choke. Cut heart in half.
Pretreatment—Water blanch 2 to 4 minutes or steam blanch 3 to 5 minutes.
Drying Temperature—140°F (60°C) for 2 hours, 130°F (55°C) until dry.
Dryness Test—Brittle.
How To Use—Rehydrated artichokes are good marinated or dipped in a batter and fried until golden and crisp. Lemon juice added to the rehydrating water helps retain color.

Asparagus

Quality When Dried—Poor to fair.
Selection—Dry only the fresh, tender, young green stalks. Before processing, store at refrigerator temperature, 35° to 40°F (1° to 3°C), to maintain highest quality.
Water Content Before Drying—92%.
Preparation—Wash spears. Trim scales and tough ends.
Pretreatment—Water blanch 2 to 3 minutes or steam blanch 3 to 5 minutes.
Drying Temperature—140°F (60°C) for 2 to 3 hours, 130°F (55°C) until dry.
Dryness Test—Very tough to brittle.
How To Use—Rehydrate asparagus and serve it in a cream sauce seasoned with lemon juice or Parmesan cheese and paprika.

Beans, Green

Dried beans are often not tender and tasty when rehydrated. It takes only a little extra effort to help them retain their tenderness and flavor.

Use only fresh beans and process them quickly. French cutting, or diagonal slicing, exposes more surface area, shortening drying time. If steamed and frozen before drying, beans will dehydrate faster and be less tough. Sulfiting lengthens their storage life.
Quality When Dried—Fair to good.
Varieties Best For Drying—Tendergreen, Blue Lake.
Selection—Dry only fresh tender beans with a dark green color and bright appearance. They should have thick walls and small seeds and be free from strings. Before processing, store only briefly at refrigerator temperature, 35° to 40° (1° to 3°C), to maintain highest quality.
Water Content Before Drying—90%.
Preparation—Wash pods and snip off pod ends. Slice lengthwise for French cut or crosswise into 1-inch segments, slanting knife diagonally to expose more surface area for drying.
Pretreatment—Water blanch 3 to 4 minutes or steam blanch 4 to 6 minutes over water containing 1 teaspoon sodium bisulfite per cup water. Place on drying tray and freeze solid, 30 to 40 minutes before drying to tenderize.
Drying Temperature—140°F (60°C) for 2 hours, 130°F (55°C) until dry.
Dryness Test—Brittle, crisp.
How To Use—Serve rehydrated green beans in a cream of mushroom sauce with almonds or in soups, stews or casseroles.

Beans, Lima

The outer skin on lima beans lengthens the drying time and the rehydration process, lowering the quality of rehydrated limas.
Quality When Dried—Fair.
Selection—Use dark green pods that are well-filled. The beans should be plump, with tender skins and a light green color. Hold for only a brief period at 45° to 50°F (5° to 10°C) before processing.
Water Content Before Drying—68%.

Preparation—Wash, shell and wash again.
Pretreatment—Water blanch 3 to 5 minutes or steam blanch 2 to 4 minutes.
Drying Temperature—140°F (60°C) for 2 to 3 hours, 130°F (55°C) until dry.
Dryness Test—Hard, brittle.
How To Use—Use rehydrated lima beans in soups, stews or in a cream sauce with other vegetables, seasoned with parsley, savory or sage.

Beets

Quality When Dried—Fair to good.
Varieties Best For Drying—Detroit Dark Red, Morse Detroit, Ohio Canner.
Selection—Dry only fresh young beets, 2-1/3 to 3 inches in diameter with fresh green tops. Beets should not be woody or tough. Dry those with a uniform dark red color, smooth skins and minimal light and dark color rings. Before processing, store only briefly at refrigerator temperature, 35° to 40°F (1° to 3°C), to maintain highest quality.
Water Content Before Drying—87%.
Preparation—Wash beets and remove tops.
Pretreatment—Steam until almost tender. Peel and cut into 1/8-inch strips or 3/8-inch dice.
Drying Temperature—160°F (70°C) for 1 hour, 130°F (55°C) until dry.
Dryness Test—Crackling brittle.
How To Use—Powder dried beets in blender to use in dry salad dressings, soups and stews or rehydrate to use in borscht or to pickle or glaze. Beets are tasty when seasoned with fresh dill, caraway seed, bay leaves, cloves, nutmeg, basil or mint. Rehydrate by soaking in a small amount of water overnight in the refrigerator.

Broccoli

Quality When Dried—Poor to fair.
Selection—Dry only fresh tender, young stalks. They should have bright green heads, leaves and stems with compact dark green or purple-green buds. Yellow flowers visible inside the buds indicate tough, old broccoli. Before processing, store only briefly at refrigerator temperature, 35° to 40°F (1° to 3°C), to maintain highest quality.
Water Content Before Drying—89%.
Preparation—Wash broccoli and trim tough stalks. Split larger stalks in half lengthwise or into quarters.
Pretreatment—Water blanch 2 to 3 minutes or steam blanch 3 to 5 minutes.
Drying Temperature—140°F (60°C) for 2 hours, 130°F (55°C) until dry.
Dryness Test—Brittle.
How To Use—Serve reconstituted broccoli with Hollandaise Sauce or cheese sauce, or season with lemon juice, nutmeg or oregano and garnish with slivered almonds.

Brussels Sprouts

Not recommended for drying.

Cabbage

Cabbage readily reabsorbs moisture from the air. It will keep well only if extremely dry. Sulfiting lengthens storage life.
Quality When Dried—Fair.
Varieties Best For Drying—Danish, Domestic, Savoy, Copenhagen.
Selection—White varieties do not dry as well. Cabbage should be solid, firm, round and heavy for its size. Before processing, store in a plastic bag at refrigerator temperatures, 35° to 40°F (1° to 3°C), to maintain the highest quality.
Water Content Before Drying—92%.
Preparation—Wash cabbage and trim outer leaves. Cut cabbage in half; core and shred into 1/4- to 3/8-inch wide pieces.
Pretreatment—Steam blanch 2 to 3 minutes over water containing 1 teaspoon sodium bisulfite per cup of water.
Drying Temperature—160°F (70°C) for 1 hour, 130°F (55°C) until dry.
Dryness Test—Crisp.
How To Use—Cook with ham in soups or reconstitute and serve with Hollandaise or cheese sauce. To lighten dried cabbage, add 1 teaspoon of fresh lemon juice per cup of reconstituting water.

Carrots

The vitamin A in carrots is easily destroyed by exposure to air during drying and storage. Color and flavor are also lost. Storage life is improved by sulfiting and coating with a cornstarch solution.
Quality When Dried—Good.
Varieties Best For Drying—Imperator, Red Cored Chantenay.
Selection—Choose smooth, well-formed, deep orange carrots that are slightly more mature than for table use and without woody fiber or a pithy core. Carrots with green areas or yellow tops are old or sunburned.
Water Content Before Drying—88%.
Preparation—Wash, trim tops and peel, if desired. Slice crosswise or diagonally no thicker than 3/8 inch or cut into 3/8-inch dice. Before processing, store at refrigerator temperature, 35° to 40°F (1° to 3°C), to maintain highest quality.
Pretreatment—Steam blanch 3 to 4 minutes over water containing 1 teaspoon sodium bisulfite per cup of water. Remove and dip in a cornstarch solution of 2 tablespoons cornstarch to 2 cups water.

Drain and place on dryer trays.
Drying Temperature—140°F (60°C) for 2 to 3 hours, 130°F (55°C) until dry.
Dryness Test—Very tough to brittle.
How To Use—Chop dried carrots in the blender for carrot flakes to use as salad sprinkles, in dry soup mixes, in baby food, in cookies or carrot cake, see Scrumptious Carrot Cake, page 143.

Cauliflower

Quality When Dried—Poor.
Selection—Dry only small white or creamy white very fresh flowerets which are firm and compact.
Preparation—Wash flowerets and remove from core, splitting stems so flowerets are not more than 1 inch thick. Before processing, store at refrigerator temperature, 35° to 40°F (1° to 3°C), to maintain highest quality.
Pretreatment—Water blanch 3 to 4 minutes in a vinegar solution of 1 tablespoon vinegar per 1 gallon of water. Drain.
Drying Temperature—140°F (60°C) for 2 to 3 hours, 130°F (55°C) until dry.
Dryness Test—Tough to brittle.
How To Use—Powder dried cauliflower in a blender and use in creamed vegetable soups. If rehydrated, serve with a Hollandaise, cheese or cream sauce and season with basil, curry powder, nutmeg, paprika, celery or poppy seed. To lighten dried cauliflower, add a teaspoonful of lemon juice per cup of reconstituting water.

Celery

Pretreating with baking soda helps preserve the green color.
Quality When Dried—Fair.
Varieties Best For Drying—Pascal.
Selection—Dry only tender, yet mature, long crisp stalks with fresh leaves. The stalk should feel smooth on the inside rather than rough or puffy. Before processing, store at refrigerator temperature, 35° to 40°F (1° to 3°C), to maintain highest quality.
Water Content Before Drying—94%.
Preparation—Trim base and wash stalks and leaves. Cut crosswise into 1/4- to 1/2-inch slices.
Pretreatment—Water blanch 30 seconds to 1 minute in a baking soda solution of 1/2 teaspoon soda per cup of water. Celery should still be quite crisp after blanching. If dried celery is to be powdered in a blender to make celery salt, blanching is optional.
Drying Temperature—150°F (65°C) for 1 hour, 130°F (55°C) until dry.
Dryness Test—Crisp.
How To Use—Dried celery slices are best in soups and stews with other vegetables. To make celery flakes, chop both dried leaves and stalks in blender. To make celery salt, add one part salt to one part powdered dry celery.

Collard Greens

See Greens, page 60.

Corn, Sweet

Quality When Dried—Good.
Varieties Best For Drying—Yellow varieties.
Selection—Tender, fresh, young sweet ears with plump kernels dry best. The kernels should be large enough so there are no spaces between rows. Do not store corn. Process it quickly.
Water Content Before Drying—73%.
Preparation—Husk ears and remove silk.
Pretreatment—Steam blanch 3 to 5 minutes over water containing 1 teaspoon sodium bisulfite per cup of water. Cut the kernels from the cob leaving about 1/4 of the kernel on the cob.
Drying Temperature—150°F (65°C) for 1 to 2 hours, 130°F (55°C) until dry.
Dryness Test—Crisp and crunchy.
How To Use—Rehydrate dried corn to use in fritters, chowders, soups and stews or to make creamed corn. To make cornmeal, grind dry corn in a blender or a food mill. For a delicious crunchy snack, see Fiesta Corn, page 141.

Cucumber

Quality When Dried—Very poor when rehydrated.
Selection—Dry only small fresh bright green cucumbers, not more than 6 inches long. Before processing, store at refrigerator temperature, 35° to 40°F (1° to 3°C), for no longer than 2 weeks to maintain the highest quality.
Water Content Before Drying—95%.
Preparation—Wash and peel, if desired. Slice crosswise 1/4 inch thick and sprinkle with seasoning salt for added flavor.
Pretreatment—None.
Drying Temperature—140°F (60°C) for 1 hour, 130°F (55°C) until dry.
Dryness Test—Crisp.
How To Use—Keep extremely dry and use within 1 or 2 weeks if stored at room temperature. Storage life of dried cucumbers will be longer if they are stored in the freezer. Chop dried cucumbers in a blender and sprinkle dry on salads. Seasoned cucumbers may be used as chips for dips.

Eggplant

Quality When Dried—Poor to fair.
Selection—Fresh, firm, young eggplant heavy for

its size, with a uniform good color, dries best. Ripe eggplant is about 4 inches in diameter and is a glossy purple-black. Store at 45°F (5°C) before processing to maintain the highest quality.
Water Content Before Drying—94%.
Preparation—Wash, peel and cut into 1/2-inch slices or 1/2-inch dice.
Pretreatment—Steam blanch 3 to 5 minutes over water containing 1 teaspoon sodium bisulfite per cup of water.
Drying Temperature—140°F (60°C) for 2 hours, 130°F (55°C) until dry.
Dryness Test—Very tough to brittle.
How To Use—Rehydrate eggplant and serve in a cream sauce with Parmesan cheese, garnished with snipped chives or parsley. The sauce may also be seasoned with allspice, chili powder, curry powder, garlic or oregano. Or dip rehydrated eggplant in a batter and fry.

Garlic

Fresh garlic keeps well but may be dried to make garlic powder.
Quality When Dried—Good.
Selection—Dry only fresh firm garlic cloves with no bruises.
Preparation—Separate and peel cloves. Cut in half lengthwise.
Water Content Before Drying—61%.
Pretreatment—None.
Drying Temperature—140°F (60°C) for 2 hours, 130°F (55°C) until dry.
Dryness Test—Crisp.
How To Use—To make garlic salt, powder dried garlic in a blender until fine. Add 4 parts salt to 1 part garlic powder and blend only a second or two. If blended longer, the salt will be too fine and will cake.

Greens

Greens include collard greens, kale, mustard greens, turnip greens and spinach. Arrange greens in one layer on drying trays. Do not clump them together. Do not dry with very moist foods as this slows the drying process too much.
Quality When Dried—Very poor when rehydrated, compared to fresh.
Selection—Dry only fresh small and tender greens.
Water Content Before Drying—Collard, 85%; Kale, 83%; Spinach, 91%; Turnip, 90%.
Preparation—Wash and trim leaves from stems.
Pretreatment—Steam blanch until slightly wilted.
Drying Temperature—130°F (55°C) for 1 hour, 120°F (50°C) until dry.
Dryness Test—Crisp, crumbles easily.
How To Use—Powder dried greens in a blender or crumble and use in creamed vegetable soups or

other soups and stews. If crumbled, remove the sharp needle-like veins and residual stems which will be tough and woody when rehydrated. Lemon juice or vinegar freshens the flavor.

Horseradish

Horseradish will smell extremely strong while drying. You may want to place the dryer outside the house.
Quality When Dried—Good.
Selection—Fresh, firm, fully mature roots are best for drying.
Preparation—Trim tops and scour roots with a stiff brush. Grate coarsely or slice 1/4 inch thick.
Pretreatment—None.
Drying Temperature—150°F (65°C) for 1 hour, 130°F (55°C) until dry.
Dryness Test—Dry and brittle.
How To Use—Powder dried horseradish in a blender. Rehydrate the powder with enough water to mix and use in cocktail sauce, fish sauce, mustard or horseradish dressing.

Kale

See Greens, this page.

Kohlrabi

Quality When Dried—Fair.
Selection—The thickened base of the stem is the edible portion which can be dried. It should be 2 to 3 inches in diameter. The young leaves can be trimmed and cooked like spinach. Before processing, store at refrigerator temperature 35° to 40°F (1° to 3°C), to maintain the highest quality.
Preparation—Wash and trim root ends and vine-like stems. Wash again and peel thinly. Cube or slice 1/4 inch thick.
Pretreatment—Water blanch 3 to 5 minutes or steam blanch 5 to 8 minutes.
Drying Temperature—140°F (60°C) for 2 hours, 130°F (55°C) until dry.
Dryness Test—Very tough to brittle.
How To Use—Serve rehydrated kohlrabi with butter, salt, pepper and a bit of prepared mustard. Use it in Oriental dishes as you would water chestnuts or add to soups or stews. Marinate rehydrated thin strips in French dressing and serve in salads or with cold meats.

Legumes

See page 51.

Lentils

See Legumes, page 51.

Mushrooms

Mushrooms are actually the "fruit" of a colorless plant called a fungus. One of the rarer species of mushrooms, but undoubtedly the choicest, is *Boletus edulis*. Drying seems to actually enhance its flavor and aroma. Dried *king bolete* is preferred by fine chefs all over the world.

Quality When Dried—Good.

Varieties Best For Drying—Dry only cultivated or wild mushrooms that are safe. Some good varieties for drying are: Boletus edulis, Chantrelles, Morels, Lactarias, Agaricus and Bisporus

Selection—Dry only clean fresh mushrooms with closed caps and visible gills under the cap. Store at 34°F (0°C) until dehydrating.

Water Content Before Drying—90%.

Preparation—Clean with a soft brush or cloth and check for evidence of worms or spoilage. Cut away any questionable parts and trim woody portion from the stem. Dry whole or slice lengthwise in half or 1/2 inch thick.

Drying Temperature—80° to 90°F (25° to 30°C) 2 to 3 hours, increase to 120° to 125°F (50°C) until dry.

Dryness Test—Crisp or brittle.

How To Use—Rehydrate dried mushrooms by soaking them in boiling water for about half a minute, stirring while soaking to loosen any dirt that may be present. Lift out gently with a slotted spoon and use in your favorite recipe.

Okra

Quality When Dried—Fair to good.

Selection—Dry only tender young fresh pods, less than 4 inches long. Freshness is determined by how easily the pods snap. A dull dry appearance frequently indicates old pods.

Water Content Before Drying—89%.

Preparation—Wash and cut off tips of stems. Slice crosswise about 1/4 inch thick. Discard any tough pithy pods.

Pretreatment—Water blanch 2 to 3 minutes or steam blanch 4 to 5 minutes.

Drying Temperature—140°F (60°C) for 2 hours, 130°F (55°C) until dry.

Dryness Test—Tough to brittle.

How To Use—Rehydrate okra, drain and toss it in cornmeal seasoned with onion salt and pepper. Fry it in oil or butter to a golden-brown. You can also use dried okra in soups and casseroles. It is especially good in dishes with tomatoes and onions. A little vinegar or lemon juice improves the flavor. Some Southern cooks maintain that the acidity of vinegar or lemon juice in the cooking water makes cooked okra less viscous.

Onions

Dried onions readily reabsorb moisture, causing deterioration during storage, so they need to be packaged with extra care. To maintain the best flavor, chop or powder onions only as needed. During the drying process, the onion smell will penetrate everything in the surrounding area, so it is wise to place the dryer outside the house.

Quality When Dried—Good to excellent.

Varieties Best For Drying—Southport White Globe, Southport Yellow Globe, White Creole, Red Creole, Australian Brown, Ebenezer and White Portugal all are recommended for drying. The white varieties have the best dried flavor.

Selection—Onion bulbs should be large, fresh and firm, heavy for their size and very pungent. Store onions in a cool dry place with good ventilation to maintain the highest quality. Do not store them with potatoes.

Water Content Before Drying—89%.

Preparation—Trim the bulb ends and remove the paper shell. Slice 1/8 to 1/4 inch thick. Onions may be cut into 3/8- to 1/2-inch dice, but will be slightly less pungent when dried.

Pretreatment—None.

Drying Temperature—160°F (70°C) for 1 to 2 hours, 130°F (55°C) until dry.

Dryness Test—Feels like paper.

How To Use—To make onion flakes, onion salt or onion powder, see pages 54 and 55.

Parsley, also see page 70

Dry parsley at lower temperatures so the flavoring oils and vitamins are not destroyed. Do not dry parsley or other herbs with very moist foods as they will absorb the excess moisture and take much longer to dry.

Quality When Dried—Good.

Varieties Best For Drying—Evergreen, Moss-Curled.

Selection—Use fresh, curly-leaved bright green parsley. Before processing, store in a plastic bag at refrigerator temperature, 35° to 40°F (1° to 3°C), to maintain the highest quality.

Water Content Before Drying—85%.

Preparation—Wash lightly under cold running water. Separate clusters and discard long or tough stems.

Pretreatment—None.

Drying Temperature—90°F (30°C) to 120°F (50°C). May be room dried.

Dryness Test—Feels like paper.

How To Use—Use the stems and leaves to make powder. Separate the leaves from the stems to make flakes; see pages 54 and 55.

Parsnips

Quality When Dried—Good.

Selection—Choose fresh, smooth small or medium-size roots. Before processing, store at refrigerator temperature, 35° to 40°F (1° to 3°C), to maintain highest quality.

Water Content Before Drying—79%.

Preparation—Wash, trim tops and peel, if desired. Slice crosswise or diagonally up to 3/8 inch thick or cut into 3/8 inch dice.

Pretreatment—Water blanch 2 to 3 minutes or steam blanch 3 to 5 minutes.

Drying Temperature—140°F (60°C) for 2 to 3 hours, 130°F (55°C) until dry.

Dryness Test—Very tough to brittle.

How To Use—Serve rehydrated parsnips in cream sauce with or without other vegetables or mashed with butter and garnished with parsley. They may be candied like sweet potatoes or yams.

Peas

The skins on peas slow their drying and rehydration. Home-dried peas are slightly inferior to commercially dried ones because at home we do not have the mechanical means to pierce the skins. Sulfiting by soaking rather than steaming increases storage life and helps retain vitamins.

Quality When Dried—Fair to good.

Varieties Best For Drying—Thomas Laxton, Dark Seeded.

Selection—Use fresh, crisp and medium-size pods. They should be bright green and well-filled. The smaller sizes do not rehydrate well and the larger ones tend to be starchy. Process immediately.

Water Content Before Drying—78%.

Preparation—Shell.

Pretreatment—Steam blanch 3 minutes. Soak in a cold solution of 1 teaspoon sodium bisulfite to 1 quart of water for 2 minutes.

Drying Temperature—130°F (55°C) until dry.

Dryness Test—Brittle and shriveled.

How To Use—Peas are good in soups and stews. You can serve them creamed with carrots, onions or mushrooms and seasoned with allspice, basil, marjoram, mint, savory, thyme or tarragon.

Peppers

Chilies are the most widely used spice and condiment in the world. They are members of the large and diverse nightshade family, in the genus *Capsicum*. Some, such as bell peppers, are sweet; others carry varying degrees of pungent spiciness.

Quality When Dried—Excellent.

Varieties Best For Drying—Peppers range from sweet to mild, medium, spicy hot, and so fiery hot that your mouth feels like dynamite has exploded in it!

There's no sure way to predict hotness, but each variety has a basic range, and the smallest varieties are generally the hottest. Climate affects hotness. Those grown in milder climates tend to be milder than those grown in hot climates. The hotness is concentrated in the enclosed veins or ribs near the seed heart, not in the seeds as commonly believed. The seeds taste hot because they are in close contact with the veins. There are hundreds (some estimate thousands…) of different varieties of peppers, all of which dry well. Some of the sweet peppers are: Bell pepper, Italian "frying" pepper, Sweet banana pepper, Sweet cherry pepper and Pimento. A few of the mild to medium varieties include: Ancho, California, Cascabel, Colorado, Fresno, Hungarian Yellow Wax, Pasilla, Poblano and Yellow Wax. Several that will make your eyes water and tongue tingle are: Cayenne, Chipotle, Guajillo, Habañero, Hontaka, Jalapeño, Mirasol and Pequin.

Selection—Look for firm, brightly colored, shiny pods with no signs of bruising or rotting. Store fresh pods in paper towels inside of a plastic bag in the refrigerator crisper for one to two weeks.

Water Content Before Drying—About 95%, depending on variety.

Preparation—Rinse and leave whole. Sweet peppers such as bell or pimento may be halved, quartered or diced prior to drying. You can slightly decrease the heat of a dried chili by removing the seeds and veins; be sure to wear rubber gloves when handling.

Drying Temperature—130°F (55°C) until dry.

Dryness Test—Tough to brittle.

How To Use—Powder or whirl in blender or food processor for seasoning meat, poultry or other dishes.

Popcorn

Quality When Dried—Good.

Varieties Best For Drying—Japanese Hulless, Hybrid South American Mushroom and Creme-Puff Hybrid.

Selection—Choose fresh ears with plump kernels.

Water Content Before Drying—73%.

Preparation—Leave the ears of popcorn on the stalks until the kernels are well-dried. Or harvest when the ears are fully ripe and hang them until thoroughly dry. Remove dry kernels from the ears and package them. If you want to hang corn decoratively, pull the husks toward the base and tie in small bunches.

Pretreatment—None.

Drying Temperature—No higher than 130°F (55°C).

Dryness Test—Dried corn will shrivel. Pop a few kernels to test. Popcorn should have about 10% moisture content in order to pop well, but it will mold if too moist.

How To Use—Follow the usual procedure for popping corn.

Potatoes

Because fresh potatoes are available all year at modest prices, it is usually not economical to dry them. Keep in mind that some vitamins are lost through steaming, rinsing and drying. If potatoes are not steamed enough, they will turn black during drying and storage. The lower the moisture content in dried potatoes, the better the storage life.
Quality When Dried—Good.
Selection—Potatoes should be mature and heavy for their size with a low sugar content and free from bruises or decay. Store potatoes in a cool, dry, dark area. Exposure to sunlight or artificial light will cause a *greening* on the surface due to the development of chlorophyll. This greening may result in a bitter taste. Refrigeration or storage below 40°F (5°C) causes the potato starch to change to sugar, making the cooked potatoes too sweet and causing them to darken more during cooking or drying.
Water Content Before Drying—80%.
Preparation—Peel, wash and slice 1/4 to 3/8 inch thick or shoestring 3/16 inch thick, or grate or dice depending on how the dried potato is to be used.
Pretreatment—Steam blanch over water containing 1 teaspoon sodium bisulfite per cup of water 4 to 6 minutes or until translucent but still firm. Rinse well in cold water to remove gelled starch.
Drying Temperature—160°F (70°C) for 1 to 2 hours, 130°F (55°C) until dry.
Dryness Test—Crisp.
How To Use—Grate slices and rehydrate for hash brown potatoes. Season with bacon fat and onion. Use diced potatoes in soups, stews and casseroles.

Pumpkin

Dried pumpkin stored longer than 1 to 2 months at room temperature develops an undesirable flavor. Keep dried pumpkin as cool and dry as possible during storage.
Quality When Dried—Fair to good.
Selection—Mature deep orange pumpkins, heavy for their size and with a fresh, glossy smooth skin dry best.
Water Content Before Drying—90%.
Preparation—Wash, cut in half and remove stems, seeds and fibrous tissues. Peel thin outer skin. Cut in 1/4-inch strips.
Pretreatment—Steam for 2 or 3 minutes or until almost tender.
Drying Temperature—140°F (60°C) for 2 to 3 hours, 130°F (55°C) until dry.
Dryness Test—Very tough to brittle.
How To Use—Rehydrate dried pumpkin and blend in a blender to use as baby food or in pumpkin pie.

Radishes

Not recommended for drying.

Rutabagas

Quality When Dried—Fair to good.
Selection—Rutabagas should be firm and heavy for their size, well-shaped, either round or elongated, and smooth. Before processing, store at refrigerator temperature, 35° to 40° (1° to 3°C), to maintain highest quality.
Water Content Before Drying—87%.
Preparation—Wash and peel thinly. Slice 1/2 inch thick or cut into 1/2-inch dice.
Pretreatment—Water blanch 2 to 3 minutes or steam blanch 3 to 5 minutes.
Drying Temperature—140°F (60°C) for 2 hours, 130°F (55°C) until dry.
Dryness Test—Very tough to brittle.
How To Use—Add to soups or stews. Or mash with butter, mix with cream and season with nutmeg, dill, thyme, onion or chives.

Shell Beans

See Legumes page 51.

Soybeans

See Legumes, page 51.

Spinach

See Greens, page 60.

Squash, Summer

Store dried squash no longer than 1 month, keeping it very cool and dry. Dried squash may be stored longer in the freezer.
Quality When Dried—Poor to fair.
Varieties Best For Drying—White, yellow, light or dark green varieties.
Selection—Choose fresh, firm, well-shaped squash with shiny smooth skin. They should be heavy for their size and fairly young. Before processing, store only briefly at refrigerator temperature, 35° to 40°F (1° to 3°C), to maintain highest quality.
Water Content Before Drying—94%.
Preparation—Wash, peel, if desired, and slice 1/4 to 3/8 inch thick. Coarsely grate zucchini or slice crosswise 3/16 to 3/8 inch thick for chips.
Pretreatment—To use rehydrated and in cooking, steam 2 to 3 minutes. For zucchini chips, do not steam, but sprinkle with a seasoned salt or dip in barbecue sauce before drying.

Drying Temperature—140°F (60°C) for 1 to 2 hours, 130°F (55°C) until dry.

Dryness Test—Tough to brittle.

How To Use—Zucchini chips stored at room temperature must be used within one week. Serve other dried squash sliced or grated in cream or cheese sauce, seasoned with onion, basil, marjoram or oregano. Grated diced zucchini may be reconstituted and used in zucchini bread.

Sweet Potatoes or Yams

Dried sweet potatoes stored longer than 1 or 2 months at room temperature develop an undesirable flavor. Keep cool and dry during storage.

Quality When Dried—Fair.

Selection—Choose thick chunky medium-size potatoes that taper toward the ends. They should be free from decay or blemishes. Before processing, store only briefly in a dry area at 55°F (12°C) to maintain highest quality.

Water Content Before Drying—71%.

Preparation—Steam blanch 2 or 3 minutes or until almost tender.

Drying Temperature—140°F (60°C) for 2 to 3 hours, 130°F (55°C) until dry.

Dryness Test—Very tough to brittle.

How To Use—Rehydrate dried sweet potatoes or yams and use to make candied yams. They may also be browned or fried. Substitute rehydrated sweet potatoes or yams for pumpkin in bread, pies, cookies or cakes.

Tomatoes

Dried tomatoes have become a very popular gourmet item in the past several years. (See *Gourmet Dried Tomatoes*, page 52.) They are easy to dry at home and have a variety of uses.

The best tomatoes for drying are the Roma or paste tomatoes because they have more flesh and less water.

Package them securely to exclude air and moisture and freeze or refrigerate to maintain high quality during storage.

Quality When Dried—Good.

Varieties Best For Drying—Plum or paste tomatoes dry best because they have a meatier flesh. These varieties are all excellent: Red Pear, Roma VF, LaRoma, Del Oro, San Marzano, Hungarian Italian, Viva Italia and Super Italian Paste. Round varieties may also be dried, but have less flavor and shrink more because they are higher in water content. Dried tomatoes occasionally turn black during drying due to low acid content or from oxidation. Dark or black dried tomatoes are not harmful but are not very appetizing. Select high acid tomatoes if possible to prevent blackening.

Selection—Choose firm, ripe, bright red tomatoes (preferably vine ripened). They should be heavy for their size, thick-walled, with a high acid content. If tomatoes are completely ripe and dark red, store at 50° to 60°F (10° to 15°C) before processing. If not fully ripe, store at 65° to 70°F (18° to 20°C) until completely ripe. Storing with an apple in a brown paper bag hastens ripening. Refrigerator storage causes breakdown of the cell structure and gives tomatoes a watery texture.

Water Content Before Drying—85 to 94%, depending on variety.

Preparation—Wash and remove center stem core. For Roma tomatoes, slice lengthwise in 1/2- to 3/4-inch slices or halve or quarter. Dry skin side-down. Skins may also be removed if desired. To peel, immerse in boiling water 30 to 45 seconds. Immediately place in cold water and peel. For round tomatoes, slice in 1/2- to 3/4-inch slices.

Drying Temperature—140°F (60°C) until dry.

Dryness Test—Tough to crisp.

How To Use—Dried tomatoes are especially nice when seasoned with Italian spices and garlic in olive oil. Store covered in the refrigerator 6 months or up to a year in the freezer. Chop dried tomatoes in a blender for seasoning salads, soups, mixed vegetables, casseroles or sauces. Tomatoes do not rehydrate well for use in salads. Use as you would stewed tomatoes. Chop just before use.

Turnips

Quality When Dried—Fair to good.

Selection—Choose smooth, round, firm turnips with fresh tops. They should be crisp and not woody. Before processing, store at refrigerator temperature, 35° to 40°F (1° to 3°C), to maintain highest quality.

Water Content Before Drying—92%.

Preparation—Wash, remove tops and peel turnips thinly. Slice 3/8 inch thick or cut into 3/8-inch dice.

Pretreatment—Water blanch 3 to 5 minutes or steam blanch 5 to 8 minutes.

Drying Temperature—140°F (60°C) for 2 hours, 130°F (55°C) until dry.

Drying Test—Very tough to brittle.

How To Use—Add rehydrated white turnips to soups or stews. Rehydrated yellow turnips are good mashed. Add 1/2 teaspoon sugar per cup of rehydrating water to improve flavor.

Yams

See Sweet Potatoes, this page.

Zucchini

See Squash, Summer, page 63.

Herbs & Spices

Herbs and spices come from a variety of plants and parts of plants. Many herbs such as basil, marjoram or mint are valued for their leaves; dill and parsley for both their leaves and stems. Cloves are flower buds, allspice comes from a berry and nutmeg comes from the fruit of a plant. And from another part of the plant come poppy, caraway or mustard seeds.

Herbs are classified as any flowering plant whose stem above the ground does not become woody. This definition includes a wide variety of vegetables and some fruits. However, for those of us who grow and use herbs, they can be defined as any plant valued for culinary flavor and aroma or medicinal properties.

Herbs are usually grown in temperate climates while many spices require a tropical climate. Some fresh herbs and spices are available seasonally. Others such as parsley, basil, dill, ginger root, fresh coriander and tarragon are more common.

Herbs and spices have little, if any, nutritive value, but their unique flavors and aromas are indispensible in creating the favorite foods of the world. Fresh herbs and spices have a stronger aroma and flavor than dried and are prized by food lovers and gourmet cooks. Dried herbs and spices are next-best and are used more often than fresh because they are available and convenient. They may lose some of their flavoring oils when dried, but drying also concentrates the flavor by removing the moisture. Most herbs contain from 70 to 85 percent water. Eight ounces of fresh herbs will yield about one ounce dried.

GROW YOUR OWN

If you have the space and time, you may want to plant an herb garden. Herbs grow fairly well with a minimal amount of care.

Plant outside herb gardens where they will get plenty of sunshine. Keep the area free of weeds. To avoid confusion about what is what, define areas for each herb with dividers or other plants. In milder climates, some perennial herbs such as mint or thyme can be harvested most of the year.

A number of herbs can be grown indoors on a sunny windowsill or covered porch. Herbs such as chervil, chives, marjoram, mint, oregano, rosemary or sage will grow indoors successfully most of the year. Nurseries and occasionally produce markets have *starts,* small plants that grow more quickly than seeds.

Drying Herbs & Spices—How to Begin

For the best flavor, use scissors to gather leaves and stems on a sunny morning just after the dew has evaporated and before the heat of the sun has dissipated the flavoring oils. The leaves of most herbs should be still green and tender and harvested just before the plant begins to flower. Harvest plants in the mint family when they are in full bloom for the best flavor. The new leaves at the tip of the plant are usually the most flavorful. After flowering, many herbs have a bitter taste and the leaves are not as aromatic because more energy has gone into the buds. Leaves and stems of several herbs may be harvested three or four times during the summer and others may be gathered year-round.

The flowers of some herbs are flavorful and should be harvested when they first open and while still very fresh.

Harvest fully mature seeds of plants such as mustard or caraway. Some seeds change from bright green to brown or gray as they mature.

PREPARATION

Lightly rinse leaves and stems with cold water, either by submerging or holding under running water; shake off excess water. Cut off dead or discolored leaves or stems.

To prepare flower petals, wash, then separate petals and trim any tough or discolored parts. If the flowers are to be used for tea, they must be dried whole.

Seed pods, depending upon how much they have dried on the plant, may be left as is until the outer covering is sufficiently dried so that it may be easily removed. When the outer covering is fairly dry, rub the seeds between the palms of your hands, blowing to remove the chaff or husks. The seeds are then dried until there is no evidence of moisture when they are crushed. Do not heat seeds to be used for planting or they will not germinate.

How to Dry Herbs

BAG DRYING

> **You Will Need:**
> Small brown paper bags
> String

Bag Drying is one of the simplest ways to dry leafy herbs with long stems. Tie the herbs in small bunches by the ends of the stems. Suspend them upside down in small brown paper bags, which have been labeled. Tie a string firmly around the top of each bag. Hanging them upside down will cause the flavoring oils from the stems to concentrate in the leaves. Cut several 1/2-inch holes in each side of the bags to let air circulate and to speed drying. Hang them in the kitchen, attic or anywhere there is a warm even temperature and good air circulation. If you are drying large quantities of herbs and hanging a number of bags in the same place, suspend them with different lengths of string to allow good air circulation between the bags.

When the leaves are sufficiently dry, usually in 5 to 10 days, they will crumble easily. Check by opening the bag and feeling the leaves. If they are dry enough, roll the bag gently between your hands so the leaves will crumble from the stems and fall to the bottom of the bag. Leaves that are not completely dry will mold during storage.

Seed pods with long stems may also be dried in bags. The seeds will fall to the bottom of the bag as they dry.

> ## No Pests Allowed
> With some seeds, there is the possibility of insect contamination. To be sure all insects are removed, cut the stalks, dip the stalks and heads in boiling water and drain on a paper towel before drying. Do not dip seeds that are going to be used for planting.

How to Bag Dry

1/After the herbs have been rinsed and the dead or discolored ones removed, tie them in small bunches at the bottom of the stems.

2/Place the herbs leaf-ends first in a paper bag which has several 1/2-inch holes on each side. The holes are for air circulation. Tie a string firmly around the top of the bag and the stems of the herbs. Hang the bag in a warm place for 5 to 10 days until the herbs are dry.

ROOM DRYING

You Will Need:
  Window screen   Cheesecloth
  Bricks or wooden blocks

Room Drying on a tray works well for herbs with large leaves, such as basil, or ones with short stems. Seeds and flowers may also be tray dried. An old window screen works well, is inexpensive and lets the air circulate. Wash it and cover it with a thin layer of cheesecloth. Place one layer of leaves, stems, flowers or seeds on the tray and cover them with another thin layer of cheesecloth to keep off dust and insects. Place the tray in a clean warm location, preferably on props, such as bricks or wooden blocks, to allow the air to circulate underneath. Turn the herbs over every day or two so they will dry evenly.

OVEN DRYING

You Will Need:
  Nylon net or window screens

Oven Drying removes much of the essential oil because a low constant temperature cannot be maintained. Most gas ovens usually generate enough heat with just the pilot light, but it is difficult to adjust electric ovens to keep the temperature below 100°F (40°C). If you use your gas oven with the pilot light, cover the oven racks with a nylon net or old window screens. Arrange the herb seeds one layer deep. Prop the oven door open slightly to let the moisture escape.

MICROWAVE-OVEN DRYING

You Will Need:
  Paper towels

Microwave Ovens may be used to dry small quantities of herbs. Place 4 or 5 stalks with leaves between paper towels. Set the microwave timer for 2 to 3 minutes. Check to see if the stems and leaves are sufficiently dry. If not, reset the timer for an additional 30 seconds and check again. Repeat the process if necessary.

DEHYDRATORS

Dehydrator drying is the most efficient and produces the highest quality dried herbs because it takes only 1 to 3 hours, has controlled temperature and good air circulation. Place the prepared herbs on the drying trays in a preheated dryer with the thermostat set for 90° to 100°F (about 35°C) and dry. Do not dry herbs with moist loads of fruits or vegetables. Not only will the increased humidity lengthen the drying time for the herbs, but fruits and vegetables are usually dried at a much higher temperature than herbs. These higher temperatures dissipate the herbs' flavoring oils.

SUN DRYING

Sun Drying is not recommended for herbs because losses in aroma, flavor and color are high.

TESTING FOR DONENESS

Herbs are dry when they crumble easily. Stems should be brittle and break when bent. Seeds will readily fall from the chaff, but usually need additional drying after they have been removed from the seed pods. Seeds should be brittle. If herbs and seeds are not sufficiently dry, they may mold.

CONDITIONING

Conditioning ensures that sufficient moisture has been removed to prevent molding during storage. Place the herbs or seeds in an airtight container for several days. Check daily for condensation on the inside of the container. If condensation appears, dry the herbs or seeds longer.

PACKAGING

Package dried herbs and seeds in any type of container which excludes air, light and moisture. Air and light result in flavor loss; moisture encourages caking, color loss or insects. Dark-colored jars with airtight lids are excellent. Paper or cardboard containers will absorb flavoring oils and will not protect herbs from air and moisture.

STORAGE

Store containers of dried herbs and seeds in the coolest place available, preferably below 60°F (15°C). A cool storage temperature will keep them from fading and will hold the flavor better. Because the temperature of the kitchen is probably much warmer than your storage area, keep only small amounts ready to use and the rest in storage. Do not store kitchen containers directly over the stove.

Crushing or grinding herbs and seeds for storage increases the loss of aroma and flavor. Whole spices have the longest shelf life; ground spices the shortest. For the fullest flavor, crush just before using. With good storage conditions, dried herbs and spices should keep well for 6 months to 1 year.

How to Use Dried Herbs & Spices

Dried herbs and spices are usually 3 to 4 times stronger than their fresh counterparts because they have been concentrated. If the recipe calls for a fresh herb or spice, you can usually use 1/3 to 1/4 as much of the dried and be safe. However, the strength of dried herbs and spices depends greatly on the conditions under which they have been stored and how old they are. Strength deteriorates with the type of herb, storage time, temperature and exposure to moisture or light. Some herbs, such as mint or basil, lose their flavor more rapidly then others when dried. It may take nearly an equal volume of some dried herbs to replace the amount of fresh called for in a recipe.

The safest way to use dried herbs and spices is to start with a small amount, taste, and add more if the flavor isn't quite strong enough. Use herbs and spices sparingly. Their influence should be subtle.

Ground spices should be added about 15 minutes before the end of the cooking period. Whole spices placed in a cheesecloth bag for easy removal can be added at the beginning of cooking so the long simmering will extract the full flavor and aroma. Whole or leaf herbs should be crumbled finely just before adding to release the flavor. Flavoring seeds may be slightly roasted before using to bring out their fullest flavor.

Many herbs and spices may be combined for seasoning. The popular blend, *fines herbes,* is equal parts chives, chervil, tarragon or rosemary, and parsley. It is used to season meats, casseroles, fish, salads or egg dishes. Another frequent blend, *bouquet garni,* is made up of thyme, bay leaf, parsley and celery leaves tied in a cheesecloth bag and used to season soup stock, soups or stews. Other combinations frequently thought of as one spice or herb, such as curry powder or chili powder, are really a blend of a number of different seasonings.

Herbs & Spices: A to Z

Anise

Anise seeds should ripen on the plant. If they are picked green they will mold during storage. When ripe, their color changes from green to grayish brown. Clip clusters into a bag or basket to prevent the seeds from scattering. Cut the stems and wash the seeds in hot water to remove insects.

Anise is grown mainly for its sweet, licorice-flavored seeds, although the small tender leaves are used in fruit and vegetable salads, soups, stews or sauces. Anise seed is used in baking cookies such as the German springerle, sweet breads and cakes. It is occasionally used in spicy meats such as sausage and in poultry and coleslaw. Anise seed will add a distinct flavor to stewed fruits and fruit compotes.

Basil

Clip basil leaves 3 to 4 inches from the top of the plant just as the first buds appear. The plants may have a second and third cutting later in the summer. The flavor and color are very perishable so handle fresh basil gently to avoid bruising. Package basil carefully and store it under the best conditions.

Basil is one of the most popular herbs in Italian and Mediterranean-style cooking. It is delicious in all tomato dishes and improves many vegetables, green salads, vegetable soups, meat, fish, poultry and egg dishes.

Borage

Borage is a mild, rather uncommon herb with leaves and flowers which can be used in seasoning. Salads and cooked vegetables are enhanced by a little borage, although it is used mainly as an ornamental plant.

Caraway

The entire caraway plant is usually dried to keep

the seeds from scattering when it matures. The seeds continue to mature after the plant dies. Caraway seeds are susceptible to aphid attacks while ripening. To destroy any hidden insects, scald ripened seeds before drying them.

Caraway seeds add refreshing flavor to heavy dishes such as pork or sauerkraut. They are frequently used in Hungarian cooking, some cabbage salads, several types of cookies, rye bread and cheeses. Try them with green beans, beets, cabbage, carrots, cauliflower, potatoes, turnips, or zucchini. Use them sparingly until you become accustomed to their flavor.

Celery

Although celery is known primarily as a vegetable, the leaves are frequently used for seasoning. Celery leaves can be used in main dishes, soups, stews, salads and vegetables.

The tiny brown celery seeds come from a different variety of celery called *smallage*. They are very strong and must be used sparingly or they will overpower accompanying flavors.

Chervil

Tender green chervil leaves are frequently used as a substitute for parsley, although their flavor is milder. Chervil is popular in French cooking and can be used with other herbs in salads, sauces, soups and fish. It should be added at the end of cooking to preserve its full flavor. Try it in cottage cheese or cream cheese for dips or sandwich spreads.

Chives

Chives have a very mild onion flavor. Drying diminishes their already delicate flavor, but dried chives may be used when fresh are not available. Dehydrator drying is recommended. When dried, the long, tubular leaves are best used in moist dishes such as cottage cheese, soups or vegetables to bring out their flavor.

Cilantro

See Coriander, below.

Coriander or Cilantro

Scald coriander seeds before drying to protect against insects. Uproot the entire plant, scald and bag dry. Although coriander and cilantro are used interchangeably, coriander is the dried seeds or fruits of the plant and cilantro is the leaves.

Coriander is extremely fragrant and will dom-inate other flavors if not used with restraint. It is popular in Mexican, Chinese and Mediterranean cooking. Use it prudently in fruit or vegetable dishes and in highly spiced foods. The crushed seeds are flavorful in sausage, pickling spices, gingerbread and cookies. Add coriander seed to apples, pears or dried fruit while cooking.

Cumin

Cumin seed, whole or ground, has a warm robust flavor and is used in spicy dishes throughout much of the world. It is a popular ingredient in curries and chili.

Dill

Drying diminishes the pleasant dill flavor so to preserve as much of it as possible, package well and store in a cool dark place. All parts of the umbrella-leaved dill plant are flavorful. The mildly flavored leaves are a pleasant addition to many salads, vegetable dishes, potatoes or fish. The seeds are stronger and are frequently used in making pickles, salad dressing and strong-flavored vegetable or meat dishes. Occasionally they may be substituted for caraway seeds in some breads such as rye.

Fennel

Although fennel is grown primarily for its licorice-flavored seed, the delicate leaves may be used in salads, vegetables, soups or stews and seafood. The strong-flavored seeds are used in cookies, cakes, breads, cheese or spicy meat dishes.

Garlic

See page 60.

Ginger

Most ginger root is imported from tropical places and is frequently available fresh in supermarkets or produce departments specializing in Oriental foods. Ginger tubers should be firm and appear fresh. The small new sprouts that appear on the sides of the ginger root have a delicate flavor and may also be used. Fresh ginger freezes well and can be grated without thawing.

Ginger can be easily rooted and grown indoors from small pieces. Set the top just below the surface of the dirt and keep the soil moist . Leave the pot in a dark place until shoots appear. Then give it plenty of light.

To dry ginger, slice it thinly or grate it. Keep it as cool as possible to retain the best flavor. If you are using dried powdered ginger, 1/8 teaspoon is equivalent to 1 tablespoon grated or shredded fresh ginger root.

Its fresh spicy flavor improves many meat, vegetable and dessert dishes. The tender aromatic ginger leaves are delicious in soups.

Horseradish

See page 60.

Marjoram

Marjoram is a variety of the mint family and is slightly milder and sweeter than oregano. It grows well indoors. Cut the leaves just as the first buds begin to appear. Marjoram may be clipped 2 or 3 times a summer.

Use marjoram in Italian dishes as well as other meat, fish, poultry or egg dishes. It goes well with various vegetables, particularly tomatoes, onions and mushrooms. Use sparingly until you become familiar with its flavor; it can overpower if used too generously. Marjoram blends well with basil, chives, parsley and thyme.

Mint

A variety of mints can be cultivated in home gardens. The fresh leaves are considerably more flavorful than the dried. Because the mint flavor is very perishable, dry quickly and store carefully.

Mild spearmint is popular in sauces and mint jelly or lamb dishes. Strong-flavored peppermint can be used in candies and some beverages or baked goods. A variety of meat dishes improve with the addition of mint. Mint blends well with a few vegetables such as beans, eggplant, peas and potatoes. Crush the leaves just before adding to food. Add at the end of cooking for best flavor.

Mustard

Two main types of mustard seeds are grown: black mustard, which has potent dark brown seeds, and the lighter variety of white mustard with its milder yellowish seeds. The seeds of both vary from mild to hot, depending on the variety. These seeds are usually ground in combination with other seasonings. Mustard seeds can also be used whole in corned beef, sauerkraut, cooked cabbage and vinegar-based salad dressings.

Onions

See page 61.

Oregano

A member of the mint family, oregano is a stronger herb than its close cousin, marjoram.

It is widely used in Italian, Greek and Mexican foods, tomato dishes and with some vegetables. Use prudently until you are accustomed to its strong flavor.

Parsley, also see page 61

Parsley has a much higher food value than most herbs and is frequently classified as a vegetable.

When cutting parsley, always remove the outer leaves rather than the inner leaves, as growth is from the center. The curly variety of French parsley is the most popular for garnishing and seasoning but it tends to diminish in flavor with drying. Italian parsley with the large flat leaves holds its flavor better when dried. Dried parsley will readily reabsorb moisture from the air, so it must be packaged extremely well.

Parsley is a popular seasoning for meats, fish, soups, casseroles or vegetable dishes.

Peppers, Green & Red

See page 62.

Peppers, Chili

See page 62.

Rosemary

Rosemary grows well indoors, is easy to dry and retains most of its flavor. Its needle-like leaves add a unique flavor to many foods. Use them in barbecue sauces, egg dishes, meats, lamb, poultry and some vegetables such as cauliflower, peas, beans or zucchini.

Sage

Sage leaves are used primarily in poultry dishes such as stuffings, soups, chicken stocks or roast poultry, but they also enhance some pork, lamb, veal, game and fish dishes. Crush or grind the dried leaves to release their full flavor.

Savory

Fresh savory has a grass-like smell and a mild peppery flavor. It maintains most of its flavor when dried. There are two seasonal varieties: summer and winter savory. The color and size vary, but the flavor is markedly similar. Savory is popular in poultry seasonings and can be used in some vegetables such as green beans or peas.

Smallage

See Celery, page 69.

Tarragon

Dried tarragon loses its pungency rather quickly, so take care in packaging and storage.

Tarragon has a characteristic flavor which makes it a valuable seasoning in vinegar, sauces, salads,

fish, lamb, poultry and veal. Only fresh tarragon should be used in making tarragon vinegar.

Thyme

Cut thyme leaves just as the buds appear but before they begin to blossom. French thyme has the best flavor when dried and is easily grown from seed.

Thyme is one of the stronger herbs with a heavy aroma and spicy taste that faintly resembles cloves. Use sparingly in meat, fish and poultry dishes. It is a good seasoning for some vegetables such as green beans, beets, carrots, potatoes and tomatoes as well as vegetable soups.

Herbs & Spices You Can Grow & Dry

Herb or Spice	When Harvested	Part of Plant Dried
Anise (annual)	Before blossoming	Leaves
	Fall	Seeds
Basil (annual)	Summer	Leaves
Borage (annual)	When mature	Leaves
	First blossoming	Flowers
Caraway (biennial)	Fall of second season	Seeds
Celery (annual)	When mature	Leaves
Chervil (annual)	When mature	Leaves
Chives (perennial)	Throughout growing season	Leaves—cut 1-1/2 to 2 inches from roots
Coriander or Cilantro (annual)	Summer	Leaves and stems
	Fall	Seeds
Cumin	When mature	Seeds
Dill (annual)	First blossoming & throughout growing season	Leaves and stems
	First blossoming	Flowers
	Fall	Seeds
Fennel (perennial)	Before blossoming	Leaves
	When mature	Seeds
Ginger	When mature	Roots
Marjoram (annual)	When mature	Leaves
Mint (perennial)	Throughout growing season	Leaves
Mustard	When mature	Seeds
Oregano (annual)	First blossoming	Leaves
	First blossoming	Flowers
Parsley (biennial)	When mature	Leaves and stems
Rosemary (perennial)	When mature	Needle-like leaves
Sage (perennial)	Before blossoming	Leaves
Savory (annual)	When mature	Leaves
Tarragon (perennial)	Before blossoming	Leaves
Thyme (perennial	When mature	Leaves

Baby Food

These recipes for making your own baby food are convenient, nutritious and real money-savers. If you want to try them today but have not yet dried your own fruit, use commercially dried fruit. Make vegetables for very young babies from powdered dried vegetables. Toddlers will appreciate added texture so make theirs with vegetable flakes. To make vegetable flakes and powders, see pages 54 and 55.

Vegetables

1/4 cup vegetable powder or flakes,
   pages 54 and 55

1/2 to 3/4 cup hot milk,
   formula or water

In a small bowl, pour hot milk, formula or water over vegetable powder. Let stand 10 to 15 minutes. Stir. Serve warm. Makes 3/4 to 1 cup baby food.

Meat-Vegetable Dinner

2 to 3 tablespoons vegetable powder or flakes
3/4 cup hot water, milk or formula

1/2 cup cubed cooked beef, ham, lamb or veal

Place vegetable powder or flakes in blender. Add hot water, milk or formula. Let stand 10 to 20 minutes. Add cubed meat. Blend until smooth. Serve warm. Makes 1-1/2 cups baby food.

How to Make Baby Food

1/Pour hot milk, formula or water over vegetable flakes. Let them stand 10 to 15 minutes to reconstitute. Serve at room temperature or warm before serving.

2/Put fruit slices or chips in a blender container. Cover them with boiling water and let them stand 20 to 30 minutes to reconstitute. Puree in the blender. You may want to strain the puree for infants. Stir the fruit into prepared baby cereal.

Fruit Puree

1/2 cup dried fruit
Boiling water

Place fruit in blender. Cover fruit with boiling water. Let stand 20 to 30 minutes. Puree. Strain if desired. Makes about 1 cup baby food.

Fruit Puree & Cereal

1/2 cup dried fruit   1 cup prepared baby cereal
Boiling water, hot milk or formula

Place fruit in blender. Cover fruit with boiling water, hot milk or formula. Let stand 20 to 30 minutes. Puree. Strain if desired. Stir into prepared baby cereal. Makes 1-1/2 to 2 cups baby food.

Chopped Fruit & Cereal

1/4 cup finely chopped dried fruit or   1/4 cup boiling water, hot milk or formula
   finely chopped fruit leather,   1 cup prepared baby cereal
   pages 36 to 43

In a small bowl, pour boiling water, milk or formula over dried fruit or fruit leather. Let stand 10 to 20 minutes. Stir into prepared baby cereal. Makes about 1-1/2 cups baby food.

Fruit Pudding

1/3 cup finely chopped dried fruit   2 egg yolks
1 cup boiling water   1/4 cup sugar
3/4 cup milk   1 tablespoon cornstarch

Place fruit in a blender. Add boiling water. Let stand 10 to 20 minutes. Blend until smooth. Add milk and egg yolks; blend. Mix sugar and cornstarch and add to fruit-egg mixture. Blend until smooth. Pour into a small saucepan. Stir over medium heat until thickened, about 10 minutes. Cool. Makes 2 cups baby food.

Vegetable Leathers & Chips

Vegetable leathers are a convenient backpacking snack and are a nice change from sweet snacks.

Vegetable leather will be smoother and easier to blend if the vegetables have been blanched first. Blanching also lengthens the shelf life of the leather. Follow pretreatment instructions for whatever vegetables you wish to include, pages 57 to 64.

Combine several of your favorite vegetables in the blender and puree until smooth. Leather may be made from a single vegetable but the flavor will not be as good.

Prepare drying trays as you would for fruit leather, page 36. Pour out the vegetable puree and dry it until it is pliable but not crisp. Roll and package it as you would fruit leather, page 37.

Vegetable leathers should be used within 2 to 3 weeks if stored at room temperature. If you wish to store them longer, refrigerate or freeze them.

VEGETABLE CHIPS

Dried thinly sliced vegetables, or vegetable chips, are a nutritious low-calorie snack. A food processor will make quick work of the slicing. Try tomato chips, cucumber chips, zucchini chips or paper-thin carrot or parsnip chips with your favorite dip. Dried vegetable chips are also good served with a variety of fresh vegetable dippers and a dip; see the photo on page 47.

Nuts & Seeds

Nuts are plant seeds or fruit encased in a *shell* or *hull* or woody fiber. The nut *kernel* is the inner edible part of the nut, also called a *nutmeat.* The *husk* is the rough outer covering which encases the shell and kernel.

Some nuts are classified as fruits or vegetables. For example, the peanut is really a member of the pea family and the almond is part of the peach family.

The kernels, or nutmeats, are extremely high in protein and fat, and contain vitamins and minerals. Nuts can be eaten fresh from the shell, roasted, or added to other foods. Their crunchy texture, high nutritive value and delicious flavor enhance appetizers, main dishes, salads, vegetables, breads, desserts and candies.

Once harvested, nuts either in the shell or out of the shell should be dried to a relatively low moisture content to store well.

Drying Nuts & Seeds—How to Begin

SELECTION

Select intact and reasonably well-shaped nuts with clean, bright shells. The nut with the shell should be heavy for its size. This usually indicates a fresh, meaty kernel.

PREPARATION

The drying of most nuts and seeds should begin soon after harvesting, usually within 24 hours.

Little preparation is needed for most nuts. To sort, immerse the nuts in water, removing and discarding those that float. This also removes dirt and insects which may have accumulated on the shells. Shelling nuts first lessens drying time, but dried shelled nuts must be refrigerated or frozen. Nuts dried and stored in the shell will keep several months at room temperature.

How to Dry Nuts & Seeds

Spread nuts in a single layer on drying trays, letting air circulate freely on all sides. The optimum drying temperature is from 90° to 100°F (30° to 40°C). Temperatures above 100°F (40°C) will shorten the storage life and affect the flavor. Shelled nuts must be protected from contamination. If you sun dry them, cover them with cheesecloth. Peanuts, page 76, and seeds, page 77, may be dried at slightly higher temperatures.

Small amounts of unshelled nuts can be dried in a furnace room, an attic, or on a radiator, as long as the temperature does not exceed 100°F (40°C). They will be dry in 24 to 48 hours. Shelled nuts may be dried the same way as long as they are covered with cheesecloth to protect them from dust. If your dehydrator can be adjusted to a low enough temperature, it is ideal for drying nuts because the air circulation is much better than in room drying. Unshelled nuts will dry in 8 to 10 hours in a dehydrator. Oven drying is not recommended for nuts because it is difficult to keep the temperature low enough.

DRYNESS TEST

Nuts are dry when their shells have hardened to a brittle state. Crack one. The nutmeat should be tender but not shriveled by overdrying.

Nuts stored in the shell should contain roughly 7 to 8 percent moisture for the best storage stability; shelled nuts about 3 to 5 percent. Depending on the amount of moisture and the weight of the shell, the yield from different nuts will vary. In general, 1 pound of unshelled nuts will yield the following: almonds, 6-1/2 ounces; Brazil nuts, 8 ounces; filberts, pecans or English walnuts, 7 ounces; or black walnuts, 3-1/2 ounces.

PACKAGING AND STORING

Nuts in the Shell—Store them in airtight plastic, metal or glass containers below 70°F (20°C). As with other dried foods, the lower the storage temperature, the longer the storage life. Because nuts contain so much oil and fat, they quickly become rancid at higher temperatures. Nuts in the shell may also be stored in airtight containers in the refrigerator or freezer, although they will take a lot of space.

Shelled Nuts—Package them in airtight plastic or glass containers or heavy plastic bags and store them in the refrigerator or freezer. Be sure they are packaged well or they will absorb odors and flavors from other foods. They will not keep longer than 1 to 2 months at room temperature. When nuts are refrigerated or frozen, let the container return to room temperature before opening. This prevents the cold nuts from drawing moisture from the air, which will cause them to mold or turn rancid more quickly.

ROASTING NUTS

Roasted or toasted nuts and seeds have a fuller flavor compared to raw dried nuts or seeds. They are heated to 250° to 300°F (120° to 150°C) and may be coated with oil, salt or other seasonings while they are being roasted.

Roasted nuts and seeds have a shorter shelf life than dried nuts and should be eaten within 2 or 3 weeks after they have been roasted.

The dried nuts and seeds best for roasting are: Filberts, see below; macadamia nuts, page 76; pumpkin seeds and sunflower seeds, page 77.

Nuts & Seeds: A to Z

Almonds

The sweeter varieties such as the Nonpareil and Jordanolo are best for eating and cooking. The more bitter varieties are used to make almond extract.

On the tree, almonds resemble small green peaches. They do not usually fall to the ground when mature as do most other nuts. When the nuts mature, the hulls split open and the shells and kernels begin to dry while still on the tree. When most of the hulls in the center of the tree have split open, the nuts can be harvested by knocking them from the tree. Remove the hulls and dry the nuts.

Beechnuts

Beechnuts usually grow wild and are found mostly in the eastern United States. They grow inside small rough burrs about as big as a cherry. Two or more of the tiny three-sided nuts are contained in each burr or husk.

The mature nuts fall from the husks to the ground. Squirrels like them, so harvest beechnuts immediately after they have fallen from the tree or the squirrels will get them before you do.

Brazil Nuts

Brazil nuts are grown wild, exclusively in the dense forests of South America. The fruit is similar to the coconut, about 4 to 6 inches in diameter, with a pod which contains from 12 to 30 of the nuts. The large three-sided nuts are white, oily and flavorful and are covered by a rough hard shell. Because of the rough shells, commercially dried nuts are usually put through a brushing process to brighten and smooth them.

Brazil nuts are excellent alone or combined with dried fruits and other nuts.

Butternuts

White walnuts is another name for butternuts. The majority are grown in the northeastern United States.

The butternut is about 1/2 inch in diameter and roughly 2 inches long with a fragile smooth shell. Dry in or out of the shell and store accordingly. Use this sweet nut with mild-flavored foods.

Cashews

Cashews are the seeds of a soft, juicy pear-shaped fruit called a *cashew apple*. The kidney-shaped cashew nut is usually about 1 inch long and is covered by a double shell. The kernel has a delicate flavor and a firm fine texture. India and East Africa are the world's foremost producers of cashers. Some are grown on the coasts of Florida.

Cashews are excellent alone or in Oriental-style main dishes. They can be used in baked goods and fruit and nut combinations.

Filberts

Filberts, or hazelnuts, are high in protein and B vitamins and contain some minerals and vitamins C and E. About 75 percent of the filberts sold in the United States come from Oregon.

The nuts usually grow in clusters of two or three with each nut covered by an open-ended husk. The husks usually open with the first frost and the mature nuts fall to the ground. They will discolor if left on the ground very long.

Commercially dried filberts are bleached by sulfuring in the shell. Because the process is strictly cosmetic and fairly complicated, it is not recommended for home use.

Filberts become spongy during the drying process but regain their firm texture when dry. The filbert kernel gradually changes from white to a creamy color. When this color change is complete throughout the kernel, it is sufficiently dry.

When using filberts in cooking or baking, bring out their flavor and texture by toasting them first. Place them in a shallow pan at 275°F (135°C) for 15 to 20 minutes until the skins crack. Remove the skins by rubbing the warm nuts between your hands.

Additional information and recipes can be obtained from the Oregon Filbert Commission, 12295 S.W. Main, P.O. Box 23126, Tigard, OR 97223.

Hazelnuts

See Filberts, page 75.

Hickory Nuts

Hickory nuts are produced by shagbark or shellbark hickory trees. These trees are members of the walnut family and grow principally in the central and northeastern United States.

The smooth-shelled nuts are enclosed in a green husk which turns brown as it matures and releases the sweet-flavored nut in the shell.

Indian Nuts

See Pine Nuts, this page.

Macadamia Nuts

Macadamia nuts are grown in California, Florida and Hawaii. When fully ripe, the thick husks split open and the hard-shelled nuts fall to the ground. They are harvested immediately, the shells removed, and the nuts are dried. The shells are difficult to crack because they are about 1/8 inch thick. This may be why they are so expensive.

The delicate mild-flavored nut is delicious eaten fresh or roasted, alone or in dried fruit and nut combinations. To roast, place them in a shallow pan at 275°F (135°C) for 15 to 20 minutes.

Peanuts

Peanuts, actually a member of the pea family, mature beneath the surface of the soil. Their shell is the softest of any of the nuts. Because they are a legume instead of a nut, they can be dried and roasted at slightly higher temperatures.

Spread peanuts on trays and dry at 130°F (55°C). Store them shelled or unshelled. To roast peanuts in the shell, place them in a shallow pan at 300°F (150°C) for 30 to 40 minutes. If they have been shelled, roast them for 20 to 25 minutes and stir frequently to prevent scorching.

Pecans

Pecans are grown mostly in the southern United States, but may be grown from southern Indiana and Iowa down into Mexico.

The nuts are mature when the green husks turn brown and open. The nuts usually fall to the ground or may be knocked down with a long pole. The smooth brown shells are usually oval-shaped, but are round in a few varieties. Their dull finish is usually polished before marketing.

They add delicious flavor to breads, cookies, candies and many fruit dishes.

Pignons

See Pine Nuts, below.

Pine Nuts

These tiny, sweet-flavored nuts, also known as Indian Nuts, Pignons and Pinons, are about the size of an orange seed. They are grown on the Nut Pine tree in the southwestern United States. Their delicious flavor makes the tedious process of cracking them worthwhile.

They are usually sufficiently dry when they fall to the ground, but should be packaged and stored to prevent additional moisture absorption.

Piñons

See Pine Nuts, above.

Pistachios

Pistachios are seeds from the fruit of the pistachio tree which is grown primarily in tropical climates. The majority of pistachios are imported, but central California is beginning to produce a new variety.

The nuts have a double shell; the outer one is red and the inner one is multicolored. Commercially, this inner shell is frequently dyed red for eye-appeal.

The long yellow-green pistachio seed is popular by itself or in candies and ice cream.

Pumpkin Seeds

Carefully wash pumpkin seeds to remove the clinging fibrous pumpkin tissue. Dry them in the sun or in a dehydrator at 115° to 120°F (45° to 50°C) until crisp. Seeds can be oven dried at 150°F (65°C) for 1 to 2 hours. Stir them frequently to prevent scorching. Dehydrator or oven drying is faster than sun drying and there is little taste difference.

Roast dried pumpkin seeds by tossing them lightly with oil and salt and placing them in a preheated oven at 250°F (120°C) for 10 to 15 minutes.

Sunflower Seeds

Sunflower seeds ripen on the flower and are usually left there to dry. If birds are enjoying the seeds, wrap cheesecloth around the flower until the seeds are dried.

The seeds may be shaken off the flower when they are mature, then dried in the sun for several days or in a dehydrator at 100°F (40°C). When dry, the seeds may be roasted in a shallow pan in a 300°F (150°C) oven for 10 to 15 minutes.

Walnuts, Black

Black walnuts grow in clusters with a thick green husk covering the shell of each nut. The dark shells have numerous coarse ridges and do not split into halves as English walnuts do. The nutmeat is very difficult to extract. They are a very flavorful nut but usually are not grown commercially.

Black walnuts will fall from the tree as they ripen. To remove the tough husks, crush them with a hammer or under your heel. Wear gloves to avoid stains from the brown dye in the shells. Dry them in the shell.

Walnuts, English

English walnuts are the most popular of the walnut family and there are several different varieties. The trees grow best in a moderate climate and the United States, mainly California and Oregon, is the world's foremost producer.

The husks of mature nuts are cracked when they fall from the tree. Harvest them immediately, leaving the uncracked nuts on the ground until they are fully ripe and the husks come off easily.

The fresh nutmeat should be white. Old or rancid kernels are a dull gray. Dry walnuts until the divider between the halves breaks with a snap. If the divider is rubbery, dry further.

Because the walnut's shell is not very appealing, the shells are frequently bleached after the nuts are completely dry to improve their appearance. Bleach only those nuts which have a closed shell to prevent the bleach solution from penetrating to the kernel.

Bleaching walnuts is an optional procedure. It does not affect the flavor of the nuts.

If you decide to bleach walnuts, use household chlorine bleach. Refer to the container for the chlorine percentage and add the amount recommended below for each gallon of lukewarm water.

Chlorine content	Amount per gallon
5%	28 fl. oz. (3-1/2 cups)
10%	14 fl. oz. (1-3/4 cups)
12%	12 fl. oz. (1-1/2 cups)
14%	10 fl. oz. (1-1/4 cups)
16%	9 fl. oz. (1-1/8 cups)
18%	8 fl. oz. (1 cup)
20%	7 fl. oz. (7/8 cup)

A tablespoon of vinegar per gallon of solution will speed the bleaching action. Hold nuts in the solution 3 to 4 minutes, then remove, drain and dry them. The bleaching action will continue for a day or two. The bleach solution may be used repeatedly with other batches of nuts.

Other Uses for Your Dryer

● *To incubate yogurt*, the temperature should be about 110°F (45°C).

● *To raise yeast breads*, use a temperature of 80° to 85°F (25° to 30°C). Cover the dough with a damp cloth to prevent it from drying out.

● *To dry flowers*, set the temperature control at 100° to 140°F (40° to 60°C). Follow your usual flower-drying procedures and flowers that usually take 3 weeks will be ready in a day!

● *To dry craft items*, use a temperature of 100° to 160°F (40° to 70°C) to shorten drying time.

● *To recrisp crackers and cookies*, heat them at 160°F (70°C) for at least 30 minutes and not more than 2 hours.

● *To decrystallize raw honey*, heat it at 120°F (48°C), in plastic or glass containers, for 2 to 3 days until no sugar crystals remain. Crystals will form again after 1 or 2 months if honey is stored at room temperature. For Creamed Honey, which will keep up to 1 year, see page 100.

Meat & Fish

Somewhere long ago, primitive man built fires to keep flies away from the drying food and to speed the drying process. He discovered that fish and meat exposed to smoke could be kept longer and had a different and enjoyable flavor. Now we know that chemicals in the smoke retard deterioration during drying by slowing bacterial growth.

Later, man discovered that heavily salting meat or fish before smoking and drying improved its flavor and storage life. It was also discovered that certain salts contained chemical compounds, now known as nitrates, which helped preserve meats and fish, and in some cases improved their color and flavor.

Seasoning, salting, smoking, drying or any combination of these became known as *curing*. Curing may also involve the use of preservatives such as sugar or vinegar, or curing salts such as sodium nitrite. Curing techniques have been improved through the ages giving us a variety of preserved meat and fish products which maintain excellent quality for long periods.

Types of Dried Meats & Fish

Jerky is raw meat or fish which has been salted, sometimes smoked, and then dried. See Meat Jerky, pages 79 to 82, and Fish Jerky, pages 87 to 88.

Dried Cooked Meat, page 82, is first cooked, then cut in small pieces and dried. Salting or smoking are unnecessary because most of the bacteria are destroyed during cooking. The meat can be reconstituted by adding water.

Smoked Fish, page 86, is salted, smoked and partially dried. Although smoked fish, with its high moisture content, cannot be stored safely at room temperature and must be refrigerated, smoking is a popular way of preserving fish for a short time.

Fish Jerky, pages 87 and 88, is raw fish which has been salted, sometimes smoked, then dried to a low moisture content.

Do not confuse fish jerky with smoked fish. Fish jerky may also be smoked but has a lower moisture content than smoked fish and can be stored at room temperature.

Equipment for Curing & Drying

A Sharp Knife or Electric Slicer is necessary to cut meat into thin strips or to clean and fillet fish.

Containers of appropriate size for curing or marinating should be made of glass, stoneware, stainless steel or plastic. Do not use containers made of wood or metals other than stainless steel.

A Commercial or Homemade Smoker is needed if you want a smoked product. There are two kinds of smokers: smokehouses and smoking ovens. The only difference between them is size.

Some of the most efficient homemade smokers are made from garbage cans or old refrigerators by adding vents, a simple heating element and wire racks. A covered outdoor barbecue grill can be used to smoke jerky. It cannot be used for drying because of the lack of temperature control. In the U.S., contact your local County Extension Service for details on making your own smoker.

Mild-Flavored Smoking Chips made of non-resinous hard wood such as alder, apple, ash, beech, hickory, maple, oak or white birch are essential for smoking.

Vegetable Oil, Mineral Oil or Non-stick Vegetable Spray will prevent food from sticking to drying trays or racks.

A Temperature-Controlled Dryer or Oven is required to dry the cured meat or fish.

Storage Containers to refrigerate or freeze the finished product differ according to the process used. See pages 80, 81, 86 and 87.

Jerky

WHAT MEATS TO USE

Use fresh or frozen lean meat for jerky. The leaner the meat, the better the quality of the finished product. **Beef**—Flank, round and sirloin tip cuts are more economical than cheaper cuts which contain more bone and fat. Rump cuts may be used but they have more gristle. For further economy, buy *good* or *utility* grades of beef rather than *choice*. The cheapest way to go is with lean ground beef. American Harvest sells a special jerky press which can be used for pressing ground meat into jerky. They also carry a fantastic jerky seasoning mix. For current prices, write or call: American Harvest, Alternative Pioneering Systems, Inc., 4064 Peavey Road, Chaska, MN 55318-9908. (800) 288-4545 FAX (612) 448-3864

Lamb—To make lamb jerky, use the leg or shoulder cuts. Lamb makes less desirable jerky because it has a higher fat content. Cutting the meat from the bone is much easier if it has been partially frozen.

Pork—Fresh pork should not be used for jerky because drying temperatures are not high enough to kill harmful bacteria or the trichinella parasite which causes trichinosis, a disease that can be fatal. Ham jerky may be made from fully cooked ham and should be used within one to two weeks.

Game Meats—Deer, elk, antelope and other game meats all make good jerky. Any cut can be used, but the loin, round and flank cuts are best. As a precaution against disease, freeze game meats for at least 60 days at 0°F (-20°C) before drying.

Poultry—Raw poultry is usually not made into jerky because the flavor and texture is much better cooked. There is also a danger of salmonella food poisoning. Smoked turkey breasts can be sliced and dried into an acceptable jerky. Fresh poultry can be cooked and then dried for use in soups and stews. See Dried Cooked Meats, page 82. **If raw or smoked poultry is made into jerky, it must be dried at 160°F (60°C) for at least one hour to destroy salmonella bacteria that can cause food poisoning.**

HOW TO BEGIN

About four pounds of lean, boneless meat will make one pound of jerky.

Do not sun dry jerky or dry at temperatures below 140°F to 160°F (60° to 70°C). The risk of spoilage and food poisoning are too great.

PREPARATION

Slice meat into long strips 3/16 to 1/4 inch thick. Uniform slices will shorten the drying time, so use a meat slicer or have your butcher slice it for you. If you slice the meat without an electric slicer, partially freeze it first to make cutting easier. Cut across the grain for increased tenderness. Remove excess fat.

SALTING & SEASONING

There are two ways to cure meat for making jerky at home.

Brine Curing uses a salt and water mixture to soak meat until the salt has been absorbed. Brines may also contain seasonings and other curing ingredients.

Dry Curing uses a mixture of salt and seasonings which are applied directly to the meat without adding water.

The amount of salt used varies with the type of meat, the method of smoking or drying, taste preference and how the meat will be stored.

Any type of fine quality sodium chloride salt intended for food use may be used. Pure pickling salt is a good choice, although it is slightly coarser

1/With a sharp knife, slice partially frozen lean meat across the grain. The strips should be no more than 1/4 inch thick.

than table salt. I don't recommend bulk salt, also called *rock salt,* because it does not dissolve easily and contains impurities.

Precise controls are difficult to maintain in home drying. For this reason, I do not recommend the use of sodium nitrite unless it is contained in a commercially prepared curing preparation such as Morton's *Tender Quick.* Follow the package instructions.

Meats dried at home without sodium nitrite should be safe when stored at room temperature if the moisture concentration is sufficiently low. If in doubt, refrigerate or freeze the dried meat.

Place the strips of meat in single layers on a clean flat surface. Liberally sprinkle both sides with a salt and seasoning mixture, see the recipes on pages 151 to 155, or use a commercial curing preparation.

Put the meat strips in a tightly covered glass, stoneware, plastic or stainless steel container and marinate in the refrigerator for 6 to 12 hours. Stir occasionally to be sure each piece is covered with the salt and seasoning mixture. Keep the meat tightly covered, particularly if liquid smoke is used, because the smell will penetrate everything in the refrigerator.

Smoke jerky for added flavor either before or after drying. Jerky doesn't have to be smoked as long before drying because the smoke penetrates undried meat better than dried.

2/Place the strips of meat in a tightly covered container with the dry cure or marinade and refrigerate the container.

If you are using a smoker to dry jerky, keep a constant temperature of 100° to 120°F (40° to 50°C) for 6 to 8 hours. Increase the temperature to 140° to 160°F (60° to 70°C) for 2 to 3 hours or until dry. The beginning temperature may be lower in a smoker when it is used for drying because the smoke inhibits the growth of surface bacteria.

Nitrites

Sodium nitrite is a compound which has long been used in the curing and preservation of meat and fish. In the presence of heat, sodium nitrite combines with muscle pigment to give the characteristic color and flavor to cured meat. Without sodium nitrite, bacon is salt pork, frankfurters are bratwurst and ham is salty roast pork. In addition to giving color and flavor, sodium nitrite prevents spoilage and the growth of harmful bacteria, particularly the bacteria which causes botulism. It also retards oxidation which gives cured meats an undesirable flavor.

Sodium nitrite is commonly used as a preservative in commercially dried jerky with the same benefits as in cured or processed meats, mainly to prevent the growth of food poisoning toxins.

The use of nitrites in processed and cured meats such as bacon, ham and jerky, is currently being investigated by the Federal Drug Administration. They must be used with very careful controls to assure safety in the prepared product. The FDA discusses their use in the home drying of meats in the Code of Federal Regulations. Title 21, Part 172.175. Further information can be found in FDA Consumer Memo Nitrates and Nitrites, DHEW Publication No. (FDA) 73-2034. It can be obtained from the US Dept. of Health, Education and Welfare, Public Health Service, Food and Drug Administration, 5600 Fishers Lane, Rockville, MD 20852.

If you want smoked flavor without going through the smoking process, there are two types of smoke-flavored seasonings available.

Liquid Smoke is made by a wood distilling process and gives a very strong smoke flavor. Use it sparingly, mixed with water and other seasonings.

Hickory-Flavored Smoked Salt is also available for seasoning meat and fish.

Neither of these seasonings has any preservative qualities and should be considered strictly as flavor enhancers.

HOW TO DRY MEAT FOR JERKY

Place the meat strips on drying racks. Do not overlap the strips to ensure good air circulation.
Dehydrator Drying—Use a temperature of 140° to 160°F (60° to 70°C) for the first 3 to 4 hours. The temperature may be reduced to as low as 130°F (55°C) after 4 hours until dry, if desired. Occasionally blot the jerky with paper towels as it dries to remove beads of oil.
Oven Drying—The temperature should be 140° to 160°F (60° to 70°C) for the first 8 to 10 hours. After that it may be lowered to 130°F (55°C) until dry. Place aluminum foil or a baking sheet underneath the drying tray to catch the drippings.

Occasionally blot the jerky with paper towels as it dries to remove beads of oil.

DRYNESS TEST

Test jerky for dryness by cooling a piece. When cool it should crack when bent but not break. There should be no moist spots.

STORING

Cool and cut jerky into 2- to 4-inch pieces with kitchen scissors before storing.

Storage is affected by the curing preparation used and the humidity and temperature of the storage area. If a commercial curing preparation containing sodium nitrite was used, store the jerky according to the package directions.

Jerky containing salt and cured without a commercial curing preparation may be stored at room temperature for 1 to 2 months. If the air humidity is low, the container should have a loose-fitting lid or one with holes punched in it. Good air circulation keeps the flavor fresher. If the humidity of the air is more than 30 percent, store jerky in an airtight container. Jerky may be refrigerated or frozen in an airtight container to increase shelf life and maintain flavor.

3/Place the meat strips on the drying trays without overlapping them.

4/The jerky is dry when a cooled piece will crack without breaking in two when you bend it.

HOW TO USE JERKY

Take jerky along on outdoor activities or anywhere you need a high-energy, lightweight snack. You can assemble an interesting snack or appetizer platter with a variety of jerky and cheeses. Spread jerky with cream cheese or serve it with slices of your favorite cheese. See the photo on page 153.

See the photo on page 153.

> ## *Salt Restrictions*
> **Consuming large quantities of heavily salted foods can be very dangerous to your health, especially if you have symptoms of high blood pressure, kidney disease or water retention during pregnancy.**

Dried Cooked Meats

Dried cooked meat is used mainly by backpackers and campers where the weight of canned meats is a disadvantage or refrigeration is not available. It is much less expensive than buying commercially prepared freeze-dried meats. Because the storage life of meats dried at home is less than 2 weeks, I do not recommend preserving meats this way for general home use.

HOW TO BEGIN

Use any type of fresh lean meat or poultry. It should be cooked thoroughly. If it is cooked in a broth, remove it from the broth and chill it. Remove any fat that forms. If you are going to dry roast the meat before drying, use a rack so the fat will drip off during cooking.

The shelf life of dried cooked pork is much shorter than that of dried cooked beef. This is because the fat in pork oxidizes and becomes rancid more quickly.

PREPARATION

Trim excess fat from the cooked meat. Cut the meat into 1/2-inch cubes for the best rehydrated quality.

HOW TO DRY COOKED MEATS

Be sure to hold meats at refrigerator temperatures prior to drying. Mishandling meats can result in bacterial growth prior to drying, and the bacteria will not be killed with normal drying temperatures. Place the cubed meat in a dryer or oven at 160° to 175°F (70° to 80°C) for 5 or more hours until completely dehydrated and crisp.

DRYNESS TEST

The meat should be hard and crisp with no evidence of moisture.

STORING

Dried cooked meat may be kept at room temperature up to 2 weeks. For better quality when rehydrated, refrigerate dried cooked meat in an airtight container up to 3 or 4 weeks, or freeze up to 2 months.

HOW TO USE

Soak the meat in boiling water or broth for 30 minutes to 1 hour or until plump. Simmer it for 15 to 20 minutes and use it in soups, stews or casseroles.

Preserving Fish

Any lean fish may be smoked or used for jerky. Varieties high in fat, such as salmon or smelt, can be smoked, but smoked fish does not keep as long as jerky. The table on pages 90 and 91 will tell you the fat content in different fish so you can decide which process is best for you.

KEEP IT COOL!

Deterioration begins almost as soon as the fish leaves the water. Hot weather hastens deterioration. Small fish are more perishable than large ones and whole fish are more susceptible to spoilage than dressed fish. To minimize the chance of spoilage, clean the fish and put it on ice or refrigerate it as soon as possible after it is caught.

CORNING

If ice or refrigeration is not available, fish can be stored temporarily by dressing and lightly salting. This is called *corning.* Corning will preserve fish up to 24 hours in cool weather. If the weather is hot, corned fish should be cooked or processed further within 6 to 12 hours.

Soon after the fish is caught, clean and dress it and wash it with fresh water. Coat the inside of the body cavity with a mixture of 1 cup of salt and 1 tablespoon pepper. Use one tablespoon of the salt and pepper mixture for every 3/4 pound of fish, rubbing a small amount on the outside of the fish.

Place the fish in a box or basket and loosely cover with several layers of damp burlap. Keep the burlap damp until you are ready to use the fish. Before cooking or processing, rinse the fish well with fresh water.

SALT CURING

Open the cleaned fish into one piece by cutting along the back. In larger fish, cut out the front half of the backbone. Smaller fish, such as smelt, may be cleaned, cured and smoked with heads attached. Wash fish thoroughly inside and out.

Brine Cure—Soak fish for 30 minutes in a brine solution of 1/2 cup of salt to 1 quart of cold water. Prepare a second brine using one of the recipes on pages 84 and 85. You may vary the spices, but use the exact amount of salt and water. A standard 8-ounce dry measure will hold about 10 ounces, by weight, of salt. Salt and sugar should be completely dissolved in the water before treating the fish.

Soak fish in the second brine for 2 to 4 hours. Use ice in plastic bags to keep the brine cold or refrigerate to maintain a temperature of 40°F (5°C). If any pieces of fish float to the top, use a serving plate to hold them under the brine. Stir the fish occasionally, particularly if the container is full. Remove surface film from the brine as it accumulates.

A *salinometer,* a floating device which measures salt concentration in a solution, may be used to determine the strength of the brine. A 70 to 80 percent saturation will properly cure the fish in the recommended time and will give an attractive glossy appearance. To measure salt strength without a salinometer, float an uncooked egg, still in the shell, in the brine. If the solution is strong enough, the egg should float with about 1/2 inch showing above the brine.

Dry Cure—To dry cure, use one of the Fish Dry Cure recipes on page 85. Coat fish inside and out with the dry cure mixture. Or layer smaller pieces of fish in the container, and generously sprinkle the mixture between each layer. The salt mixture should be about 1/4 inch thick on each layer of fish, inside and out, to ensure adequate curing. Fish must be kept under refrigeration, 40°F (5°C), during dry curing to minimize chances of spoilage.

HOW LONG TO CURE?

The time required to cure fish will vary according to the following factors:

Taste Preference—The longer the cure, the heavier the salt content will be in the cured fish.

Size—Larger fish or thicker pieces require longer curing.

Fat Content—The higher the fat content, the longer it should be cured. See Fat Content in Fish, pages 90 and 91.

Fresh or Frozen—Thawed frozen fish absorb salt faster than fresh fish. The fresher the fish, the slower the rate of salt absorption and the longer the curing time.

Fish Brines

Pickled Fish Brine

Something to make you pucker up!

1 lb. salt (about 1-1/2 cups)
1 cup sugar
1 cup lemon juice
1 teaspoon garlic powder
1 teaspoon onion powder

1/3 cup mixed pickling spices
1 teaspoon pepper
2 cups cider vinegar
1-1/2 qts. water

Combine all ingredients in a 4- to 5-quart glass, stoneware, plastic, or stainless steel container. Stir until sugar and salt are dissolved. Follow directions for Salt Curing, Brine Cure, page 83. Makes brine for 4 to 6 pounds of fish.

Teriyaki Fish Brine

Soy sauce and ginger add a pungent flavor.

1 lb. salt (about 1-1/2 cups)
2 cups brown sugar, firmly packed
2 garlic cloves, crushed
1 tablespoon ground ginger

1 teaspoon pepper
2 cups soy sauce
1-1/2 qts. water

Combine all ingredients in a 4- to 5-quart glass, stoneware, plastic, or stainless steel container. Stir until sugar and salt are dissolved. Follow directions for Salt Curing, Brine Cure, page 83. Makes brine for 4 to 6 pounds of fish.

Gourmet Fish Brine

With just a hint of tarragon.

1 lb. salt (about 1-1/2 cups)
1 cup sugar
1/2 cup lemon juice
3 garlic cloves, crushed
1 teaspoon pepper

2 teaspoons tarragon, crushed
2 tablespoons parsley flakes, crushed
2 cups dry white wine
1-1/2 qts. water

Combine all ingredients in a 4- to 5-quart glass, stoneware, plastic, or stainless steel container. Stir until sugar and salt are dissolved. Follow directions for Salt Curing, Brine Cure, page 83. Makes brine for 4 to 6 pounds of fish.

Spiced Fish Brine

Molasses and garlic add a full rich flavor.

2 lbs. salt (about 3 cups)
2 cups brown sugar, firmly packed
1 cup molasses
1-1/2 cups lemon juice

3 garlic cloves, crushed
2 medium onions, cut in rings
1 tablespoon pepper
1 gal. water

Combine all ingredients in a 8- to 10-quart glass, stoneware, plastic, or stainless steel container. Stir until sugar and salt are dissolved. Follow directions for Salt Curing, Brine Cure, page 83. Makes brine for 8 to 10 pounds of fish.

Successful Brine or Dry Curing

- Use the recommended amount of salt.
- Use the correct proportions of brine or cure to the amount of fish.
- Keep the fish cold during the curing process, (40°F (5°C).

- Cure the same size fish or fish pieces together.
- Cure the same types of fish together.
- Stir occasionally so that all pieces are covered with the brine or dry cure.

Hot & Spicy Fish Dry Cure

Cayenne pepper is the secret ingredient.

1 lb. salt (about 1-1/2 cups)
2 cups brown sugar, firmly packed
1 tablespoon onion powder
1 tablespoon garlic powder

1 tablespoon paprika
1 teaspoon black pepper
1 teaspoon cayenne pepper

Combine all indredients in a large bowl. Mix well. Follow directions for Salt Curing, Dry Cure, page 83. Makes dry cure for 3 to 4 pounds of fish.

Slightly Spiced Fish Dry Cure

Smoking and a gentle blend of spices delicately season the fish.

1 lb. salt (about 1-1/2 cups)
2 cups brown sugar, firmly packed
1 teaspoon ground allspice

1 teaspoon ground cloves
2 teaspoons bay leaves, crushed
1 tablespoon onion powder

Combine all ingredients in a large bowl. Mix well. Follow directions for Salt Curing, Dry Cure, page 83. Makes dry cure for 3 to 4 pounds of fish.

Hot-Smoked Fish

Smoking fish at home is a simple, economical way to preserve a large catch for later use.

As with smoked or dried meat, bacteria-related food poisoning can develop if fish is improperly processed or stored. Carefully follow the precautions for smoking, storage and moisture content. Smoked fish must be refrigerated or frozen if it is to be stored.

HOW TO BEGIN

Follow the cleaning, cool storage or corning procedures on page 83 before processing fish to minimize spoilage.

PREPARATION

Prepare a salt cure seasoning mixture from the Fish Brines or Fish Dry Cures, pages 84 and 85.

Thoroughly rinse the fish in fresh water but do not soak them. Cover the fish with netting or cheesecloth and hang them outdoors in a cool, shady, well-ventilated spot for 3 hours. Smaller fish or fish pieces may be placed on a drying tray. This initial drying will form a thin shiny coating or *pellicle* on the fish which helps seal in the natural flavors and provides a smooth surface which receives the smoke evenly.

HOW TO HOT-SMOKE FISH

Salted fish which has been flavored with natural or artificial smoke and slightly dried is known as *hot-smoked* or *kippered fish.*

Smoking temperatures of 130° to 150°F (55° to 65°C) will kill harmful bacteria or inhibit their growth, but hot-smoked fish is still a perishable product and must be refrigerated. Holding the fish at temperatures of 35° to 40°F (0° to 5°C) before and after smoking, eliminates the danger of botulism poisoning. Freezing the smoked fish will extend the shelf life.

Use a temperature-controlled smokehouse or smoking oven to smoke fish. Lightly smoke about 8 hours at 80° to 90°F (25° to 30°C) with the draft and flue open. Densely smoke the fish 4 hours more, gradually increasing the temperature to 130° to 150°F (55° to 65°C). Hold at this temperature an additional 2 to 3 hours until the fish has a shiny brown surface.

Place a meat thermometer in the thickest part of the fish. Increase the temperature to 225°F (105°C) and check the internal temperature of the fish. It should register 180°F (85°C) for 30 minutes. If your smoker won't reach that temperature, finish processing the fish in the oven. **The fish must remain at 180° (85°C) for 30 minutes to inhibit growth of bacteria which could cause food poisoning.**

Cool smoked fish for 2 or 3 hours. While still warm, lightly brush the surface with vegetable oil for a glossier appearance.

STORAGE

For refrigerator storage, wrap the smoked fish in paper towels, then in newspaper and place it in an airtight container or plastic bag. Use it within 2 weeks. Check occasionally for signs of mold. If mold forms, discard the fish.

To freeze, wrap the fish or fish pieces individually in heavy wax paper, then in moisture-proof freezer paper. Depending on the fat content, smoked fish may be stored in the freezer up to 6 months. The higher the fat content, the shorter the storage time.

HOW TO USE

Hot-smoked fish has a strong flavor and is best when served with bread or cheese or other lunch and snack foods. For a delicious dip recipe, see page 150.

COLD-SMOKING

In this process, the fish is not heated, but salt cured, then slowly smoked and dried at 80° to 100°F (27° to 38°C). Cold-smoking requires exact salt and moisture concentrations, temperature controls and timing and is not as safe or convenient to do at home as hot-smoking. If you decide to cold-smoke at home, follow the Fish Dry Cure recipes, pages 87 and 88, very closely and refrigerate or freeze the smoked fish as a safety precaution.

> ## *Don't Overdo It*
> **Smoked foods should be eaten in moderation. In countries where the diet consists mainly of smoked foods eaten daily, there appears to be an increase in the incidence of cancer in the esophagus and stomach.**

Fish Jerky

Fish jerky is a lightly salted product, usually smoke-flavored, and has a very low moisture content.

The amount of moisture remaining in fish jerky should be 15 to 20 percent. This low-moisture content is sufficient to inhibit the growth of harmful bacteria without added preservatives. If there is any doubt whether the moisture content of fish jerky prepared at home is low enough, refrigerate or freeze it to be safe.

HOW TO BEGIN

Follow the cleaning, cool storage or corning procedures on page 83 before processing fish to minimize risk of spoilage.

PREPARATION

Cut the fish in strips 1/4 to 3/8 inch thick. Soak the strips for 30 minutes in a cold brine, 40°F (5°C), consisting of 1/2 cup of salt to 1 quart water. Prepare a dry cure seasoning mixture from the recipes below. Rinse the fish strips in fresh water and place them on a clean flat surface.

Liberally sprinkle both sides of each fish strip with the dry cure seasoning mixture, using about 1 tablespoon salt mixture per 2 pounds of fish. Place the seasoned strips in an airtight glass or plastic container. Refrigerate 4 to 8 hours so fish will absorb the salt.

HOW TO DRY FISH JERKY

Place the fish strips on drying racks or trays without overlapping pieces.

Dehydrator or Oven Drying—Dry the fish strips for 12 to 14 hours at 140° to 160°F (60° to 70°C) until dry.

Smoker Drying— Smoke the fish strips for 3 to 4 hours at 140° to 160°F (60° to 70°C). Maintain the temperature, although smoke may not be present, until dry.

DRYNESS TEST

Feel and squeeze the fish to check for moisture. Fish with a high fat content will not appear or taste as dry as fish with a low fat content. High fat content fish may show signs of oily moisture which won't evaporate. Fish jerky should feel firm, dry and tough, but it should not crumble. There should be no moist spots.

STORING

Store fish jerky in airtight containers in a cool place, or refrigerate or freeze it. Use fish jerky within 3 months if it is stored cool place or at refrigerator temperature. It will keep 6 months or longer if frozen.

TO USE

Serve fish jerky for snacks or pack it for hiking and camping.

Fish Jerky Dry Cures

Pickled Dry Cure

If you like fish and pickles, here's the recipe for you.

1 tablespoon salt	2 bay leaves, crushed
1 teaspoon ground allspice	2 medium onions, cut in rings
1 tablespoon mixed pickling spices	2 tablespoons distilled white vinegar

Combine salt, allspice, pickling spices and bay leaves in a small bowl. Follow directions for Fish Jerky, above, distributing the salt mixture, onion rings and vinegar equally over each layer of fish. Remove onion rings before drying fish. Makes dry cure for 2 pounds of fish.

Lemon Dry Cure

Use freshly squeezed lemon juice; you'll need only two to four lemons.

4 teaspoons salt
2 teaspoons onion powder

2 tablespoons parsley flakes, crushed
1/4 cup lemon juice

Combine salt, onion powder and parsley flakes in a small bowl. Follow directions for Fish Jerky, page 87, distributing the salt mixture and lemon juice equally over each layer of fish. Makes dry cure for 2 pounds of fish.

Basic Dry Cure

Especially for strong-flavored fish.

1 tablespoon salt
1 teaspoon onion powder
1 teaspoon garlic powder

2 tablespoons liquid smoke
2 tablespoons soy sauce
3 drops Tabasco sauce

Combine salt, onion and garlic powder in a small bowl. Combine liquid smoke, soy sauce and Tabasco sauce in another small bowl. Follow directions for Fish Jerky, page 87, distributing both the salt mixture and liquid smoke mixture equally over each layer of fish. Makes dry cure for 2 pounds of fish.

Herbed Dry Cure

Subtly blended herbs and wine please a gourmet's palate.

1 tablespoon salt
1/2 teaspoon celery salt
2 tablespoons parsley flakes, crushed
1/2 bay leaf, crushed

1/2 teaspoon cracked pepper
1/8 teaspoon thyme
1 medium onion, cut in rings
2 tablespoons dry white wine

Combine salt, celery salt, parsley flakes, bay leaf, cracked pepper and thyme in a small bowl. Follow directions for Fish Jerky, page 87, distributing the salt mixture, onion rings and wine equally over each layer of fish. Remove onion rings before drying fish. Makes dry cure for 2 pounds of fish.

Guide to Preserving Meats & Fish

PROCESS	IF YOU ARE MAKING:			
	Meat Jerky	**Dried Cooked Meat**	**Hot-Smoked Fish**	**Fish Jerky**
Preparation	Cut in strips.	Cook, remove fat, cut in cubes.	Clean fish, corning process if necessary, slice.	Clean fish, corning process if necessary, cut in strips, soak in brine.
Seasoning or Curing Salts	Options: Salt and pepper only. Seasoning recipes. Commercial curing preparation. If jerky is not to be smoked, add smoke flavor, if desired.	No	**Salt Cure Options:** Brine cure recipes. Dry cure recipes.	**Salt Cure Options:** Salt and pepper only. Dry cure recipes. If jerky is not to be smoked, add smoke flavor, if desired.
Drying	Options: Dehydrator Oven Smoker	Options: Dehydrator Oven	Partially dry outdoors for 3 hours to form pellicle.	Options: Dehydrator Oven Smoker
Smoking	If desired, before or after drying for flavor.	No	Yes	If desired, before or after drying for flavor.
Packaging	Options: Depending on humidity or curing preparation, see page 81, store in containers with loose-fitting lids or in airtight containers.	Airtight container.	Options: Refrigerate in paper towels, newspapers and airtight containers. Freeze in wax paper and freezer paper.	Airtight containers.
Storing	Options: With commercial curing preparation, store according to package directions. With recipes on pages 151 to 155, store at room temperature for 1 to 2 months. May be refrigerated or frozen.	Options: Room temperature—2 weeks. Refrigerator—4 weeks. Freezer—2 months.	Options: Refrigerator—2 weeks. Freezer—6 months.	Options: Cool place—3 months if jerky is completely dry. Refrigerator—3 months. Freezer—6 months or longer.
Use	Snacks or backpacking and camping.	Backpacking and camping. Must be reconstituted by soaking and simmering.	Lunches and snacks.	Snacks or backpacking and camping.

Characteristics of High-Quality Fish

FRESH FISH	• Firm and flexible flesh. • Clean, fresh, mild odor. • Glistening clear eyes, protruding slightly. • Bright red, clean gills. • Shiny, bright skin. • Pink, fresh and clean intestinal cavity.
HOT SMOKED (KIPPERED) FISH	• Bright glossy appearance. A dull surface indicates poor-quality fish before processing or incorrect curing methods. • Uniform color with no salt crystals. Salt crystals indicate the fish were too heavily brined or not rinsed before smoking. • Firm and rigid texture compared to fresh fish. Soft, flabby fish indicates incorrect curing or smoking or poor quality before processing. • Mild fresh-smoked odor. Stale smoked fish has an objectionable smell. • Good taste and smoky flavor with no traces of rancidity.
FISH JERKY	• Uniform color with a dry texture. • Resilient but firm or tough texture when chewed. • Jerky should not crumble or be crunchy. • Mild- or smoked-fish flavor with no trace of rancidity.

Fat Content in Fish

SPECIES	ALSO KNOWN AS	GENERAL LOCATION United States unless indicated.	FAT CONTENT
Catfish	Bullhead, Blue Channel	Great Lakes, other U.S. lakes, inland rivers, ponds, creeks	Low
Chub		Great Lakes	High
Cod	Codfish, Scrod (small) Baby Snapper	New England, Middle Atlantic, Pacific Coast	Low
Croaker	Hardhead	New Jersey, Atlantic Coast to Texas Gulf	Low
Flounder	Sole, Fluke, Blackback	Northwest Coast, Gulf Coast, New England, Middle Atlantic, Canada	Low
Grouper	Red, Black, Yellowfin, Speckled Hind, Gag, Scamp	South Atlantic, Gulf	Low
Haddock	Scrod (small), Baby Snapper	New England, Canada	Low
Hake	White, Red, Squirrel, Ling, Deep-Sea	Gulf of St. Lawrence south, to North Carolina	Low
Halibut		Pacific Coast, Alaska, New England	Low
Yellow Perch	Lake Perch	Great Lakes, other U.S. lakes, rivers	Low
Lake Trout		Cold lakes of North America	High
Mackerel	Blue, American, Cero, Kingfish	New England, South Atlantic, Gulf	High
Mullet	Striped, White, Jumping, Silver	Atlantic (Florida to North Carolina), Gulf (Florida to Texas	High
Ocean Perch	Redfish	New England, Northwest Coast, Canada	Low
Pollock	Boston Bluefish	Cape Cod to Cape Breton	Low

Fat Content in Fish (continued)

SPECIES	ALSO KNOWN AS	GENERAL LOCATION United States unless indicated.	FAT CONTENT
Rainbow Trout		Throughout the U.S., Canada	Low
Red Snapper		Gulf, Middle Atlantic	Low
Sable		Pacific	High
Salmon		Pacific Coast, Alaska, North	High
Sockeye	Red	Atlantic, Great Lakes	
Chinook	Spring, King		
Silver	Silversides, Coho		
Pink	Humpback		
Chum	Fall		
Scup	Porgy, Paugy	Southern New England to North Carolina	Low
Sea Bass			
Black & White		Pacific Coast	Low
Common	Blackfish, Black Sea Bass	New England, Middle and South Atlantic	
Sea Herring	Atlantic or Pacific Herring	New England, Middle Atlantic, California, Alaska	High
Sea Trout			
Gray	Weakfish, Squeteagues	Middle and South Atlantic	Low
Spotted	Speckled Trout	Middle and South Atlantic, Gulf	
White	White or Sand Trout	Gulf	
Shad	Buck, Roe or White Shad	Coastal rivers from Maine to Florida, Washington to California	High
Smelt	Whitebait, Surf Smelt, Silverside, Jacksmelt, Bay Smelt	North Atlantic, Pacific Coast, Columbia River and bays from Mexico to Canada, Great Lakes	Medium
Sole	Rex, Pentrale, Sand, Crey, Lemon Sole	Pacific Coast, Alaska, Canada, Atlantic Coast	Low
Spot	Goody, Lafayette	New Jersey to Florida	Low
Striped Bass	Rock, Rock Bass, Rock Fish	Atlantic Coast, Pacific Coast	Low
Swordfish	Broadbill	New England, Middle Atlantic, Pacific Coast	Low
Tuna		Atlantic and Pacific Coast, Southern waters	High
Whitefish		Great Lakes, Minnesota, Canada	High
Whiting	Hake, Silver	New England	Low

Adapted from *Seafood Species Chart,* National Fisheries Institute, 111 East Wacker Drive, Chicago, IL 60601.
Additions from Northeast Fisheries Center, Gloucester Laboratory, Emerson Avenue, Gloucester, MA 01930.

Recipes

Fruits

When the winter doldrums settle in, all that's left of the carefree summer and crisp autumn are golden memories, but if your shelves are packed with containers of dried fruits, you can warm and brighten the darkest day. For a starter, make Apple Rhuberry Pie, page 116. The incredible Flaky Pie Crust and the fresh tasting fruit filling will inspire compliments from the fussiest pie critics.

If it's your turn to put on the next neighborhood coffee hour, outdo them all with Cinnamon Crumble Coffeecake, page 98, and Pineapple Doughnuts, page 101. And to keep your luncheon menu in style, page 121 has a recipe for the gourmet delight—Scandinavian Fruit Soup.

As soon as your family is ready for an afternoon of cookie baking, make the batter for Filled Drop Cookies, page 109, and mix up several different fillings, such as Golden Apricot Filling, page 106, Prune-Orange Filling, page 107, and Cherry Filling, page 108. If the young crowd wants more variety, let them assemble Fruit-Filled Chimichangas and Fruit Won Ton, page 113. Everyone will want to get in on mixing and matching the fillings and wrappings.

Tips for Reconstituting Dry Foods

• The lower the moisture content, the longer the reconstituting time. Vegetables are dried to a very low moisture content, 5 percent or less, and take much longer to rehydrate than dried fruits which are dried to about 20 percent.

• Vegetables which have been blanched for the correct amount of time reconstitute more rapidly than underblanched vegetables. Overblanched vegetables are mushy when reconstituted.

• The smaller the piece of dried fruit or vegetable, the shorter the reconstituting time. Food that has been shredded, grated or powdered takes the shortest time; whole pieces take the longest time.

• Dried fruits and vegetables will take longer to reconstitute in hard water than in soft water.

• Boiling water shortens reconstituting time.

• Reserve liquid from reconstituting fruits and vegetables to use in the recipe. If the recipe calls for milk, use evaporated or powdered milk with the drained liquid as part of the required water.

• Add salt, sugar and seasonings *after* the food has fully rehydrated.

• Most dried fruits and vegetables measure about half as much as when they are fresh. Finely chopped or powdered, their dried volume is about 1/4 of their volume when fresh.

Sweet & Sour Fruit

Try this: Wrap filled fruit in a slice of bacon and bake at 375°F (190°C) until the bacon is crisp.

40 to 48 large slices dried apricots, dates, figs,
   peaches, pears or prunes
1 cup pineapple juice
1/2 cup red wine vinegar

1/4 cup brown sugar
1/2 teaspoon ground ginger
Suggested not-so-sweet fillings, see below
Garnishes, see below

Suggested not-so-sweet fillings:
Blanched almonds
Cheddar cheese, finely shredded
Sautéed chicken livers
Chutney
Crabmeat and mayonnaise
Cream cheese and almonds

Deviled ham
Whole shrimp
Sautéed Vienna sausage slices
Walnut halves
Water chestnuts

Garnishes:
Blanched almonds, slivered or chopped
Unsweetened grated coconut

Crumbled crisp bacon

In a small saucepan, combine pineapple juice, vinegar, brown sugar and ginger. Bring to a boil. Add fruit and bring to a boil again. Remove from heat. Refrigerate fruit in marinade 12 to 24 hours. Drain fruit and rinse. Dry on dryer trays at 130°F (55°C) 2 to 3 hours or until chewy but not sticky. Fill with one or more suggested not-so-sweet fillings. Garnish, if desired. Makes 40 to 48 appetizers.

Fruit Pillows

A delightful hors d'oeuvre or satisfying snack.

40 to 48 large slices dried apricots, dates, figs,
   peaches, pears or prunes
1/2 cup cream cheese (4 oz.), room
   temperature
1/4 cup small curd cottage cheese
2 tablespoons dairy sour cream
2 tablespoons honey
1 teaspoon vanilla extract

2 tablespoons toasted sesame seeds
1/4 cup wheat germ
1/3 cup sunflower seeds
2 tablespoons finely chopped almonds
1/2 cup shredded unsweetened coconut,
   if desired
Raisins or whole unblanched almonds

In a medium bowl, beat cream cheese and cottage cheese until fluffy. Add remaining ingredients except coconut and raisins or almonds. Stir until mixed. Spoon 1 heaping teaspoon filling into pit cavity of each piece of dried fruit. Gently dip filled side of fruit in coconut, if desired. Garnish with a raisin or a whole blanched almond. Makes 40 to 48 appetizers.

Fruit-Cheese Hors d'Oeuvres

Easy to make and a delight to eat!

20 to 24 halved drained apricots, dates, figs,
    peaches, pears or prunes
2 tablespoons cream cheese, room
    temperature
2 tablespoons dairy sour cream

1/8 teaspoon paprika
1/2 cup finely shredded Cheddar cheese,
    lightly packed
1/4 cup finely shredded raw carrots
1/3 cup finely chopped almonds

If dried fruit has hardened, steam over boiling water 5 to 10 minutes to soften. In a small bowl, beat cream cheese until fluffy. Stir in sour cream, paprika, Cheddar cheese and carrots, mixing well. Spoon 1 teaspoon filling into pit cavity of each piece of dried fruit. Gently dip filled side of fruit into chopped almonds. Makes 20 to 24 appetizers.

How to Make Fruit-Cheese Hors d'Oeuvres

1/Let the cream cheese soften at room temperature so it will be easier to beat to a fluffy consistency. Have the paprika, shredded Cheddar cheese and shredded carrots ready to mix into the cream cheese. Prepare the almonds for dipping.

2/Spoon the cream cheese mixture into the pit cavity of each piece of dried fruit before dipping each hors d'oeuvre into the chopped almonds.

Banana Bread

Mmmmm, good. Serve it warm or cool.

1/ 2 cup shortening	3/4 teaspoon salt
3/4 cup brown sugar, firmly packed	1 cup mashed banana
2 eggs	1/4 cup milk
1 teaspoon grated orange peel	3/4 cup chopped nuts
2 cups all-purpose flour	3/4 to 1 cup chopped dried apricots, dates,
2 teaspoons baking powder	pears, prunes, raisins or packaged currants
1/2 teaspoon baking soda	

Preheat oven to 350°F (175°C). Generously grease and flour a 9" x 5" loaf pan; set aside. In a large bowl, cream shortening with brown sugar. Add eggs and orange peel; beat well. Set aside 1/4 cup flour to coat fruit and nuts. Sift together remaining flour, baking powder, baking soda and salt. Add flour mixture to creamed mixture alternately with mashed banana and milk. Beat well. In a small bowl, mix nuts and chopped fruit with reserved 1/4 cup flour. Stir into batter. Pour into prepared loaf pan. Bake in preheated oven about 1 hour, until a wooden pick inserted in center comes out clean. Cool 10 minutes in pan. Remove from pan and cool on a cooling rack. Makes 1 loaf.

Orange-Date Bread

You'll be proud to serve this when guests drop in for brunch.

1/4 cup butter or margarine	1 teaspoon baking soda
1/2 cup brown sugar, firmly packed	3/4 teaspoon salt
1/2 cup granulated sugar	1 tablespoon grated orange peel
1 egg	1 cup chopped dates (8-oz.)
2-1/4 cups all-purpose flour	1/2 cup coarsely chopped pecans
1 teaspoon baking powder	1 cup strained fresh orange juice

Preheat oven to 350°F (175°C). Grease and flour a 9" x 5" loaf pan or an 8-inch square baking pan; set aside. In a medium bowl, cream butter or margarine with brown sugar and granulated sugar. Add egg. Beat well. Set aside 1/4 cup flour to coat fruit and nuts. Sift together remaining flour, baking powder, baking soda and salt in a medium bowl. In a small bowl, mix orange peel, dates and pecans with reserved 1/4 cup flour. Alternately add sifted flour mixture and orange juice to egg mixture. Beat until blended. Stir in fruit-nut mixture. Pour into prepared pan. Bake in preheated oven in loaf pan 40 to 50 minutes or in square pan 25 to 30 minutes. Cool 5 minutes in pan. Remove from pan and cool completely on a cooling rack. Makes 1 loaf.

German Pancake

Puffy and elegant.

Boiling water
1/2 to 3/4 cup chopped dried apples, apricots,
    cherries, dates, figs, pears, raisins or
    dried currants
6 tablespoons butter
6 eggs
1 cup milk

1/4 teaspoon salt
1 teaspoon sugar
1/2 teaspoon vanilla extract
1 cup flour
Lemon juice and powdered sugar or
    berry jam or jelly, if desired

Pour boiling water over dried fruit to cover. Let stand to soften 5 to 15 minutes; drain. Preheat oven to 400°F (205°C). In preheating oven, melt butter in a 13" x 9" baking pan, checking frequently to avoid scorching. In blender, combine eggs, milk, sugar and vanilla. Blend lightly to mix. Add flour. Mix well in blender. With a wooden spoon or rubber spatula, stir in chopped dried fruit. Pour into baking pan containing melted butter. Bake 20 to 25 minutes until puffy and golden brown. If desired, sprinkle with lemon juice and powdered sugar or serve with berry jam or jelly. Serve immediately. Makes 4 to 6 servings.

Buttermilk Pancakes

Serve these moist, tender pancakes with Cinnamon Butter, page 126, or Creamed Honey, page 100.

Boiling water
1/2 to 3/4 cup chopped dried apples, apricots,
    cherries, dates, pears or whole dried
    blueberries
1 cup all-purpose flour
1 tablespoon sugar

1/2 teaspoon salt
1/2 teaspoon baking soda
1 teaspoon baking powder
1 egg
1-1/2 cups buttermilk
3 tablespoons vegetable oil

Pour boiling water over dried fruit to cover. Let stand to soften 5 to 15 minutes; drain. Preheat a lightly oiled griddle or skillet. Sift together flour, sugar, salt, baking soda and baking powder. In a medium bowl, beat egg. Blend in buttermilk. Add flour mixture to egg mixture, mixing lightly. Stir in oil and chopped dried fruit. Batter will be slightly lumpy. Drop batter from a large cooking spoon onto hot griddle or skillet. Turn pancakes when surface bubbles begin to break. Serve immediately. Makes eighteen to twenty 2-inch pancakes.

Cinnamon Crumble Coffeecake

Moist and delicious with a surprise fruit filling.

Nut Topping, see below
1/4 cup butter or margarine
1/4 cup brown sugar, firmly packed
1/4 cup granulated sugar
1 egg
1 teaspoon vanilla extract
1 cup all-purpose flour

1 teaspoon baking powder
1/4 teaspoon baking soda
1/8 teaspoon salt
1/2 cup dairy sour cream
1 cup chopped dried apples, apricots, dates,
   prunes or sweet cherries

Nut Topping:
1/3 cup light brown sugar, firmly packed
2 tablespoons all-purpose flour
3/4 teaspoon cinnamon

3 tablespoons butter or margarine
1/3 cup chopped nuts

Grease and flour an 8-inch square baking pan; set aside. Preheat oven to 350°F (175°C). Prepare Nut Topping; set aside. In a medium bowl, cream butter or margarine with brown sugar and granulated sugar. Stir in egg and vanilla. Sift together flour, baking powder, baking soda and salt. Alternately add flour mixture and sour cream to egg mixture. Spread batter in bottom of prepared pan. Sprinkle chopped dried fruit over batter. Sprinkle Nut Topping over dried fruit. Bake in preheated oven 25 to 30 minutes. Cool 10 to 15 minutes in pan. Makes 6 servings.

Nut Topping:
In a small bowl, combine brown sugar, flour, cinnamon and butter or margarine. Blend well with pastry blender or 2 knives. Stir in nuts.

Bran Muffins

They taste too good to be so nutritious!

1 cup whole-wheat flour
1/2 cup all-purpose flour
1/2 cup bran flakes
1 teaspoon baking soda
1/4 teaspoon salt
1/2 to 3/4 cup chopped dried apples,
   apricots, bananas, cherries, dates,
   prunes, pineapple or raisins

1/3 cup chopped nuts, if desired
1 egg, beaten
1-1/4 cups buttermilk
1/2 cup honey
1/4 cup butter or margarine melted

Preheat oven to 350°F (175°C). Grease 12 to 14 muffin pan cups; set aside. Place whole-wheat and all-purpose flours and bran flakes in a large bowl. Add baking soda and salt. Stir. Add dried fruit and nuts. Mix to coat well with flour mixture. In a medium bowl, mix egg, buttermilk, honey and melted butter or margarine. Pour all at once into flour and fruit mixture. Stir only until moistened. Fill muffin pan cups 3/4 full. Bake in preheated oven 20 to 25 minutes. Makes 12 to 14 muffins.

Pear Fritters

Not as sweet as a doughnut—but so delicious!

3/4 cup chopped dried pears
1 tablespoon lemon juice
2 egg yolks, beaten
1/4 cup milk
1/3 cup dairy sour cream
1/2 teaspoon vanilla extract
1-1/3 cups all-purpose flour
2 teaspoons baking powder

1/2 teaspoon salt
1/2 teaspoon nutmeg
1/4 teaspoon cinnamon
2 egg whites
2 tablespoons sugar
Oil or shortening for frying
Cinnamon Sugar, see below, if desired
Powdered Sugar, if desired

Toss dried pears with lemon juice; set aside. In a large bowl, blend egg yolks, milk, sour cream and vanilla. In a medium bowl, sift together flour, baking powder, salt, nutmeg and cinnamon. In another medium bowl, beat egg whites until frothy. Gradually add sugar and continue beating until stiff peaks form. Add flour mixture to egg yolk mixture and blend. Fold stiffly beaten egg whites and dried pears tossed with lemon juice into batter. In a heavy pan or deep fryer, heat 2 inches of oil or shortening to 375°F (190°C). Drop batter by slightly rounded teaspoonfuls into hot oil or shortening. Larger fritters will be doughy in the center. Fry until crisp and golden brown, turning once. Drain on paper towels. If desired, place in a paper bag and shake with Cinnamon Sugar or powdered sugar. Makes 35 to 40 small fritters.

Variations

Substitute other dried fruit such as apples, apricots, bananas, cherries, dates, peaches, pineapple or prunes for pears.

Cinnamon Sugar

Shaking doughnuts and fritters in this spicy coating makes them even tastier.

1/2 cup sugar
1 teaspoon cinnamon

Mix sugar and cinnamon in a small bowl. May be stored in a covered jar. Makes about 1/2 cup.

Hot Cross Buns

Traditionally English, these buns have been a favorite for over 600 years!

1 cup milk
3 tablespoons butter or margarine
1/3 cup sugar
1 pkg. active dry yeast
1/4 cup warm water (110°F, 45°C)
3/4 teaspoon salt
3/4 teaspoon cinnamon
1/2 teaspoon nutmeg
1/4 teaspoon ground cloves

3-1/2 to 4 cups all-purpose flour
2 eggs, beaten
3/4 cup dried currants
1/4 cup finely diced candied orange peel,
  citron or pineapple
1 tablespoon oil
1 egg yolk diluted with 1 teaspoon water
Lemon Glaze, see below

Lemon Glaze:
1 cup powdered sugar
1/2 teaspoon grated lemon peel

1 tablespoon lemon juice

In a small saucepan, scald milk by heating until bubbles form around the edges. Add butter or margarine and sugar. Stir until sugar is dissolved. Cool to lukewarm, about 110°F (45°C). In a large bowl, dissolve yeast in warm water. Stir in lukewarm milk mixture, salt, cinnamon, nutmeg and cloves. Stir in 2 cups flour and beaten eggs. Beat until smooth. In a small bowl, mix currants and candied fruit with 1/2 cup flour. Stir into milk mixture. Gradually add enough flour to make a stiff dough. Turn out onto a floured surface and knead until smooth and elastic, about 10 minutes. Add only enough flour to prevent stickiness. Dough should be soft. Coat the inside of a large bowl with 1 tablespoon oil. Place dough in bowl, turning once to oil top. Cover with a cloth. Set in a warm place free from drafts and let rise until doubled in bulk, about 1-1/2 hours. Punch down in bowl. Shape dough into 1-1/2-inch balls and place on a baking sheet. Cut a cross in top of each ball with a sharp knife or scissors. Cross should be no more than 1/8 inch deep. Brush lightly with diluted egg yolk. Cover and let rise in a warm place until doubled in bulk, 30 to 45 minutes. Preheat oven to 400°F (205°C). Bake about 10 minutes or until lightly browned. Cool slightly on cooling racks. Prepare Lemon Glaze. Pour glaze into crosses on buns. Makes 30 to 35 buns.

Lemon Glaze:
Combine powdered sugar, grated lemon peel and lemon juice in a small bowl. Mix until smooth.

Creamed Honey

You can substitute this creamy honey for regular honey.

10 oz. prepared creamed honey
8 cups decrystallized honey, page 77

Combine prepared honey and decrystallized honey in a large bowl. Beat with electric mixer 10 to 15 minutes until thoroughly blended. Cover the honey and let it stand at room temperature for 2 weeks. After the 2-week period, the honey is ready to use and may be stored at room temperature up to 1 year. Makes about 9 cups.

Pineapple Doughnuts

If you freeze these, thaw them at room temperature and reheat in a 350°F (175°C) oven.

1-1/2 cups buttermilk
1 pkg. active dry yeast
1/4 cup sugar
1/2 cup riced cooked potatoes
2 eggs
3/4 teaspoon salt
1 teaspoon cinnamon

1/3 cup butter or margarine, melted
1 teaspoon grated lemon peel
1 medium apple, peeled and shredded
3-1/4 cups all-purpose flour
1-1/2 cups chopped dried pineapple
Oil or shortening for frying
Cinnamon Sugar, page 99

In a small saucepan, warm buttermilk to 105° to 115°F (40° to 45°C). Pour into a warmed large bowl and sprinkle with yeast. Add sugar and stir until dissolved. Let stand 5 to 10 minutes. Add potatoes, eggs, salt, cinnamon, melted butter or margarine, lemon peel and apple. Mix well. Add 1-1/4 cups flour. Beat until smooth and elastic. Gradually stir in remaining 2 cups flour. Beat until very smooth. Fold in pineapple. Batter will be sticky. Cover and let rise in a warm place 1 hour or until doubled in bulk. In a heavy pan or deep fryer heat 3 inches of oil or shortening to 375°F (190°C). Drop batter by heaping tablespoonfuls into hot oil or shortening. To make flat doughnuts, let batter slide off spoon, pushing slightly with a second spoon. If batter is dropped by rounded spoonfuls, doughnuts may be doughy in center. Fry until golden brown, turning once. Remove from oil. Drain on paper towels. Shake in paper bag with Cinnamon Sugar. Serve immediately. Makes 36 to 48 doughnuts.

How to Make Pineapple Doughnuts

1/After folding the dried pineapple into the batter, let the batter rise 1 hour until it's doubled in bulk.

2/Let the batter slide off the spoon into the hot oil, pushing it slightly with a second spoon. When doughnuts have been fried to a golden brown, drain on paper towels and shake in a brown paper bag with Cinnamon Sugar.

Golden Crunch Balls

A high-energy, slightly tart fruit snack.

1/2 cup dried apricots	1/2 teaspoon cinnamon
1/2 cup dried apples	3 tablespoons honey
1/2 cup dried peaches	3 tablespoons orange juice
1/2 cup finely grated unsweetened coconut	1 tablespoon lemon juice
1/4 cup blanched almonds	Powdered sugar, if desired
1 teaspoon grated lemon peel	

Grind apricots, apples and peaches in meat grinder or blender until pieces are the size of rock salt or finer, about 1/8 inch in diameter. Place in a medium bowl. Stir in coconut, almonds, lemon peel and cinnamon. In a small saucepan, slightly warm honey, orange juice and lemon juice. Stir to mix well. Slowly pour honey mixture over fruit mixture, stirring until mixture sticks together evenly. Form into small balls about 3/4 inch in diameter. Place on baking sheets. Dry at 120°F (50°C) until no longer sticky to touch, up to 6 hours on a dry day. If desired, roll balls in powdered sugar. Makes 48 balls.

Fruit Balls

These snacks are perfect for backpacking or lunch boxes.

1/4 cup dried apricots	1/3 cup finely shredded coconut
1/2 cup dried cherries or figs	1/3 cup sunflower seeds
1 cup dried dates	1 cup finely chopped nuts
1/2 cup dried prunes	3 tablespoons lemon juice
1/4 cup raisins	2 to 3 tablespoons white corn syrup

In blender or food grinder, finely chop apricots, cherries or figs, dates, prunes and raisins. In a medium bowl, mix finely chopped dried fruit with coconut, sunflower seeds and nuts. Stir in lemon juice. Add white corn syrup gradually and mix well. Shape into 1-inch balls. Dry on screens in food dryer at 130°F (55°C) 4 to 6 hours until firm to touch. Wrap individually in plastic wrap and store in an airtight container in a cool dry place. Use within 2 to 3 weeks. Makes 36 balls.

To warm a serving dish or bowl for raising yeast dough, pour very warm water over the outside of the dish or bowl just before using it.

Apricotlets

Chewy apricot candy is a year-round favorite.

1-3/4 cups boiling water
About 1-1/3 cups dried apricots
2 cups granulated sugar
2 tablespoons white corn syrup
1/8 teaspoon salt

2 tablespoons unflavored gelatin
1/2 cup apple juice
1 tablespoon lemon juice
3/4 cup chopped nuts
Powdered sugar

Lightly coat an 8-inch square baking pan with butter or margarine; set aside. Pour boiling water over apricots. Let stand until apricots are plump, about 30 minutes. Blend water and apricots to a pulp in blender. Put through a sieve; discard bits of fiber and skin. Simmer pulp in a medium saucepan over low heat, stirring occasionally to prevent scorching. Measure 2 cups pulp. Reserve remaining pulp for another use. Return 2 cups pulp to saucepan. Add granulated sugar, corn syrup and salt. Cook over low heat until thickened, about 30 minutes to 1 hour, stirring frequently to prevent scorching. Dissolve gelatin in apple juice. Stir into pulp mixture and again cook until thickened, about 10 minutes. Stir in lemon juice and chopped nuts. Pour mixture into prepared pan. Let stand at room temperature 24 hours. Cut in 1" x 1/2" bars. If knife sticks, dip it in hot water. Place bars on tray in food dryer. Dry at 120°F (50°C) until pieces are dry to touch. Or let stand in warm place until dry to touch. Roll in powdered sugar. Makes 36 pieces.

Variation

Applets: Substitute 2 cups apple pulp for apricot pulp. Apple pulp may be made from dried, canned or fresh tart apples. Skim off any foam which forms on top. Add 1/4 teaspoon cinnamon to pulp mixture with nuts and lemon juice.

How to Make Apricotlets

1/Cut the cooked and hardened apricot mixture into 1-1/2" x 1" bars and place them on drying trays.

2/When the bars are dry to touch, roll them in powdered sugar.

Danish Pastry

Make 20 small pastries with half the dough and a braided wreath with the other half.

1-1/2 cups butter, room temperature
1/4 cup all-purpose flour
2 pkgs. active dry yeast
1/2 cup warm water, (110°F, 45°C)
3/4 cup milk
1/4 cup sugar
1 teaspoon salt

1/2 teaspoon ground cardamom, if desired
1 egg, beaten
3-3/4 cups all-purpose flour
Any fruit filling, pages 106 to 108, or
    Almond Crunch Filling, page 148
Sugar Glaze, see below
Chopped nuts or candied cherries

Sugar Glaze:
2 cups powdered sugar
3 to 4 tablespoons milk

1/2 teaspoon vanilla extract

Cover a wet 16-1/2" x 13-1/2" baking sheet with a piece of wax paper. Draw a 16" x 8" rectangle on the wax paper; set aside. In a small bowl, beat butter and 1/4 cup flour until fluffy. Spread on wax paper to outline of rectangle; refrigerate. In a large bowl, sprinkle yeast over warm water. Stir to dissolve. Heat milk to lukewarm. Add sugar, salt and cardamom, if desired. Stir to dissolve. Stir milk mixture into yeast mixture. Add eggs and 2 cups flour. Beat until smooth. Stir in remaining flour with a wooden spoon until dough pulls away from sides of bowl. On a floured surface, lightly knead dough 1 minute. Place in an ungreased bowl. Cover and refrigerate 30 minutes. Turn out onto a lightly floured surface and roll out to a 16-inch square. Invert wax paper with chilled butter mixture over half of dough. Remove wax paper. Gently fold other half of dough over butter mixture, pinching edges to seal. With a rolling pin, lightly pound dough to a 12" x 16" rectangle. If butter breaks through dough, brush lightly with flour. Fold 1/3 of dough into center, then fold in remaining 1/3, making 3 layers. Seal edges. Wrap in foil or wax paper. Refrigerate 1 hour. Repeat rolling and folding; seal edges. Chill 30 minutes. Repeat rolling, folding, sealing and chilling once or twice more. Wrap and refrigerate 3 hours or overnight. Line baking sheets with brown wrapping paper. Cut dough in half. Roll out one half to a 20-inch square. Cut into four 5-inch wide strips. Cut each strip into 4 squares, making sixteen 5-inch squares. Place 1 tablespoon filling in center of each square. Fold together 2 opposite corners; seal edges. Place pastries on prepared baking sheets. Repeat with other half of dough. Let rise in warm place 45 minutes. Bake at 375°F (190°C) 15 to 20 minutes. Cool slightly on a cooling rack. Mix ingredients for glaze. Drizzle glaze over warm pastry. Garnish with chopped nuts or candied cherries. Makes 40 pastries.

Variation

To make a wreath, roll out half the dough to a 20" x 9" rectangle. Cut dough into thirds lengthwise. Fill center of each strip with 1/3 cup filling. Fold strips over filling, pinching edges to seal. Seal ends. Place filled strips of dough on prepared baking sheet. Starting from center, braid to each end. Shape into a circle, pressing ends together. Bake 25 to 30 minutes. Cool slightly before glazing and garnishing.

1/Prepare a large baking sheet by wetting it and placing a piece of wax paper on the wet baking sheet. Spread the butter mixture on the wax paper to a 16" x 8" rectangle. Then put it in the refrigerator to chill.

2/Roll out the dough to a 16-inch square. Invert the wax paper with the chilled butter mixture over half the dough and peel off the wax paper. Gently fold the other half of the dough rectangle over the butter mixture. Pinch the edges to seal the dough.

How to Make Danish Pastry

3/After pounding the dough to a 16" x 12" rectangle, fold 1/3 of the dough to the center, then fold over the remaining 1/3 of the dough to make 3 layers. Seal the edges, wrap the dough in foil or wax paper and chill. Repeat the pounding, folding and chilling two or three more times.

4/Cut dough in half. Roll out each half to a 20-inch square. Cut the square into four 5-inch wide strips and cut each strip into 4 squares. You will have 16 squares. Place the filling in the center of each square. Fold each square in half diagonally over the filling to make a triangle. Pinch the edges of each triangle together to seal.

Peanut Butter & Granola Bars

If these delicious bars are too chewy, put them in a food dryer for a few hours.

1-1/2 cups Crunchy Granola, page 144	1 teaspoon oil
2 tablespoons instant nonfat dry milk	2 tablespoons honey
2 tablespoons bran flakes	1/2 teaspoon vanilla extract
1/4 teaspoon cinnamon	1-1/2 teaspoons water
1/8 teaspoon salt	1/3 cup crunchy peanut butter
1/4 cup raisins	1 egg, well-beaten

Preheat oven to 250°F (120°C). Generously grease and flour an 8" x 8" x 2" baking pan; set aside. In a medium bowl, mix Crunchy Granola, dry milk, bran flakes, cinnamon, salt and raisins. In a large bowl, combine oil, honey, vanilla, water and peanut butter. Stir to mix well. Gradually stir granola mixture into peanut butter mixture. Add egg and mix well. Press mixture into prepared baking pan. Bake 25 minutes. Cool 10 to 15 minutes in pan before cutting into 2" x 1" bars. For less chewy bars, place them in a food dryer at 130°F (55°C) 2 to 3 hours or, if climate is dry, let bars stand uncovered at room temperature overnight. Makes 32 bars.

Peanut Butter & Fruit Spread

A nutritious after-school snack.

1 cup peanut butter, smooth or crunchy	1 tablespoon lemon juice
2 tablespoons butter or margarine, softened	2 tablespoons honey, if desired
1/3 cup finely chopped dried fruit	

In a small bowl, combine all ingredients until smooth and mixed well. Serve on crackers or bread. Makes 1-1/2 cups.

Golden Apricot Filling

Tangy fruit flavor is especially good in Filled Drop Cookies, page 109.

1/2 cup water	3/4 cup sugar
1 cup orange or pineapple juice	1 teaspoon lemon juice
1-1/2 cups chopped dried apricots	

In a small saucepan, combine water and orange or pineapple juice. Add apricots. Cook over medium heat until thickened, 20 to 25 minutes, stirring frequently. Stir in sugar and lemon juice. Cook and stir until sugar is dissolved and mixture is thickened. Makes 1-3/4 cups filling.

Prune-Orange Filling

Delicious in Fruit-Filled Chimichangas and Fruit Won Ton, page 113.

2 cups chopped prunes
1/2 cup water
1/2 cup orange juice

1/2 cup sugar
1 teaspoon grated orange peel
2 tablespoons lemon juice

In a medium saucepan, combine prunes, water, orange juice and sugar. Cook over low heat until thickened, 30 to 35 minutes, stirring occasionally. When thickened, add orange peel and lemon juice. Cool. Makes 2 cups filling.

Old-Fashioned Date Filling

Perfect for filled cookies, pastries or fruit leathers.

1-1/2 cups finely chopped dates
1/2 cup water
1/2 cup sugar

1 teaspoon lemon juice
1/2 teaspoon grated lemon peel
1/3 cup chopped nuts, if desired

In a medium saucepan, combine dates, water and sugar. Cook over low heat until thickened, 20 to 25 minutes, stirring frequently. When thickened, add lemon juice, lemon peel and nuts, if desired. Cool. Makes 1-3/4 cups filling.

Variation

Substitute figs or raisins or 1-3/4 cups chopped cooked prunes (about 2 cups dried) for dates.

Waikiki Pineapple Filling

Try it in Sweet & Spicy Fruit, page 117, or Danish Pastry, page 104.

1 cup sugar
1/2 cup pineapple juice
3 tablespoons lemon juice
1/2 teaspoon grated lemon peel
1/4 teaspoon nutmeg

2 tablespoons tapioca
1-1/2 cups drained crushed fresh pineapple or
    1-1/2 cups drained crushed canned pineapple
1 tablespoon butter or margarine

Combine all ingredients except butter or margarine in a medium saucepan. Let stand 15 minutes. Stir constantly over medium heat until thickened, 10 to 15 minutes. Stir in butter or margarine. Cool. Makes 2 cups filling.

Cherry Filling

Dried cherries make a tasty filling.

2-1/2 cups boiling water
2 cups pitted tart dried cherries
3/4 cup sugar
2 tablespoons cornstarch

1 teaspoon red food coloring
1/2 teaspoon almond extract
1 tablespoon butter or margarine

Pour boiling water over dried cherries to cover. Let stand to soften 1 to 2 hours; drain and reserve juice. In a medium saucepan, mix sugar and cornstarch. Gradually stir in 1/2 cup reserved juice and red food coloring. Stir constantly over medium heat until mixture thickens and boils. Continue to boil and stir 1 minute. Stir in drained cherries, almond extract and butter or margarine. Cool. Makes 2-1/4 cups filling.

Pear-Lemon Squares

Crunchy on the bottom, chewy on top.

1 cup plus 2 tablespoons all-purpose flour
1/4 cup powdered sugar
2 teaspoons grated lemon peel
1/4 cup butter or margarine
2 eggs
3/4 cup granulated sugar

3 tablespoons lemon juice
1 teaspoon baking powder
1/4 teaspoon salt
1 cup finely chopped dried pears
Additional powdered sugar, if desired

Preheat oven to 350°F (175°C). Grease and flour a 9-inch square baking pan; set aside. In a medium bowl, combine 1 cup flour, 1/4 cup powdered sugar, 1 teaspoon grated lemon peel and butter or margarine. With a pastry blender or 2 knives, cut mixture until it resembles coarse cornmeal. Press mixture into bottom of prepared pan. Bake in preheated oven 15 minutes. Remove from oven. In a medium bowl, combine eggs and granulated sugar, beating until fluffy. Stir in lemon juice and remaining lemon peel. Add remaining 2 tablespoons flour, baking powder and salt. Mix well. Stir in dried pears. Pour mixture over partially baked layer and spread evenly to sides of pan. Bake 20 minutes until top is bubbly and very lightly browned. Cool before cutting into squares. Lightly sprinkle with powdered sugar before serving, if desired. Makes thirty-six 1-1/2-inch squares.

Variations

Substitute 1 cup finely chopped dried apricots, dates, pineapple or light cherries for pears.

Filled Drop Cookies

You choose the surprise fruit filling.

Any fruit filling, pages 106 to 108, or
   Almond Crunch Filling, page 148
1/4 cup shortening
1/4 cup butter or margarine
1 cup brown sugar, firmly packed
1 egg
1/4 cup buttermilk

1 teaspoon vanilla extract
1-3/4 cups all-purpose flour
1/2 teaspoon salt
1/2 teaspoon baking soda
1/4 teaspoon cinnamon
1/4 cup raisins or dried currants
1/4 cup chopped nuts

Prepare fruit or nut filling. Preheat oven to 400°F (205°C). Grease baking sheets; set aside. In a large bowl, cream shortening and butter or margarine with brown sugar. Stir in egg, buttermilk and vanilla. In a medium bowl, mix flour, salt, baking soda, cinnamon, raisins or currants and nuts. Add to creamed mixture and stir until mixed. Drop dough from a teaspoon onto prepared baking sheets. Coat the bottom of a 1/4 teaspoon measure with butter or margarine. Press on each cookie to make a small indentation. Place 1/2 teaspoon filling in each indentation. Cover filling with a small piece of dough. Bake in preheated oven 7 to 8 minutes until edges are light golden brown. Remove from baking sheets; place on a cooling rack. Makes about 36 cookies.

Apple-Pear Cookies

This refrigerator cookie has a soft texture and a mild fruit flavor.

Boiling water
3/4 cup finely chopped dried apples and pears
1 cup butter or margarine
1 cup sugar
2 eggs

1 teaspoon vanilla extract
3 cups all-purpose flour
1/2 teaspoon salt
1/2 teaspoon baking soda
1/2 cup finely chopped nuts

Pour boiling water over dried fruit to cover. Let stand to soften 5 to 15 minutes; drain. In a medium bowl, cream butter or margarine with sugar. Add eggs and vanilla. Beat well. In another medium bowl, mix flour, salt, baking soda, dried fruit and nuts. Add to creamed mixture and mix well. Shape into two 2" x 1-3/4" rolls. Wrap well in wax paper. Refrigerate 4 hours or overnight. Preheat oven to 400°F (205°C). Grease baking sheets. Cut rolls in 1/4-inch slices. Place slices on prepared baking sheets. Bake 7 to 8 minutes until edges are golden. Remove from baking sheets; place on a cooling rack. Makes about 96 cookies.

Don't hold or soak cut fruits to be dried in saltwater. It will give an off flavor and gray color to the fruit.

Date Pinwheels

A crisp cookie with a rich date flavor.

Old-Fashioned Date Filling, page 107
1/2 cup butter or margarine
1/2 cup brown sugar, firmly packed
1/2 cup granulated sugar
1 egg

1 teaspoon vanilla extract
2 cups all-purpose flour
1/4 teaspoon baking soda
1/4 teaspoon salt

Prepare Old-Fashioned Date Filling, increasing nuts to 1 cup, if desired. In a medium bowl, cream butter or margarine with brown sugar and granulated sugar. Add egg and vanilla. Beat well. In a medium bowl, mix flour, baking soda and salt. Add to creamed mixture and mix well. Cut dough in half. Generously flour a large sheet of wax paper. Roll out each half of dough on floured wax paper to a 12" x 9" rectangle. Spread with filling. Starting with longer edge, roll up tightly to make a 12-inch long roll. Wrap roll in wax paper. Refrigerate 4 hours or overnight. Preheat oven to 375°F (190°C). Grease baking sheets; set aside. Cut chilled roll into 1/4-inch slices. Place slices on prepared baking sheets. Bake in preheated oven 8 to 10 minutes until edges are golden. Remove from baking sheets; place on a cooling rack. Makes about 80 cookies.

How to Make Date Pinwheels

1/Spread the dough rectangle with Old-Fashioned Filling. Starting with the longer edge, roll up the rectangle tightly to make a 12-inch long roll. Wrap the roll in wax paper and refrigerate it.

2/Cut the chilled roll into 1/4-inch slices. Bake the slices until the edges are golden.

Appledoodles

These cookies puff up in the oven but flatten to a crisp chewy cookie as they cool.

1/2 cup butter or margarine
1/2 cup shortening
1-1/2 cups plus 3 tablespoons sugar
2 eggs
2-1/2 cups all-purpose flour

2 teaspoons cream of tartar
1/4 teaspoon salt
3 teaspoons cinnamon
1 cup coarsely chopped dried apple

Preheat oven to 400°F (205°C). Grease baking sheets; set aside. In a large bowl, cream butter or margarine and shortening with 1-1/2 cups sugar. Add eggs. Beat well. In a medium bowl, mix flour, cream of tartar, salt and 1/2 teaspoon cinnamon. Add to creamed mixture. Mix well. Stir in dried apple. In a wide, shallow bowl, mix remaining 3 tablespoons sugar and remaining 2-1/2 teaspoons cinnamon. With hands, roll dough into 1-inch balls. Roll balls in cinnamon-sugar mixture to coat well. Place balls at least 2 inches apart on prepared baking sheets. Bake in preheated oven 7 to 8 minutes until edges are slightly golden. Do not overbake. Cookies will puff up as they bake and look slightly underdone when removed from the oven. Remove from baking sheets; place on a cooling rack. Makes about 60 cookies.

Variations

Peardoodles: Substitute 1 cup coarsely chopped dried pears for apples.
Pineappledoodles: Substitute 1 cup coarsely chopped dried pineapple for apples.

Easy Oatmeal Cookies

Fruit pieces add a surprise.

1/2 cup butter or margarine
1/2 cup shortening
1 cup brown sugar, firmly packed
1 cup granulated sugar
2 eggs
1 teaspoon vanilla extract
1-1/2 cups all-purpose flour

1 teaspoon salt
1 teaspoon baking soda
3 cups uncooked rolled oats
1/2 cup chopped nuts
1 cup chopped dried fruit such as apples,
    apricots, cherries, dates, pears and prunes

Preheat oven to 350°F (175°C). Grease baking sheets; set aside. In a medium bowl, cream butter or margarine and shortening with brown sugar and granulated sugar. Add eggs and vanilla. Beat well. In a small bowl, mix flour, salt and baking soda. Add to creamed mixture and mix well. Stir in oats, nuts and dried fruit. Drop by rounded teaspoonfuls onto prepared baking sheets. Dough rounds should be about 1 inch in diameter. Bake in preheated oven 7 to 8 minutes. When done, cookies will appear slightly moist in center. Cool slightly, about 30 seconds, on baking sheets before placing on a cooling rack. Makes about 60 cookies.

Divine Date Roll

Serve this dessert at a luncheon or tea.

2-1/2 cups miniature marshmallows
1/2 cup half-and-half or light cream
1/4 teaspoon vanilla extract
1/2 cup chopped pecans or walnuts
1 cup chopped dates

12 (2-1/4" x 5") double graham crackers,
    crushed
1/3 cup finely chopped pecans or walnuts
Whipped cream

In a medium bowl, combine marshmallows, half-and-half and vanilla. Let stand 15 minutes. Stir in 1/2 cup nuts and dates. Let stand 10 more minutes. Add crushed graham crackers, stirring until mixture clings together. Shape into a 10" x 2-1/2" roll. Roll in 1/3 cup finely chopped nuts. Wrap well in wax paper. Refrigerate 2 to 3 hours. Cut into 1-inch slices and garnish with whipped cream. Makes 8 to 10 servings.

Mom's Apple Pudding-Cake

If you didn't shred the apples before drying, use your blender or food processor to shred them.

Boiling water
1-1/2 cups dried shredded apple
1/4 cup butter or margarine
1 cup sugar
1 egg
1 teaspoon vanilla extract
1 cup all-purpose flour

1 teaspoon baking soda
1/2 teaspoon salt
1 teaspoon cinnamon
1/4 teaspoon ground allspice or nutmeg
1/2 cup chopped dates or prunes
1/2 cup chopped walnuts or pecans
Vanilla ice cream or whipped cream

Pour boiling water over dried apple to cover. Let stand to soften 10 to 15 minutes. Preheat oven to 350°F (175°C). Generously grease and flour an 8"x 8"x 2" pan; set aside. In a large bowl, cream butter or margarine with sugar. Drain apple and add with egg and vanilla to creamed mixture. Mix well. In a medium bowl, combine flour, baking soda, salt, cinnamon, allspice or nutmeg, dates or prunes and nuts. Stir to mix well. Gradually add to creamed mixture, beating well. Pour into prepared pan. Bake in preheated oven 40 to 50 minutes or until a wooden pick inserted in center comes out clean. Serve with vanilla ice cream or whipped cream. Makes 6 to 8 servings.

Fruit-Filled Chimichangas

You'll adore this Northern Mexican dessert.

1-1/2 to 2 cups any fruit filling, pages 106 to
   108
8 small fresh flour tortillas

1 egg white, beaten with 1 teaspoon water
Oil or shortening for frying
Powdered sugar

Prepare fruit filling. Preheat oven to 300°F (150°C). Moisten top and bottom tortillas in tortilla stack with a few drops of water and wrap stack in aluminum foil. Heat 10 to 15 minutes in preheated oven until tortillas are pliable. Fill one tortilla at a time, keeping the rest wrapped to prevent them from drying and becoming brittle. Place tortilla on work surface. Brush with egg white and water mixture. Place 3 to 4 tablespoons fruit filling over the lower third of tortilla. Fold the bottom edge of tortilla up over filling. Fold both sides toward the center and roll into a cylinder. Secure seam by brushing with egg white and water mixture. Place seam-side down on paper towels. In a heavy pan deep-fat fryer or mini fryer, heat 2 inches of oil to 375°F (190°C). Fry 2 chimichangas at a time, seam-side down, about 2 minutes until golden and crisp, turning once. Drain on paper towels. Sprinkle with powdered sugar and serve warm. Makes 8 servings.

Fruit Won Ton

These are scrumptious served with ice cream or pudding!

1/2 cup any fruit filling, pages 106 to 108
20 to 25 won ton skins or wrappers

Oil or shortening for frying
Powdered sugar

Prepare fruit filling. Place about 1 teaspoon fruit filling in center of each won ton skin. Moisten edges of skin with water. Fold 2 opposite corners together to make a triangle. Seal by pressing edges firmly with fingers. Pull the right and left corners of folded triangle down and below folded edge so they slightly overlap. Moisten overlapping corners and press firmly together. Heat 2 inches of oil or shortening in mini-fryer or wok to 375°F (190°C). Fry filled won ton about 1 minute until crisp and golden. It is not necessary to turn the won ton if you are cooking enough at the same time to keep the oil bubbling over the won ton edges. Drain on paper towels. Lightly sift powdered sugar over won ton. Serve warm. Makes 20 to 25 won ton.

Covering dried fruit with boiling water is only one method for softening dried fruit. For other methods, see page 92.

Orange-Prune Mold

Heavenly gelatin like this can be a salad or dessert.

1 (3-oz.) pkg. orange-flavored gelatin	1/2 cup miniature marshmallows
1 cup boiling water	1/2 cup chopped prunes
1/4 cup sugar	1/4 cup walnuts or pecans
1 cup cold water	1/2 cup whipping cream
1 (11-oz.) can mandarin orange segments	

In a large bowl, dissolve gelatin in boiling water. Stir in sugar until dissolved. Add cold water. Refrigerate until gelatin mixture has the consistency of unbeaten egg white. Reserve 6 to 8 mandarin orange segments for garnish. Fold remaining mandarin orange segments, marshmallows, prunes and nuts into chilled gelatin. In a small bowl, beat whipping cream until stiff. Fold into gelatin mixture. Spoon into a 1-quart mold and refrigerate until set. To unmold, dip bottom of mold in warm water before inverting over platter. Remove mold. Garnish gelatin with reserved mandarin orange segments. Makes 4 to 6 servings.

Schnitz Pie

This recipe for dried-apple pie has been handed down from the Pennsylvania-Dutch settlers.

Hot apple juice or boiling water	1 cup sugar
3-1/4 cups dried apple slices	1 teaspoon cinnamon
Flaky Pie Crust, page 116	1/2 teaspoon nutmeg
1/4 cup fresh lemon juice	3 tablespoons butter or margarine
1/4 cup flour	

Pour hot apple juice or boiling water over apple slices to cover. Let stand to reconstitute 20 to 30 minutes. Prepare dough and bottom pie crust. Preheat oven to 425°F (220°C). Drain apples and toss with lemon juice. In a small bowl, combine flour, sugar, cinnamon and nutmeg. Sprinkle flour mixture over apples, stirring to coat. Fill pie crust heaping full with apple mixture. Dot with butter or margarine. Roll out top crust. Cutting decorative slits to let steam escape while baking. Roll dough onto rolling pin and unroll on top of filling. Trim dough to extend 3/4 inch over pie plate rim. Fold top crust under bottom crust and flute edges. Place a 1-1/2-inch wide piece of aluminum foil around the edge of crust to prevent excessive browning during baking. Bake in preheated oven 15 minutes. Reduce heat to 375°F (190°C) and bake 25 to 30 minutes longer until crust is golden. Foil may be removed during last 10 minutes of baking. Makes one 9-inch double-crust pie.

Apple Rhuberry Pie

Homemade freezer jam adds really fresh flavor.

Boiling water
2 cups dried rhubarb slices
Flaky Pie Crust, see below
2 cups dried apple slices
1/2 cup homemade strawberry freezer jam or
   prepared strawberry jam

2 tablespoons lemon juice
1/2 to 3/4 cup sugar, depending on tartness
   of apples
1/4 cup quick-cooking tapioca
3 tablespoons butter or margarine
1 teaspoon sugar

In a large bowl, pour boiling water over dried rhubarb. Let stand to reconstitute 45 to 60 minutes. Prepare dough and bottom crust for Flaky Pie Crust; set aside. In a medium bowl, pour boiling water over apples. Let stand to reconstitute 15 to 20 minutes. Drain reconstituted fruit. Toss with lemon juice and strawberry jam in a large bowl. Preheat oven to 400°F (205°C). In a small bowl, mix sugar and tapioca. Pour over fruit mixture and toss to mix. Fill pie crust heaping full with fruit mixture. Dot with butter or margarine. Roll out top crust, cutting decorative slits to let steam escape while baking. Roll dough onto rolling pin and unroll on top of filling. Trim dough to extend 3/4 inch over pie plate rim. Fold top crust under bottom crust and flute edges. For a crunchy top crust, brush very lightly with melted butter or margarine and sprinkle with 1 teaspoon of sugar. Place a 1-1/2-inch wide piece of aluminum foil around edge of crust to prevent excessive browning during baking. Bake in preheated oven 40 to 50 minutes until crust is golden. Foil may be removed during last 10 minutes of baking. Makes one 9-inch double-crust pie.

Flaky Pie Crust

For a 9-inch double-crust pie. So flaky and tender you won't believe it!

2/3 cup vegetable shortening
2 cups all-purpose flour
1 teaspoon salt

1/2 cup to 1/2 cup plus 1 tablespoon
   cold milk

With a pastry blender or 2 knives, cut shortening into flour and salt in a large bowl. Mixture should resemble small peas. Sprinkle cold milk over mixture a spoonful at a time, tossing with a fork until dough clings together. Shape into 2 balls and flatten on a lightly floured surface. Roll out 1 ball to an 11-inch circle. Roll onto rolling pin. Place carefully over a 9-inch pie plate. Do not stretch dough as this causes shrinkage. Fill crust with filling. Roll out dough for top crust to an 11-inch circle. Cut decorative slits in top crust to let steam escape while baking. Roll dough onto rolling pin and unroll on top of filling. Trim dough to extend 3/4 inch over pie plate rim. Fold top crust under bottom crust and flute edges. Makes crust for one 9-inch double-crust pie.

Apricot Fluff

This light dessert has a creamy texture with apricot bits mixed in.

1/2 cup chopped dried apricots	1/4 cup granulated sugar
1-1/4 cups hot apricot nectar	1 cup whipping cream (1/2 pint)
1 (3-oz.) pkg. orange-flavored gelatin	1 tablespoon powdered sugar
1 cup boiling water	

Place apricots in a small bowl. Cover with hot apricot nectar. Let stand 5 minutes. In a medium bowl, dissolve gelatin in boiling water. Add granulated sugar and apricot nectar mixture. Refrigerate until partially set, 1 to 1-1/2 hours. In a large bowl, whip cream with powdered sugar until stiff. Fold chilled apricot mixture into whipped cream. Spoon into parfait glasses or sherbet dishes. Refrigerate until set. Makes 6 servings.

Sweet & Spicy Fruit

Here's an appetizer you can serve as a dessert!

1 cup water	40 to 48 large slices whole dried apricots,
1/3 cup brown sugar or honey	dates, figs, peaches, pears or prunes
4 lemon slices	Sweet fillings, see below
1 stick cinnamon	Garnishes, see below
4 whole cloves	

Suggested sweet fillings:

Chocolate kisses	Miniature marshmallows
Chopped dates	Mints
Fondant	Nuts
Fruit fillings, pages 106 to 108	Peanut butter
Crunchy Granola, page 114, or	Chopped dried pineapple
Easy Granola, page 146	Raisins

Garnishes:

Blanched almonds, slivered or chopped	Powdered sugar
Grated coconut	Raisins

In a small saucepan, combine water, brown sugar or honey, lemon slices, cinnamon and cloves. Bring to a boil. Add fruit and bring to a boil again. Remove from heat. Refrigerate fruit in marinade 12 to 24 hours. Drain fruit and rinse. Dry on drying trays at 130°F (55°C) 2 to 3 hours or until chewy but not sticky. Fill with one or more suggested sweet fillings. Garnish, if desired. Makes 40 to 48 appetizers.

Best Baked Apples

Served warm with vanilla ice cream, they're irresistible!

6 large baking apples
1/2 cup finely chopped dates
1/2 cup finely chopped prunes
1/4 cup brown sugar, firmly packed
1 teaspoon cinnamon
2 tablespoons chopped nuts

2 tablespoons butter or margarine, melted
2 teaspoons lemon juice
1/3 cup water
1/2 cup light corn syrup
Vanilla ice cream

Wash apples, remove cores and peel the upper 1/3 of each apple to prevent the skin from splitting while baking. With a large knife, cut across each apple 4 times through the peeled top to the peel, making 8 even sections. In a small bowl, mix dates, prunes, brown sugar, cinnamon, nuts, butter or margarine and lemon juice. Evenly distribute date mixture in centers of apples. Pour 1/3 cup water into a baking pan that will hold the filled apples. Place apples in water. Pour corn syrup over apples. Bake at 350°F (175°C) 50 to 60 minutes, basting occasionally with syrup-water from bottom of pan. Place apples in individual serving dishes. Pour syrup-water mixture from bottom of baking pan into a small saucepan. Boil over medium heat to the consistency of light syrup. Pour over apples. Serve warm with vanilla ice cream. Makes 6 servings.

How to Make Best Baked Apples

1/Cut each prepared apple 4 times across the peeled top to make 8 even sections. Fill the centers with the date mixture. Place apples in a baking pan with 1/3 cup water.

2/Pour the corn syrup over the apples. While the apples are baking, occasionally baste them with the syrup-water mixture from the bottom of the pan.

Baked Fruit Custard

A soothing custard I remember from my childhood and now make for my children.

2 eggs
2 cups milk
1 teaspoon vanilla extract
1/3 cup sugar
1/8 teaspoon salt

1/2 cup chopped dried fruit such as apples,
   apricots, pears or prunes
Nutmeg
5 dried fruit slices

Preheat oven to 350°F (175°C). Combine eggs, milk, vanilla, sugar and salt in blender. Blend until mixed. Distribute dried fruit equally in bottom of 5 (6-oz.) custard cups. Pour custard mixture over dried fruit and sprinkle top of each custard with nutmeg. Place cups in a large baking pan. Place pan in preheated oven. Pour boiling water into baking pan to about 1 inch from tops of cups. Bake 45 minutes or until knife inserted in center of a custard comes out clean. Serve warm or cold garnished with a slice of dried fruit. Makes 5 servings.

Fruit Crisp

Always a family favorite and so easy to make.

Boiling water
3 cups dried apples, sweet cherries, peaches
   or pears
2 tablespoons lemon juice
1/3 cup raisins, if desired
1/3 cup all-purpose flour

2 tablespoons wheat germ
3/4 cup brown sugar, firmly packed
1 teaspoon cinnamon
1/3 cup butter or margarine
1/2 cup uncooked rolled oats (not instant)
Vanilla ice cream or whipped cream

Pour boiling water over dried fruit to cover. Let stand to reconstitute about 30 minutes. If using sweet cherries, let stand 45 minutes to 1 hour. Drain. Preheat oven to 375°F (190°C). Generously butter an 8" x 8" x 2" baking pan. Place reconstituted dried fruit in prepared pan. Sprinkle lemon juice and raisins over fruit. In a medium bowl, blend flour, wheat germ, brown sugar, cinnamon and butter or margarine until crumbly. Toss with rolled oats. Sprinkle flour-oat mixture evenly over fruit in pan. Bake in preheated oven 25 to 30 minutes until golden brown. Serve warm with vanilla ice cream or whipped cream. Makes 6 to 8 servings.

Variations

Substitute 3 cups dried rhubarb or tart cherries for fruit. Allow 45 minutes to 1 hour to reconstitute. Sprinkle 1/3 cup granulated sugar over fruit before topping with flour-oat mixture.

Scandinavian Fruit Soup

Fresh fruit and juices mixed with dried fruits make a refreshing dessert.

2 cups water
2 slices fresh lemon
1 slice fresh orange
1 cinnamon stick
3 whole cloves
2 cups (1- to 1-1/2-inch pieces) mixed dried
  fruit such as apples, apricots, cherries, figs,
  peaches, pineapple, prunes and raisins
1 cup water

1 cup orange juice
1 cup fresh or canned pineapple chunks,
  drained
1/2 cup honey
1 tablespoon lemon juice
1/16 teaspoon salt
2 tablespoons tapioca
Sour cream, whipped cream or vanilla yogurt

In a medium saucepan, combine 2 cups water, lemon and orange slices, cinnamon stick, cloves and dried fruit. Bring to a boil. Remove from heat. Cover and let stand 30 minutes. While fruit is soaking, combine remaining ingredients except sour cream, whipped cream or yogurt in a medium bowl. Let stand at least 15 minutes. Drain fruit. Remove and discard cinnamon stick, cloves and lemon and orange slices. Add orange juice and pineapple mixture to drained fruit in saucepan. Bring to a boil and simmer 15 minutes or until thickened. Serve hot or chilled with sour cream, whipped cream, or vanilla yogurt. Makes 6 to 8 servings.

Good Morning Prunes

Refrigerate the prunes in apple juice overnight; add honey and cinnamon in the morning.

3 cups whole prunes
1-1/2 cups apple juice or cider
2 tablespoons honey

1/8 teaspoon cinnamon
6 orange slices

The night before, place prunes in a medium bowl with apple juice or cider; refrigerate. Before serving the next morning, place in a medium saucepan with honey and cinnamon. Cover and bring to a boil. Lower heat and simmer 5 to 10 minutes. Garnish with a thin slice of fresh orange. Serve hot. Makes 6 servings.

Tangy Stewed Fruit

Here's a dessert that doubles as a topping for ice cream, sherbet, cake, custard or pudding.

2 cups boiling water
2 to 3 cups dried fruit such as apples,
  apricots, cherries, figs, nectarines, peaches,
  pears, pineapple or prunes
1/2 cup orange juice

1 tablespoon lemon juice
2 tablespoons sugar
1/4 cup maple syrup or honey
Dairy sour cream or yogurt

In a medium saucepan, pour boiling water over dried fruit. Let stand to soften 5 to 15 minutes. Add orange juice and lemon juice. Bring to a boil. Lower heat and simmer 20 minutes. Stir in sugar and maple syrup or honey. Mix well. Serve hot or cold. Garnish each serving with a teaspoon of sour cream or yogurt. Makes 5 to 6 servings.

Stuffed Pork Chops

Thick juicy pork chops with spicy apple stuffing and a tangy fruit glaze.

2 tablespoons butter or margarine
6 (1-inch thick) pork chops with pockets
1/2 cup chopped dried apples
2 tablespoons raisins
3/4 cup apple cider or apple juice
1-1/2 teaspoons lemon juice
2 tablespoons onion flakes, pages 54 and 55
1/4 cup chopped celery
1/4 teaspoon salt

1/4 teaspoon nutmeg
1/4 teaspoon cinnamon
1/4 teaspoon paprika
1/4 teaspoon poultry seasoning
1 tablespoon parsley flakes, pages 54 and 55
2 cups day-old 1/2-inch bread cubes
1 egg, beaten
Apple-Lemon Glaze, see below

Apple-Lemon Glaze:
1 tablespoon cornstarch
1 tablespoon sugar
1/4 teaspoon nutmeg

1 cup apple cider or apple juice
1 teaspoon lemon juice

Preheat oven to 350°F (175°C). In a large skillet, melt butter or margarine. Add pork chops. Brown on both sides and remove from skillet. In a small bowl, combine dried apples, raisins, cider or apple juice and lemon juice. Let stand to soften fruit. Lightly brown onion flakes and celery in remaining butter or margarine in skillet. Stir in apple-raisin mixture. Add remaining ingredients except Apple-Lemon Glaze. Toss lightly. Stuff pork chop pockets with stuffing. Place stuffed pork chops in a 13" x 9" baking pan. Prepare Apple-Lemon Glaze. Pour over pork chops. Cover and bake in preheated oven 30 minutes. Uncover and baste with glaze. Bake uncovered 25 to 30 minutes longer. Makes 6 servings.

Apple-Lemon Glaze:
In a small saucepan, combine cornstarch, sugar and nutmeg. Stir in apple cider or apple juice and lemon juice. Stir over medium heat until glaze thickens and boils.

Fried Apple Rings

Delicious for brunch with sausage and scrambled eggs.

Hot apple juice or boiling water to cover
20 to 24 dried apple rings
1/3 cup butter or margarine

1/4 cup sugar
1 teaspoon cinnamon

In a medium bowl, pour hot apple juice or boiling water over apple rings to cover. Let stand to soften 15 to 20 minutes; drain. Heat butter or margarine in a large skillet. Add apples. Cover and cook over low heat 15 to 20 minutes. In a small bowl, mix sugar and cinnamon. Uncover apples and sprinkle with cinnamon-sugar mixture. Cook uncovered 15 to 20 minutes longer, basting occasionally with juice in saucepan. Serve hot. Makes 4 to 6 servings.

1/Stuff the pocket of each browned pork chop with the apple stuffing. Place the stuffed pork chops in a baking pan or dish.

2/Pour the Apple-Lemon Glaze over the pork chops before baking and baste once during baking.

How to Make Stuffed Pork Chops

Cynthia's Best Baked Beans

Everyone always asks for seconds.

8 slices bacon
1 cup chopped onion
1/4 cup chopped green pepper, if desired
2 (16-oz.) cans pork and beans
1 (8-oz.) can tomato sauce
1/2 cup water

1/4 cup brown sugar, firmly packed
1 garlic clove, minced
2 teaspoons Worcestershire sauce
1/2 cup chopped dried apricots
1/2 cup grated Cheddar cheese

Preheat oven to 350°F (175°C). Butter a 2-quart casserole; set aside. In a large skillet, fry bacon until crisp. Remove and drain on paper towels; reserving 1/4 cup bacon drippings. Sauté onion and green pepper in reserved drippings until tender. Stir in pork and beans, tomato sauce, water, brown sugar, garlic, Worcestershire sauce and dried apricots. Crumble and add 5 slices of bacon, reserving 3 slices for garnish. Pour into prepared casserole. Bake 45 to 50 minutes until bubbly. During the last 5 minutes of baking, sprinkle grated Cheddar cheese over top. Just before serving, crumble 3 reserved slices of bacon on top of cheese. Serve hot. Makes 4 to 6 servings.

Country Sausage & Eggs

If you don't have a ring mold, shape the mixture into a ring with your hands.

1-1/2 lbs. bulk pork sausage
1 egg, beaten
1/3 cup milk
3 tablespoons onion flakes, pages 54 and 55
1 cup soda cracker crumbs

1/2 cup chopped dried apple
Scrambled Eggs, see below
1/2 cup grated Cheddar cheese
Paprika

Scrambled Eggs:
1 tablespoon butter or margarine
6 to 8 eggs
2 tablespoons milk or light cream

1/2 teaspoon salt
1/4 teaspoon pepper

Preheat oven to 350°F (175°C). Grease a ring mold; set aside. In a medium bowl, mix sausage, egg, milk, onion flakes, cracker crumbs and dried apple. Press into prepared ring mold. Turn out onto a shallow baking sheet with rim. Bake 30 to 40 minutes until golden brown. Remove from oven. With 2 spatulas remove from baking sheet and place on a heat-resistant platter. Absorb excess grease on platter with paper towels. Prepare Scrambled Eggs and place in center of ring. Sprinkle grated Cheddar cheese over top. Place in oven 2 to 3 minutes to melt cheese. Sprinkle with paprika. Makes 4 to 6 servings.

Scrambled Eggs:
In a medium skillet, melt butter or margarine. In a large bowl, beat eggs with milk or light cream, salt and pepper. Cook eggs in skillet over low heat, stirring frequently.

Old-Fashioned Applesauce

Popular since pioneer days, it's still a treat!

5 cups boiling water
4 cups coarsely chopped dried apples

1/2 to 3/4 cup sugar
1 teaspoon cinnamon, if desired

In a medium saucepan, pour boiling water over dried apples. Let stand to soften 15 minutes. Cover and bring to a boil. Lower heat and simmer until thickened to desired consistency, 30 to 45 minutes. Stir in sugar and cinnamon, if desired. Serve cool or warm. Makes 3-1/2 to 4 cups applesauce.

Golden Fruitcake

A not-too-rich fruitcake that uses golden dried fruits.

1-1/2 cups dried apricots or peaches, cut into 1/2-inch pieces	1/2 teaspoon salt
2 cups water	1/2 teaspoon soda
3/4 cup butter or margarine	1 cup whole red candied cherries
3/4 cup sugar	1 cup slivered almonds
4 eggs	1-1/2 cups golden raisins
2 cups all-purpose flour	1/2 teaspoon grated lemon peel

Preheat oven to 300°F (150°C). Generously grease and flour or line with waxed paper 2 (8" x 4") loaf pans; set aside. In a medium saucepan, simmer, uncovered, apricots or peaches in water until tender, about 2 minutes. Cool; drain off any remaining water. Cream butter or margarine until fluffy in a medium bowl. Beat in eggs, one at time, beating after each addition. In a separate bowl, combine 1-1/2 cups of the flour, salt and soda. Stir into creamed mixture. Combine cooled apricots or peaches, cherries, almonds, raisins, lemon peel and remaining 1/2 cup flour. Add to batter and blend well. Spoon batter into prepared loaf pans. Bake in preheated oven about 1-1/4 hours, until a wooden pick inserted in center comes out clean. Cool 10 to 20 minutes in pan. Remove from pan and cool on a rack. Makes 2 large loaves.

Lunch Box Health Bars

Keep these in your desk at work when you have to skip lunch.

1 cup water	1/2 teaspoon ground cloves
1-1/2 cups chopped mixed dried fruits	1 cup chopped walnuts or pecans
2 tablespoons butter or margarine	*Crust:*
2 eggs, slightly beaten	1/4 cup butter or margarine, softened
1/2 cup packed brown sugar	1/4 cup packed brown sugar
1/2 cup whole-wheat flour	2 tablespoons honey
1/4 cup wheat germ	2 tablespoons light molasses
1/4 cup unprocessed wheat bran	2 cups quick-cooking rolled oats
1-1/2 teaspoons ground cinnamon	1/4 cup whole-wheat flour
1/2 teaspoon salt	

Preheat oven to 350°F (175°C). Generously grease and flour a 13" x 9" baking pan; set aside. Bring water to a boil in a small saucepan, add fruit and 2 tablespoons butter or margarine and remove from heat. Let stand 5 minutes. Stir in eggs, brown sugar, whole-wheat flour, wheat germ, wheat bran, cinnamon, salt and cloves. Add nuts. Stir until well mixed. Make Crust. Spread fruit mixture over prebaked crust. Bake 25 to 30 minutes more. Cool on a rack. Cut into 3" x 1-1/2" bars. Makes 30 bars.

Crust:
Cream butter or margarine, sugar, honey and molasses in a large bowl until fluffy. Stir in oats and whole-wheat flour. Press into the bottom of greased pan. Bake 5 minutes.

Creamy Apricot Dressing

Fruit salad becomes an elegant dessert topped with this creamy dressing.

3/4 cup pineapple juice
1 teaspoon lemon juice
1/2 cup coarsely chopped dried apricots

1 cup whipping cream
3 tablespoons powdered sugar
1/2 teaspoon vanilla extract

In blender container, pour pineapple juice and lemon juice over dried apricots. Let stand to soften 30 minutes. Blend until smooth. Chill. Before serving, whip cream in a medium bowl. Stir in powdered sugar and vanilla. Fold apricot mixture into whipped cream. Serve over fruit salad, chilled pudding or ice cream. Makes about 2 cups dressing.

Raisin Sauce

Fill the gravy boat with this flavorful sauce the next time you serve baked ham or pork roast.

2 cups boiling water
1 cup raisins
1/3 cup brown sugar, firmly packed
2 tablespoons cornstarch

1/4 teaspoon cinnamon
1/4 teaspoon ground cloves
1/2 teaspoon dry mustard
1 teaspoon vinegar

In a medium saucepan, pour boiling water over raisins. Let stand to soften 5 minutes. In a small bowl, mix brown sugar, cornstarch, cinnamon, cloves and dry mustard. Stir into raisin mixture. Cook over low heat until mixture thickens and boils, about 5 minutes. Stir in vinegar. Makes 2 cups sauce.

Variation

Substitute chopped apricots or dried currants for raisins.

Easy Indian Chutney

Sweet and spicy flavor enhances curry, meat or rice dishes.

1/4 cup boiling water
1 cup chopped dried apricots, peaches, pears
  or pineapple
1/4 cup raisins or dried currants
3 tablespoons honey
1 tablespoon red wine vinegar

1/4 teaspoon ground ginger
1/4 teaspoon ground coriander
Dash cayenne pepper
Dash ground cloves
1/3 cup chopped cashews

In a medium saucepan, pour boiling water over dried fruit. Cover and bring to a boil. Remove from heat and let stand 10 minutes or until water is absorbed. Add raisins or currants to fruit mixture. In a small bowl, combine honey, vinegar, ginger, coriander, cayenne pepper and cloves. Stir to mix well. Stir into dried fruit mixture. Add cashews; stir. Store in refrigerator up to 2 weeks. Makes 1-1/2 cups chutney.

Gelatin & Dried Fruits

If you like gelatin salads or desserts, try the taste-tempting flavor blends from this Mix & Match table.

Mix & Match with Gelatin & Dried Fruit

GELATIN FLAVOR	Apples	Apricots	Cherries	Peaches	Pears	Prunes	Raisins
Apricot	*	*					*
Blackberry	*		*			*	
Cherry	*		*			*	*
Lemon	*	*	*	*	*	*	*
Lime	*				*	*	*
Orange	*	*	*	*	*	*	*
Orange/Pineapple	*	*	*	*	*	*	*
Peach				*		*	
Raspberry	*		*		*	*	
Strawberry	*				*	*	

You can vary your own gelatin-fruit blends even more by adding one or more foods from the following list to the slightly thickened gelatin-fruit mixture:

Diced cream cheese
Miniature marshmallows
Chopped nuts
Chopped celery

Grated carrots
Whipping cream
Cottage cheese
Canned mandarin oranges

Fresh fruits such as chopped apples, sliced bananas, berries, orange or grapefruit sections or seedless grapes

Pineapple is not included because dried pineapple, like fresh pineapple, prevents gelatin from thickening. If you want to add pineapple to gelatin, use cooked or canned pineapple.

Easy Fruit Gelatin

Dried fruit in this gelatin will be soft rather than chewy.

1/2 cup dried fruit, see Mix & Match table, above
Boiling water
Cold water

1 (3-oz.) pkg. any flavored gelatin, see Mix & Match table, above
1 cup boiling water

In a medium bowl, cover dried fruit with boiling water. Let stand to soften 10 to 15 minutes. Drain water from fruit into a measuring cup. Add cold water to make 1 cup. In another medium bowl, dissolve gelatin in 1 cup boiling water. Add drained fruit. Stir in mixture of reserved liquid and cold water. Refrigerate until set. Makes 4 servings.

Easier Fruit Gelatin

With this method, the dried fruit in the gelatin will be chewy.

1 (3-oz.) pkg. any flavored gelatin, see Mix & Match table, above
1-1/2 cups boiling water

3/4 cup chopped dried fruit, see Mix & Match table, above
1 cup cold water

In a medium bowl, dissolve gelatin in boiling water. Add dried fruit. Stir in cold water. Refrigerate until set. Makes 4 servings.

Vegetables

Whether you're preparing tonight's supper or next week's camping trip, you'll find the recipes in this section can make the difference between just another meal and a nutrition-packed feast. Meat Loaf Italiano, page 138, will remind you of Beef Wellington. The difference is in the Italian seasonings and the pastry crust sprinkled with sesame seeds. If you bring out Scrumptious Carrot Cake, page 143, for dessert, your reputation as an outstanding cook will soar to impressive heights! To follow one sensational dinner with another, serve Breaded Chicken Supreme, page 140, and Squash Parmesan, page 130. Dessert could be Schnitz Pie, page 114, or Mom's Apple Pudding Cake, page 112.

It's impossible to keep raw vegetables fresh on a camping trip and canned vegetables are heavy and inconvenient to carry. But if you take lightweight packets of dried vegetables, you'll be ready to prepare a delicious and nutritious hot meal to end each exciting day. If you want a three-course meal around the campfire, it takes only a few minutes to make Cream of Vegetable Soup, page 133. Tangy Stewed Fruit, page 121, is a delightful dessert and, if you're backpacking, you don't need to top it with sour cream or yogurt—it's delicious by itself.

Old-Fashioned Corn & Ham Fritters

Dress up a platter of scrambled eggs with these hearty fritters.

Boiling water
3 tablespoons dried corn
2 egg yolks
1/4 cup milk
1/3 cup dairy sour cream
1-1/3 cups all-purpose flour
3/4 teaspoon salt
2 teaspoons baking powder

1/4 teaspoon paprika
1/4 teaspoon dry mustard
1 tablespoon parsley flakes, pages 54 and 55
2 tablespoons onion flakes, pages 54 and 55
3/4 cup diced cooked ham
2 egg whites, stiffly beaten
Oil or shortening for frying

Pour boiling water over corn. Let stand to reconstitute 1 to 2 hours. In a medium bowl, blend egg yolks, milk and sour cream. In another medium bowl, combine flour, salt, baking powder, paprika, dry mustard, parsley flakes and onion flakes. Stir into egg yolk mixture. Drain reconstituted corn. Stir corn and ham into batter. Fold stiffly beaten egg whites into batter. In a heavy pan, deep-fat fryer or mini fryer, heat 2 to 3 inches of oil or shortening to 375°F (190°C). Drop batter by level tablespoonfuls into hot oil or shortening. Large rounded fritters will not cook well in the center. Fry until crisp and golden brown, turning once. Makes 15 to 18 fritters, enough for 4 to 6 servings.

Italian Dried Tomatoes in Olive Oil

Store in the refrigerator for up to six months.

1/2 cup extra-light olive oil
4 garlic cloves, crushed
1 tablespoon fresh rosemary or 2 tablespoons
   dried rosemary
1 small dried red pepper

2 cups dried Roma tomatoes
Boiling water
1 tablespoon dried leaf parsley
1 tablespoon dried leaf oregano
About 2 cups extra-light olive oil

Heat the 1/2 cup olive oil over medium heat in a medium saucepan. Add garlic, rosemary and red pepper. Remove from heat and let stand 1 hour. Soak dried tomatoes in boiling water to cover in a medium bowl. Let stand until softened, about 30 minutes. Drain tomatoes well and pat dry with paper towels. Pack tomatoes, parsley and oregano into clean 1-pint jars. Pour in flavored oil through a strainer, discarding seasonings. Add additional olive oil to cover tomatoes. Close jar with a canning lid and keep refrigerated up to 6 months or freeze up to a year. Makes 2 pints.

Tomato Pesto

Use this on your favorite pasta dish.

1 cup drained dried tomatoes, page 130,
   reserving 1 cup oil
2 cups boiling water
1/2 cup pine nuts
3 garlic cloves

1/2 teaspoon salt
1/4 teaspoon freshly ground black pepper
1 tablespoon chopped fresh basil
2/3 cup grated Parmesan cheese (2 ounces)

Place drained tomatoes in a medium saucepan and cover with boiling water. Simmer, covered, over low heat 10 minutes. Drain and reserve cooking liquid. In a food processor with the metal blade, process tomatoes until finely diced. Add oil from the dried tomatoes, the pine nuts, garlic, salt, pepper, basil and Parmesan cheese. Process until blended. Stir in enough cooking liquid to make a sauce-like consistency. Serve over hot cooked pasta. May be stored in airtight container in the refrigerator up to 1 week. Makes 2-1/2 cups.

Dried Tomato Salad Dressing Italiano

A tangy dressing to go with your favorite salad!

1 cup drained dried tomatoes, page 130,
   reserving 1 cup oil
1/4 cup red-wine vinegar
1/4 cup capers, drained

1/2 teaspoon freshly ground pepper
2 tablespoons chopped fresh Italian parsley leaves
1 tablespoon chopped fresh basil
1 teaspoon dried leaf oregano

Process drained tomatoes until finely minced in a food processor with the metal blade. Add oil, vinegar, capers, pepper, parsley, basil and oregano. Process to combine. Serve over mixed green salad or cucumber and onions. Makes about 2 cups.

Country Corn

This recipe has been popular in the Midwest for generations.

2 cups boiling water
1 cup dried corn
3 tablespoons light or heavy cream

1/4 teaspoon salt
1 tablespoon sugar
2 tablespoons butter or margarine

In a medium saucepan, pour boiling water over dried corn. Let stand to reconstitute 1 to 2 hours. Do not drain. Add cream, salt, sugar and butter or margarine. Simmer over low heat 1 hour. Serve hot. Makes 4 to 6 servings.

Tender Glazed Carrots

Carrots cut diagonally before drying have extra eye appeal.

Boiling water
1-1/2 cups dried carrots
2 tablespoons butter or margarine
2 tablespoons brown sugar

3 tablespoons Dijon-style mustard
1/4 teaspoon salt
1 tablespoon parsley flakes, pages 54 and 55

In a medium saucepan, pour boiling water over dried carrots to cover. Let stand to reconstitute 45 minutes or until plump. Simmer over low heat only until tender, about 10 minutes. Drain. Stir in butter or margarine, brown sugar, mustard and salt. Stir over medium heat until glazed, 1 or 2 minutes. Sprinkle with parsley and serve hot. Makes 4 to 6 servings.

Leather Britches With Ham

The pioneers called dried green beans leather britches *and put them in hearty soups.*

2 cups boiling water
2 cups dried green beans
2 tablespoons vegetable oil
2 cups cubed smoked ham
1 cup chopped onion
1/4 cup chopped celery

1 garlic clove, minced
4 cups water
1/4 teaspoon pepper
2 cups diced potatoes
1 to 2 tablespoons cider or wine vinegar

In a medium bowl, pour 2 cups boiling water over dried green beans. Let stand to reconstitute 1 to 2 hours. In a large heavy kettle, heat oil. Lightly brown ham. Stir in onion, celery and garlic. Sauté until vegetables are golden. Add 4 cups water. Simmer 1 hour. Add undrained reconstituted green beans and pepper. Cover and simmer 1 to 1-1/2 hours. Add diced potatoes and vinegar. Simmer uncovered 1/2 hour or until potatoes are tender. Serve hot. Makes 6 servings.

Beefy Hobo Stew

You don't have to be a hobo to love this meal-in-one stew!

4 to 5 tablespoons vegetable oil
1/4 cup all-purpose flour
1/2 teaspoon salt
1/4 teaspoon pepper
1/2 teaspoon thyme
1/2 teaspoon marjoram
2 tablespoons parsley flakes, pages 54 and 55
2 to 3 lbs. stew beef, cut in 1-inch cubes

1 qt. water
3 beef bouillon cubes
2 cups boiling water
2 cups mixed dried vegetables such as
    green beans, carrots, corn and peas
2 cups potatoes, cut in 1-inch cubes
2 medium onions, quartered
1/2 cup cold water

In a large heavy kettle, heat oil. Combine flour, salt, pepper, thyme, marjoram and parsley flakes in a brown paper bag. Shake beef cubes in bag to coat with flour mixture; reserve remaining flour mixture. Brown beef cubes in hot oil. Add 1 quart water and bouillon cubes. Cover and simmer 2 to 3 hours or until meat is tender. While meat is cooking, pour 2 cups boiling water over dried vegetables. Let stand to reconstitute up to 1 or 2 hours, depending on type of vegetables and size of pieces. Add potatoes, onions and reconstituted vegetables to beef mixture. Simmer 20 to 30 minutes longer or until vegetables are tender. Dissolve 2 to 3 tablespoons reserved flour mixture or flour in 1/2 cup cold water; strain and slowly add to stew, stirring constantly until stew thickens. Makes 6 to 8 servings.

Cream of Vegetable Soup

To make Cream of Mixed-Vegetable Soup, combine a variety of vegetable flakes and powders.

1-1/2 cups Vegetable Puree, see below
3 tablespoons butter or margarine
1 tablespoon onion flakes, pages 54 and 55
2 tablespoons all-purpose flour
1/2 teaspoon salt

1/4 teaspoon pepper
1/4 teaspoon crushed basil, if desired
3 cups milk
1-1/2 teaspoons parsley flakes,
    pages 54 and 55

Vegetable Puree:
6 to 8 tablespoons vegetable powder or
    flakes, such as asparagus, green bean,
    carrot, cauliflower, celery, pea or potato,
    pages 54 and 55

1-1/2 cups boiling water

Prepare Vegetable Puree. In a 1-1/2-quart saucepan, melt butter or margarine over medium heat. Add onion flakes. Sauté until golden. Stir in flour, salt, pepper and basil, if desired. Gradually add milk, stirring constantly over low heat to prevent lumping. Do not boil. Stir in Vegetable Puree. Heat to serving temperature. Garnish with parsley flakes. Makes 4 servings.

Vegetable Puree:
In a small bowl, pour boiling water over vegetable powder or flakes. Let stand to reconstitute 10 to 15 minutes.

Country Chicken-Vegetable Soup

Great on a cold evening with hot French bread and a gelatin salad.

2 cups boiling water
2 cups mixed dried vegetables such as
    green beans, carrots, corn and peas
2 tablespoons butter or margarine
2 tablespoons vegetable oil
1 cup chopped onion
1/2 cup chopped celery
1 (3- to 4-lb.) chicken, cut up
2 cups water
2 chicken bouillon cubes

1/2 cup chopped carrot
1/4 teaspoon basil
1 bay leaf
2 tablespoons parsley flakes, pages 54 and 55
1/4 teaspoon thyme
1 (2-lb.) can tomatoes, undrained
1/2 teaspoon paprika
1/2 teaspoon salt
1/8 teaspoon pepper
2 cups cooked noodles, if desired

Pour 2 cups boiling water over dried vegetables. Let stand to reconstitute up to 1 or 2 hours, depending on the type of vegetables and size of pieces. In a large skillet, heat butter or margarine and oil. Sauté onion and celery until tender. Remove from skillet. Brown chicken in same skillet. In a large kettle, combine browned chicken, 2 cups water, bouillon cubes, sautéed onion and celery, carrots, basil, bay leaf, parsley flakes, thyme and tomatoes. Simmer 45 minutes to 1 hour or until chicken is tender, skimming foam from top and discarding. Remove chicken from skillet to cool. Strain broth through a large-mesh sieve; discard spices and vegetables. Remove bones from chicken. Place chicken in kettle with broth, undrained reconstituted vegetables, paprika, salt and pepper. Simmer 15 minutes. If desired, add cooked noodles to soup. Serve hot. Makes 6 to 8 servings.

Homestead Vegetable Soup

With crusty bread it's a hearty one-dish meal.

2 beef bouillon cubes
2 cups boiling water
2 cups mixed dried vegetables such as
    green beans, carrots, corn, peas or potatoes
3 cups homemade broth or consommé or
    2 (10-3/4-oz.) cans consommé
1 (1-lb.) can tomatoes, undrained
3/4 cup pearl barley

1/2 teaspoon salt
1/8 teaspoon pepper
1/2 teaspoon basil
1/2 teaspoon thyme
1 tablespoon dried parsley
3 tablespoons butter or margarine
1/2 cup chopped celery
1/2 cup chopped onion

Dissolve bouillon cubes in boiling water. Pour over dried vegetables and let stand to reconstitute up to 1 or 2 hours, depending on type of vegetables and size of pieces. In a large kettle, heat broth or consommé and tomatoes. Add barley, salt, pepper, basil, thyme and parsley. Simmer uncovered 30 minutes. In a small skillet, melt butter or margarine. Sauté celery and onion. Add to broth. Stir in undrained reconstituted vegetables. Simmer 15 to 20 minutes longer or until vegetables are tender. Makes 8 cups of soup or 6 to 8 servings.

Tomato Corn Chowder

Don't forget which recipe you used because this chowder will be in demand.

5 cups boiling water	**1 teaspoon sugar**
1-1/4 cups dried corn	**1/2 teaspoon paprika**
Additional boiling water	**1/2 teaspoon salt**
1/2 cup dried onion	**1/8 teaspoon pepper**
1/4 cup dried celery	**1 tablespoon parsley flakes, pages 54 and 55**
2 tablespoons dried green pepper	**1-1/2 cups diced potatoes**
6 slices bacon	**1 cup milk**
1 (1-lb.) can tomatoes, chopped	

In a large heavy saucepan, pour 5 cups boiling water over corn. Let stand to reconstitute 2 hours. Pour additional boiling water over onion, celery and green pepper to cover. Let stand to reconstitute 30 minutes. Drain. In a medium skillet, fry bacon until crisp. Remove bacon and drain on paper towel. Crumble and set aside. Pour off all but 1/3 cup bacon drippings. Sauté drained reconstituted onion, celery and green pepper in bacon drippings until tender. Add sautéed vegetables and bacon drippings to corn mixture. Stir in tomatoes, sugar, paprika, salt, pepper and parsley flakes. Cover and simmer over low heat 1 hour. Add diced potatoes. Cover and simmer 30 minutes. Stir in milk. Heat until almost boiling. Garnish with crumbled bacon. Serve hot. Makes 4 to 6 servings.

How to Make Tomato Corn Chowder

1/Pour boiling water over the corn and let it reconstitute for 2 hours. Reconstitute the other vegetables before sautéing them in bacon drippings.

2/Combine all ingredients except dried potatoes, milk and crumbled bacon. After simmering for 1 hour, add the potatoes. Simmer 30 minutes longer. Before serving, stir in the milk. Heat the chowder to serving temperature and garnish it with crumbled bacon.

Plantation Chowder

It's even better the second day, if there's any left.

3 chicken-flavor bouillon cubes	1/2 teaspoon salt
3-1/2 cups boiling water	1/8 teaspoon pepper
1-1/4 cups dried corn	1/2 bay leaf
6 slices bacon	2 cups diced potatoes
Additional boiling water	1/2 cup water
1/2 cup dried onion	2 tablespoons flour
1/2 teaspoon sugar	2 cups milk

Dissolve bouillon cubes in 3-1/2 cups boiling water. Pour mixture over dried corn in a large sauce-pan. Let stand to reconstitute 2 hours. Pour additional boiling water over onion to cover. Let stand to reconstitute 10 to 15 minutes. Drain. In a medium skillet, fry bacon until crisp. Remove bacon and drain on paper towel. Sauté drained, reconstituted onion in bacon drippings until tender. Add onion and bacon drippings to corn mixture. Stir in sugar, salt, pepper and bay leaf. Cover and simmer over low heat 1 hour. Add diced potatoes. Cover and simmer 30 minutes or until potatoes are tender. Mix 1/2 cup water with 2 tablespoons flour until smooth. Stir into vegetable mixture. Add milk, stir. Heat until almost boiling. Garnish with crumbled crisp bacon. Serve hot. Makes 4 to 6 servings.

Vegetable Meat Loaf

Meat and vegetables layered in a ring surround fluffy mashed potatoes.

Boiling water	1 tablespoon parsley flakes, pages 54 and 55
2 cups chopped mixed dried vegetables such as green beans, carrots, corn and peas	1/2 teaspoon salt
	1/8 teaspon pepper
1-1/2 lbs. lean ground beef	1/2 cup breadcrumbs
1/2 pkg. onion soup mix	4 cups mashed potatoes
1 egg, beaten	Parsley sprigs
2 tablespoons ketchup	

Pour boiling water over dried vegetables to cover. Let stand to reconstitute up to 1 to 2 hours. Preheat oven to 350°F (175°C). In a large bowl, mix ground beef, onion soup mix, egg, ketchup, parsley flakes, salt, pepper and breadcrumbs. Press half of meat mixture into a 10-inch ring mold which can be used for baking. Drain reconstituted vegetables. Press vegetables on top of meat mixture. Press remaining meat mixture over vegetable layer. Bake in preheated oven 1 hour. Let stand in pan 5 minutes after removing from oven. Place a platter upside down over baking pan. Invert platter and pan. Remove pan. Fill center of loaf with mashed potatoes. Garnish with parsley sprigs. Makes 4 to 6 servings.

Mexican Meat Pie

Mildly spiced meat pie and a green salad make a complete dinner.

Boiling water
1/3 cup dried corn
Cornmeal Pastry, see below
1 tablespoon vegetable oil
1 lb. lean ground beef
3 tablespoons onion flakes, pages 54 and 55
3 tablespoons dried chopped green pepper
1 teaspoon chili powder
3/4 teaspoon oregano
1/2 teaspoon salt

1/3 teaspoon black pepper
1 (4-oz.) can diced green chilies
1 teaspoon Worcestershire sauce
1/2 cup chili sauce or ketchup
1 (8-oz.) can tomato sauce
1 cup water
Picante Topping, see below
Crisp crumbled bacon
Sliced black or green pimiento-stuffed olives

Cornmeal Pastry:
1 cup all purpose flour
1/2 cup cornmeal
1/2 teaspoon salt
1/2 teaspoon paprika

1/3 cup grated Cheddar cheese
1/2 cup shortening
4 to 5 tablespoons ice water

Picante Topping:
1 egg, beaten
2 tablespoons milk
1/2 teaspoon dry mustard

1 teaspoon Worcestershire sauce
1 cup grated Cheddar cheese

Pour boiling water over dried corn. Let stand to reconstitute 1 to 2 hours. Prepare Cornmeal Pastry; set aside. Preheat oven to 425°F (220°C). Heat oil in a medium skillet. Add ground beef, breaking into pieces with a spatula. Cook until browned. Drain excess fat. Add onion flakes, green pepper and reconstituted corn. Cook until vegetables are lightly browned. Stir in remaining ingredients. Simmer over medium heat 10 to 15 minutes. Let mixture cool to warm or room temperature. Press into unbaked Cornmeal Pastry. Bake in preheated oven 20 to 25 minutes. Prepare Picante Topping. Remove pie from oven. Spread with Picante Topping. Bake 5 minutes or until cheese is slightly bubbly. Garnish with crisp crumbled bacon and sliced olives.

Cornmeal Pastry:
In a medium bowl, combine flour, cornmeal, salt, paprika and cheese. With a pastry blender or 2 knives, cut in shortening until mixture resembles small peas. Sprinkle with ice water 1 tablespoon at a time, tossing rapidly with a fork. Dough should clump together. Press into a ball and flatten on a lightly floured surface. Roll out to a circle 11 inches in diameter. Roll onto rolling pin or fold in quarters. Place carefully over a 9-inch pie plate. Do not stretch dough. Trim pastry to extend 1 inch over pie plate rim. If necessary, patch pastry with excess pieces. Fold edge under and crimp.

Picante Topping:
Combine egg, milk, dry mustard and Worcestershire sauce in a small bowl. Toss with grated cheese.

Meat Loaf Italiano

Pizza-seasoned meat loaf covered with a crusty sesame seed bread.

1 teaspoon active dry yeast
2/3 cup warm water (110°F, 45°C)
2 teaspoons sugar
1 teaspoon salt
2 to 2-1/4 cups all-purpose flour
1 tablespoon vegetable oil

2 tablespoons cornmeal
Italian Herb Filling, see below
1 cup grated mozzarella cheese (8 oz.)
1/4 cup grated Parmesan cheese
Water
Sesame seeds

Italian Herb Filling:

1 lb. lean ground beef
1 tablespoon all-purpose flour
2 tablespoons onion flakes, pages 54 and 55
2 tablespoons dried chopped green pepper
3 tablespoons dried mushrooms or
   1 (4-oz.) can mushrooms
1 fresh garlic clove, crushed
1/2 teaspoon oregano

1/2 teaspoon basil
1 teaspoon paprika
1/4 teaspoon salt
1/3 cup chopped pitted black olives
1 tablespoon Worcestershire sauce
1 (8-oz.) can tomato sauce
1 cup water

In a medium bowl, dissolve yeast in warm water. Add sugar, salt and 1 to 1-1/2 cups flour. Beat until smooth. Gradually add enough remaining flour to make a stiff dough. Turn out onto a floured surface and begin kneading, adding only enough flour to prevent dough from sticking to surface. Knead until satiny, 5 to 10 minutes. Coat the inside of a large bowl with 1 tablespoon oil. Place dough in bowl, turning once. Cover with a cloth. Set in a warm place free from drafts and let rise until doubled in bulk, about 1 hour. Preheat oven to 400°F (205°C). Sprinkle a jelly-roll pan or large baking sheet with cornmeal; set aside. Prepare Italian Herb Filling. In a small bowl, mix mozzarella cheese and Parmesan cheese. Punch down dough. Roll dough into a 16" x 12" rectangle. Place on prepared pan. Place filling lengthwise down center third of dough. Sprinkle cheese mixture on top of filling. Make diagonal cuts 2 inches apart from edge of dough to filling. Crisscross diagonal strips over filling. Lightly spray top of loaf with water and sprinkle with sesame seeds. Bake in preheated oven 20 to 25 minutes or until golden brown. Makes 6 to 8 servings.

Italian Herb Filling:
In a large skillet, brown ground beef, breaking it into pieces with a spatula. Drain excess fat. Stir in flour. Stir in remaining ingredients. Simmer over low heat 10 minutes or until thickened. Let mixture cool to warm or room temperature.

Breaded Chicken

Use paper bags and you won't have to wash as many dishes!

1/2 to 3/4 cup Seasoned Breading Mix,
  see below
1 (2-1/2- to 3-lb.) frying chicken
1/4 cup flour

1 egg
2 tablespoons whole or evaporated milk
1/4 cup butter or margarine, melted

Prepare Seasoned Breading Mix. Preheat oven to 325°F (165°C). Cut chicken in serving pieces. Put chicken pieces and flour in a medium brown paper bag. Shake to coat chicken with flour. In a small bowl, beat egg and milk together. Pour into a clean paper bag. Quickly put chicken in bag and shake to coat with egg mixture. Place chicken pieces and breading mix in another bag; shake to coat chicken with breading mix. Arrange breaded chicken in an 11" x 7" x 2" baking pan. Spoon melted butter or margarine over chicken. Bake uncovered in preheated oven 1 hour and 20 minutes. Makes 4 servings.

Seasoned Breading Mix

You'll find dozens of uses for this easy mix.

2-1/2 cups Fine Dry Breadcrumbs, see below
1/2 cup onion flakes, pages 54 and 55
1 teaspoon garlic powder
2 tablespoons parsley flakes, pages 54 and 55
1/2 teaspoon basil

1/2 teaspoon marjoram
1 tablespoon powdered celery or
  celery flakes, pages 54 and 55
1 teaspoon salt
1/2 teaspoon pepper

Fine Dry Breadcrumbs:
5 slices day-old bread

Prepare Fine Dry Breadcrumbs. Combine with other ingredients in a small brown paper bag and shake to mix well. Store in an airtight container in a cool dry place. Use within 2 to 3 months. Makes about 3 cups breading mix.

Fine Dry Breadcrumbs:
Dry bread until crisp in a dehydrator at 160°F (70°C) or an oven at 200°F (95°C). Crush in a food chopper, blender or food processor or put in a plastic bag and crush with a rolling pin. Store in a tightly covered container in a cool dry place. Use within 3 months.

Savory Salad Sprinkles

Toss over crisp greens, potato salad, macaroni salad and egg salad.

1/2 cup grated Parmesan cheese
2 tablespoons sesame seeds
2 tablespoons carrot flakes, pages 54 and 55
2 tablespoons onion flakes, pages 54 and 55
1 tablespoon cucumber flakes, pages 54 and 55
2 teaspoons parsley flakes, pages 54 and 55

1 teaspoon tomato flakes, pages 54 and 55
1/2 teaspoon garlic salt
1/2 teaspoon monosodium glutamate, if desired
1/2 teaspoon paprika
1/4 teaspoon freshly ground black pepper

Combine all ingredients in a small bowl. Mix until evenly distributed. Put in a 1-cup container. Label and store in a cool dry place. Use within 1 month. Makes about 1 cup.

Fiesta Corn

You can have it both ways, as a crunchy flavorful dried snack or a delicious cooked vegetable.

4 cups fresh blanched corn,
   see Corn, Pretreatment, page 59
1 cup finely chopped onion
1 cup finely chopped red or green pepper

1 teaspoon cornstarch
1/2 teaspoon chili powder
1/2 teaspoon salt
1/8 teaspoon pepper

In a large bowl, toss blanched corn with onion and red or green pepper. In a small bowl, mix cornstarch, chili powder, salt and pepper. Toss with corn mixture until evenly distributed. Spread on drying trays. Dry at 150°F (65°C) for 1 to 2 hours, then at 130°F (55°C) until dry. Eat dry as a snack or reconstitute with boiling water and cook until tender. Makes 2-1/2 cups dried corn.

Seasoned Salt

Does wonders for eggs, cheese, fish and meat dishes.

1 teaspoon tomato powder, pages 54 and 55
1 teaspoon green pepper powder, pages 54 and 55
1 teaspoon onion powder or 1 tablespoon onion flakes, pages 54 and 55
1-1/2 teaspoons garlic powder

2 teaspoons paprika
1 teaspoon dry mustard
1 teaspoon oregano
3/4 teaspoon thyme
1 teaspoon celery salt
3/4 cup pickling salt

Blend all ingredients except pickling salt in blender until fine. Add pickling salt. Blend only 1 or 2 seconds to mix. If mixture is too fine, it will cake during storage. Store in a shaker container that has an airtight lid. Makes 1 cup.

Scrumptious Carrot Cake

No one will believe it's made with dried carrots!

Boiling water
1-1/2 to 3 cups dried shredded carrots
2 cups all-purpose flour
1 cup granulated sugar
1 cup brown sugar, firmly packed
2 teaspoons baking powder
1 teaspoon salt

2 teaspoons baking soda
2 teaspoons cinnamon
1/2 teaspoon nutmeg
4 eggs
1-1/2 cups vegetable oil
1 cup chopped walnuts or pecans
Cream-Cheese Frosting, see below

Cream-Cheese Frosting:
1 (8-oz.) pkg. cream cheese, room
  temperature
1/2 cup butter or margarine, room
  temperature

2 teaspoons vanilla extract
1 (1-lb.) box powdered sugar
1 cup chopped walnuts or pecans, if desired

Pour boiling water over dried carrots. Let stand to reconstitute 20 to 25 minutes. Drain and measure 3 cups reconstituted carrots. Preheat oven to 350°F (175°C). Generously grease and flour two 9-inch, round cake pans or 1 large 9" x 12" x 2" baking pan; set aside. In a large bowl, combine flour, granulated sugar, brown sugar, baking powder, salt, baking soda, cinnamon and nutmeg. In a small bowl, beat eggs and oil. Add to flour mixture. Stir 300 strokes or mix with electric mixer on low speed until blended. Fold in carrots and chopped nuts. Pour into prepared baking pans. Bake 25 to 30 minutes or until wooden pick inserted in center comes out clean. Cool in pans on rack 10 minutes. Turn out onto rack to cool completely. When cool, frost with Cream-Cheese Frosting. Makes 8 to 10 servings.

Cream-Cheese Frosting:
In a medium bowl, beat cream cheese and butter or margarine until fluffy. Blend in vanilla. Gradually add powdered sugar. Beat until smooth and creamy. Fold in chopped nuts, if desired, reserving 2 tablespoons to garnish top of cake. Spread frosting over sides and top of cake. If desired, sprinkle remaining nuts on top.

Don't mince fresh or dried herbs on a cutting board or in a food processor. Much of the natural aromatic oil in the leaves will be lost. Instead, snip with scissors or crumble with your hand to desired fineness to maintain the best flavor.

Nuts and Seeds

What would granola or gorp be without nuts and seeds? Can there be a more perfect pair than cream cheese and nuts? And only the most hardened ingrate would be unmoved by a holiday tin filled with spiced roasted nuts.

Every pantry should have a choice of granolas. Below and on page 146 you'll find both Easy Granola and Crunchy Granola. It doesn't matter if your family isn't enthusiastic about the great out-doors—gorp is just as delicious while you're watching TV, reading, playing Chinese checkers or building models. You'll find three basic gorp recipes on page 147. Read them all. Then combine what strikes you as best of all three and you'll have your own individualized gorp.

A favorite snack at my house is Cream Cheese Spread, page 146. It is especially good with a fruit bread like Orange-Date Bread, page 95. Try it with a cup of refreshing herb tea.

For this year's gift-giving, decorate several small containers with paints, paper cut-outs and ribbons. Fill them with roasted nuts from the recipes on pages 148 and 149. Be sure to make enough so your family can enjoy them too.

Crunchy Granola

More nutritious, fresher and less expensive than the granola you buy.

4 cups uncooked rolled oats (not instant)	2 tablespoons oil
1 cup wheat germ	1/2 cup honey
1/2 cup bran flakes	1/2 cup apple juice or water
1 cup shredded unsweetened coconut	1/2 cup brown sugar, firmly packed
1/4 cup sesame seeds	2 tablespoons vanilla extract
1/2 cup sunflower seeds	2 cups chopped dried fruit, if desired
1/2 teaspoon cinnamon	1 cup chopped nuts, if desired
1/8 teaspoon salt	

Preheat oven to 300°F (150°C). In a large bowl, mix oats, wheat germ, bran flakes, coconut, sesame seeds, sunflower seeds, cinnamon and salt. In a small saucepan, heat oil, honey, apple juice or water and brown sugar until warm, stirring until brown sugar is dissolved. Remove from heat and stir in vanilla. Pour oil mixture over oat mixture, stirring to mix well. Pour mixture into a shallow 9" x 13" or larger baking pan. Bake 25 to 30 minutes or until golden brown, stirring every 10 minutes. During last 5 minutes of baking, stir in dried fruit and nuts, if desired. Cool and store in airtight containers at room temperature. Use within 4 weeks. Makes about 9 cups.

Sunflower seeds and dried apples are two of the energy-packed ingredients in Crunchy Granola.

Easy Granola

For good nutrition and delicious flavor try this easy-to-make breakfast or snack treat.

4 cups uncooked rolled oats (not instant)
1 cup wheat germ
1/3 cup instant nonfat dry milk
1 cup flaked coconut
1/2 cup sesame seeds
1 cup sunflower seeds
1/2 teaspoon salt

1 cup blanched slivered almonds
1/4 cup vegetable oil
1/2 cup honey
1/2 cup brown sugar, firmly packed
1-1/2 teaspoons vanilla extract
1-1/2 cups chopped dried fruit, if desired

Preheat oven to 300°F (150°C). In a large bowl, mix oats, wheat germ, dry milk, coconut, sesame seeds, sunflower seeds, salt and almonds. In a small saucepan, heat oil, honey and brown sugar until warm, stirring until brown sugar is dissolved. Remove from heat and stir in vanilla. Pour oil mixture over oat mixture, stirring to mix well. Pour into a shallow 9" x 13" or larger baking pan. Bake in preheated oven 25 to 30 minutes until golden brown, stirring every 10 minutes. During last 5 minutes of baking, stir in dried fruit, if desired. Cool and store in airtight containers at room temperature. Use within 4 weeks. Makes 9 to 10 cups.

Hearty Cereal Topping

Ordinary cold or hot cereal isn't ordinary with this topping.

1/4 cup wheat germ
1/2 cup bran cereal
1/2 cup brown sugar, firmly packed
1/2 teaspoon cinnamon

1/4 cup butter or margarine
1/4 cup sunflower seeds
1/4 cup finely chopped nuts
1/2 cup chopped dried fruit

Preheat oven to 300°F (150°C). In a large bowl, combine wheat germ, bran cereal, brown sugar and cinnamon. Mix well. With a pastry blender, cut in butter or margarine until evenly distributed. Stir in sunflower seeds and chopped nuts. Mix well. Spread mixture in a 9-inch square pan. Bake 10 minutes. Stir in dried fruit. Cool and store in an airtight container in a cool dry place. Use within 4 to 6 weeks. Makes about 3 cups.

Cream Cheese Spread

It will disappear just as fast at an afternoon tea as it will as an after-school snack.

1 (8-oz.) pkg. cream cheese
2 to 3 tablespoons milk or cream
1/4 cup finely chopped nuts such as almonds,
   filberts, pecans, sunflower seeds or walnuts

1/3 cup chopped dried fruit such as apples,
   apricots, cherries, dates, figs, peaches,
   pears, pineapple, prunes, raisins,
   strawberries or packaged currants

Let cream cheese stand at room temperature until softened. In a small bowl, beat cream cheese with milk or cream to a spreading consistency. Add nuts and dried fruit. Spread on crackers or bread. Makes about 1-1/2 cups.

Light Gorp

Keep a close watch or it may disappear before you hit the trail!

1/2 cup dried apples	1/2 cup dried pineapple
1/2 cup dried apricots	1/4 cup coconut flakes
1/4 cup dried peaches	1/2 cup golden raisins
1/2 cup dried pears	1/2 cup cashews or blanched almonds

Cut apples, apricots, peaches, pears and pineapple into 1/2-inch pieces. Combine all ingredients in a medium bowl. Package in airtight plastic bags and store in a cool dry place. Use within 3 to 4 weeks. Makes about 3-1/2 cups.

Mixed Gorp

Create your own gorp snacks with a variety of dried fruit, nuts and candy.

1/2 cup dried apples	1/2 cup chopped dates
1/2 cup dried apricots	1/2 cup raisins
1/2 cup dried prunes	1/4 cup butterscotch chips
1/4 cup coconut flakes	1/2 cup mixed nuts

Cut apples, apricots and prunes into 1/2-inch pieces. Combine all ingredients in a medium bowl. Package in airtight plastic bags and store in a cool dry place. Use within 3 to 4 weeks. Makes about 3-1/2 cups.

Variations

Other ingredients you'll enjoy in gorp are: dried currants, chopped figs, pecans, walnuts, peanuts, "M&M's" plain or peanut chocolate candies, carob stars, chocolate chips, jelly beans and gum drops.

Dark Gorp

Hikers aren't the only ones who will enjoy this version of the famous trail snack.

1/2 cup prunes	3/4 cup "M&M's" plain chocolate candies
1/2 cup dried cherries	1/4 cup sunflower seeds
1/2 cup chopped dates	1/2 cup cashews
1/2 cup raisins	

Cut prunes into 1/2-inch pieces. Combine all ingredients in a medium bowl. Package in airtight plastic bags and store in a cool dry place. Use within 3 to 4 weeks. Makes about 3-1/2 cups.

Almond Crunch Filling

Use this in Filled Drop Cookies, page 109, for a delicious change.

1 cup almond paste (8-oz.)
1/2 cup butter or margarine, melted
1 egg

1/2 teaspoon almond extract
3/4 cup zwieback crumbs (8 pieces)
1/4 cup finely chopped almonds

In a medium bowl, combine almond paste, melted butter or margarine, egg and almond extract. Beat until smooth. Stir in zwieback crumbs and almonds. Makes 2 cups filling.

Sugar & Spice Nuts

Fill a pretty tin with sweet spiced nuts, top it with a bow and give it to a friend.

1 egg white
1 tablespoon butter or margarine, melted
3 cups nuts such as almonds, cashews, filberts, peanuts, pecans, sunflower seeds and walnuts
3/4 cup sugar

2 tablespoons cornstarch
1-1/2 teaspoons cinnamon
1/2 teaspoon ground allspice
1/2 teaspoon nutmeg
1/4 teaspoon salt

Preheat oven to 275°F (135°C). In a small bowl, slightly beat egg white. Stir in melted butter or margarine. Add nuts; stir to coat with egg white mixture. In a medium bowl, mix sugar, cornstarch, cinnamon, allspice, nutmeg and salt. Add nuts to spice mixture. Stir until all nuts are coated. Spread mixture in a shallow baking pan. Bake in preheated oven 45 minutes. Break apart while still warm. Makes 3-1/2 cups.

Spicy Cocktail Nuts

Company coming? Serve these with a cool drink.

3 tablespoons butter or margarine, melted
1/2 teaspoon seasoned salt
1/4 teaspoon garlic salt
1/4 teaspoon paprika
1/8 teaspoon onion powder

Dash Tabasco sauce
3 cups nuts such as almonds, peanuts, cashews, filberts, pecans, sunflower seeds and walnuts

Preheat oven to 275°F (135°C). In a medium bowl, mix melted butter or margarine, seasoned salt, garlic salt, paprika, onion powder and Tabasco sauce. Add nuts; mix well. Spread mixture in a shallow baking pan. Bake in preheated oven 20 to 25 minutes, stirring occasionally. Drain on paper towels. Makes 3 cups.

Tangy Sunflower Seeds

Soy sauce adds salt and extra flavor.

2 tablespoons vegetable oil
1 tablespoon soy sauce
1/4 teaspoon paprika

1/2 teaspoon celery salt
Dash cayenne pepper
2 cups raw shelled sunflower seeds

Preheat oven to 300°F (150°C). In a medium bowl, mix oil, soy sauce, paprika, celery salt and cayenne pepper. Add sunflower seeds. Stir until seeds are evenly coated. Spread mixture in a shallow baking pan. Bake in preheated oven 20 minutes, stirring frequently. Drain on paper towels. Makes 2 cups.

Mexican Nuts

Add a little more chili powder if you like hotter flavor.

1/4 cup butter or margarine, melted
1-1/4 teaspoons chili powder
1/2 teaspoon coriander
1/2 teaspoon paprika
1/4 teaspoon salt

Dash cumin
4 cups nuts such as almonds, cashews, filberts,
    peanuts, pecans, sunflower seeds and
    walnuts

Preheat oven to 275°F (135°C). In a medium bowl, mix melted butter or margarine, chili powder, coriander, paprika, salt and cumin. Add nuts; stir well. Spread mixture in a shallow baking pan. Bake in preheated oven 20 to 25 minutes, stirring occasionally. Drain on paper towels. Makes 4 cups.

Smoky Nuts

A mild hickory-smoked flavor.

1 tablespoon vegetable oil
1-1/2 teaspoons Worcestershire sauce
1-1/4 teaspoons hickory salt
1/2 teaspoons garlic powder
1/2 teaspoon paprika

1/4 teaspoon onion powder
4 cups nuts such as almonds, cashews, filberts,
    peanuts, pecans, sunflower seeds and
    walnuts

Preheat oven to 275°F (135°C). In a medium bowl, mix oil, Worcestershire sauce, hickory salt, garlic powder, paprika and onion powder. Add nuts; stir well. Spread mixture in a shallow baking pan. Bake in preheated oven 20 to 25 minutes, stirring occasionally. Drain on paper towels. Makes 4 cups.

Meat and Fish

If you like jerky but think it comes in only one flavor—jerky-flavored jerky—the recipes beginning on this page will be a pleasant surprise. They combine flavoring the jerky with the curing process. While the meat is marinating in the seasoning mixture, it is also being cured.

First of all, there's Great Jerky which is a tasty but very basic recipe. From then on, making and sampling jerky can be almost as exciting as a trip around the world!

Western Barbecue Jerky blends the flavors that cowboys and ranch hands flourished on. Hawaiian Jerky introduces exotic flavors which also occur in the Far East variations, Teriyaki Jerky and Sweet & Sour Jerky. The aromas of India are more pungent, as you'll find with Curried Jerky. Middle Eastern Jerky is subtle but intriguing.

Returning to the treats of the Western Hemisphere, you'll enjoy Fiesta Jerky if you like highly spiced foods. If not, Mild Mexican Jerky is for those who like Mexican-style food that's light on the chili.

The Sour Cream Dip, below, is not only a gourmet treat, but a sensational way to use smoked fish. People who don't usually care for fish will discover they like it with this blend of appetizing ingredients.

Recipes for flavoring and curing fish are on pages 84 and 85.

Sour Cream Dip

Blend smoked or smoke-flavored dried fish with sour cream to make a superb dip .

1 cup dairy sour cream
1/4 cup mayonnaise
2 tablespoons lemon juice
1 garlic clove, crushed

1/4 teaspoon pepper
1 tablespoon parsley flakes, page 54 and 55, ed crushed
3/4 to 1 cup crumbled smoked fish, page 86

In a medium bowl, stir together sour cream, mayonnaise, lemon juice, garlic, pepper and parsley flakes until blended. Stir in crumbled fish. Serve with crisp crackers, potato chips or raw vegetables. Makes 2-1/4 cups dip.

If jerky is too brittle, brush on a little Worcestershire sauce or soy sauce to soften it.

Great Jerky

Our family's favorite.

3/4 teaspoon salt
1/4 teaspoon cracked pepper
1 tablespoon brown sugar
1 garlic clove, crushed

2 tablespoons soy sauce
1 tablespoon Worchestershire sauce
1 lb. lean meat, thinly sliced
   (3/16 to 1/4 inch thick)

In a small bowl, combine all ingredients except meat. Stir to mix well. Place the meat slices in a single layer on a clean flat surface. Generously spread both sides with the salt mixture. Place the meat strips on a tightly covered glass, stoneware, plastic or stainless steel container. Marinate 6 to 12 hours in the refrigerator, stirring occasionally and keeping the mixture tightly covered. Follow directions on pages 79 to 82 for smoking, drying and storing. Makes 1/4 pound jerky.

Teriyaki Jerky

One piece will whet your appetite for more.

1/2 teaspoon salt
1/8 teaspoon pepper
1/2 teaspoon ground ginger
2 tablespoons brown sugar

1 garlic clove, crushed
1/4 cup soy sauce
1 lb. lean meat, thinly sliced
   (3/16 to 1/4 inch thick)

In a small bowl, combine all ingredients except meat. Stir to mix well. Place meat 3 or 4 layers deep in a glass, stoneware, plastic or stainless steel container, spooning soy sauce mixture over each layer. Cover tightly. Marinate 6 to 12 hours in the refrigerator, stirring occasionally and keeping the mixture tightly covered. Follow directions on page 79 to 82 for smoking, drying and storing. Makes 1/4 pound jerky.

Sweet & Sour Jerky

You'll be pleasantly surprised.

1 teaspoon salt
1/4 teaspoon pepper
1/2 teaspoon onion powder, pages 54 and 55
1 garlic clove, crushed
3 tablespoons brown sugar

1 tablespoon soy sauce
1/4 cup red wine vinegar
1/4 cup pineapple juice
1 lb. lean meat, thinly sliced
   (3/16 to 1/4 inch thick)

In a small bowl, combine all ingredients except meat. Stir to mix well. Place meat 3 or 4 layers deep in a glass, stoneware, plastic or stainless steel container, spooning vinegar mixture over each layer. Cover tightly. Marinate 6 to 12 hours in the refrigerator, stirring occasionally and keeping the mixture tightly covered. Follow directions on pages 79 to 82 for smoking, drying and storing. Makes 1/4 pound jerky.

Curried Jerky

A gourmet's delight!

1 teaspoon salt	1-1/2 teaspoons curry powder
1/4 teaspoon pepper	1/2 teaspoon garlic powder
1/8 teaspoon cinnamon	1 teaspoon ground ginger
1/16 teaspoon ground cloves	1 lb. lean meat, thinly sliced
1/8 teaspoon ground cumin	(3/16 to 1/4 inch thick)

In a small bowl, combine all ingredients except meat. Stir to mix well. Place the meat slices in a single layer on a clean flat surface. Generously sprinkle both sides with the salt mixture. Place the meat strips in a tightly covered glass, stoneware, plastic or stainless steel container. Marinate 6 to 12 hours in the refrigerator, stirring occasionally and keeping the mixture tightly covered. Follow directions on pages 79 to 82 for smoking, drying and storing. Makes 1/4 pound jerky.

Frontier Jerky

Something to nibble on as you tell stories around the campfire.

1 teaspoon salt	2 tablespoons liquid smoke
1/4 teaspoon pepper	1 lb. lean meat, thinly sliced
1 teaspoon garlic powder	(3/16 to 1/4 inch thick)
2 tablespoons Worcestershire sauce	

In a small bowl, combine all ingredients except meat. Stir to mix well. Place meat 3 or 4 layers deep in a glass, stoneware, plastic or stainless steel container, spooning liquid smoke mixture over each layer. Cover tightly. Marinate 6 to 12 hours in the refrigerator, stirring occasionally and keeping the mixture tightly covered. Follow directions on pages 79 to 82 for smoking, drying and storing. Makes 1/4 pound jerky.

Western Barbecue Jerky

A tasty reminder of the Old West.

1 teaspoon salt	3 tablespoons brown sugar
1/4 teaspoon pepper	1/3 cup red wine vinegar
1/8 teaspoon cayenne pepper	1/3 cup ketchup
1 teaspoon onion powder	1 lb. lean meat, thinly sliced
1/2 teaspoon garlic powder	(3/16 to 1/4 inch thick)
1 teaspoon dry mustard	

In a small bowl, combine all ingredients except meat. Stir to mix well. Place meat 3 or 4 layers deep in a glass, stoneware, plastic or stainless steel container, spooning vinegar mixture over each layer. Cover tightly. Marinate 6 to 12 hours in the refrigerator, stirring occasionally and keeping the mixture tightly covered. Follow directions on pages 79 to 82 for smoking, drying and storing. Makes 1/4 pound jerky.

Clockwise from the top: Teriyaki Jerky, page 151, topped with cream cheese and a green or red pepper strip; Frontier Jerky, above; Fish Jerky made with Basic Dry Cure, page 88; and Curried Jerky, above.

Hot & Tangy Jerky

For those who like to try something different.

1 teaspoon salt	2 garlic cloves, crushed
1/4 teaspoon cracked pepper	2 tablespoons A-1 Sauce
1/4 teaspoon cayenne pepper	3 tablespoons Worcestershire sauce
1 teaspoon onion powder	1 lb. lean meat, thinly sliced
1/2 teaspoon paprika	(3/16 to 1/4 inch thick)

In a small bowl, combine all ingredients except meat. Stir to mix well. Place meat 3 or 4 layers deep in a glass, stoneware, plastic or stainless steel container, spooning Worcestershire sauce mixture over each layer. Cover tightly. Marinate 6 to 12 hours in the refrigerator, stirring occasionally and keeping the mixture tightly covered. Follow directions on pages 79 to 82 for smoking, drying and storing. Makes 1/4 pound jerky.

Middle Eastern Jerky

A good snack to take on a camel ride—or anywhere else.

1 teaspoon salt	1/4 teaspoon turmeric
1/8 teaspoon pepper	1/8 teaspoon ground cumin
1-1/2 teaspoons coriander	1 lb. lean meat, thinly sliced
1/4 teaspoon chili powder	(3/16 to 1/4 inch thick)
1/4 teaspoon ground ginger	

In a small bowl, combine all ingredients except meat. Stir to mix well. Place the meat slices in a single layer on a clean flat surface. Generously sprinkle both sides with the salt mixture. Place the meat strips in a tightly covered glass, stoneware, plastic or stainless steel container. Marinate 6 to 12 hours in the refrigerator, stirring occasionally and keeping the mixture tightly covered. Follow directions on pages 79 to 82 for smoking, drying and storing. Makes 1/4 pound jerky.

Fiesta Jerky

Hot and spicy!

1 teaspoon salt	1 teaspoon onion powder
1/4 teaspoon pepper	1/4 teaspoon ground cumin
1 tablespoon chili powder	1 lb. lean meat, thinly sliced
1 teaspoon garlic powder	(3/16 to 1/4 inch thick)

In a small bowl, combine all ingredients except meat. Stir to mix well. Place the meat slices in a single layer on a clean flat surface. Generously sprinkle both sides with the salt mixture. Place the meat strips in a tightly covered glass, stoneware, plastic or stainless steel container. Marinate 6 to 12 hours in the refrigerator, stirring occasionally and keeping the mixture tightly covered. Follow directions on pages 79 to 82 for smoking, drying and storing. Makes 1/4 pound jerky.

Mild Mexican Jerky

Flavorful, but not too hot.

1 teaspoon salt
1/4 teaspoon pepper
1 teaspoon chili powder
1/2 teaspoon garlic powder

1/2 teaspoon oregano, crushed
1 teaspoon paprika
1 lb. lean meat, thinly sliced
   (3/16 to 1/4 inch thick)

In a small bowl, combine all ingredients except meat. Stir to mix well. Place the meat slices in a single layer on a clean flat surface. Generously sprinkle both sides with the salt mixture. Place the meat strips in a tightly covered glass, stoneware, plastic or stainless steel container. Marinate 6 to 12 hours in the refrigerator, stirring occasionally and keeping the mixture tightly covered. Follow directions on pages 79 to 82 for smoking, drying and storing. Makes 1/4 pound jerky.

Hawaiian Jerky

Pineapple juice gives jerky an island flavor.

1 teaspoon salt
1 teaspoon ground ginger
1 tablespoon brown sugar
1/4 teaspoon pepper
1/8 teaspoon cayenne pepper

1 garlic clove, crushed
1/4 cup pineapple juice
1/4 cup soy sauce
1 lb. lean meat, thinly sliced
   (3/16 to 1/4 inch thick)

In a small bowl, combine all ingredients except meat. Stir to mix well. Place meat 3 or 4 layers deep in a glass, stoneware, plastic or stainless steel container, spooning soy sauce mixture over each layer. Cover tightly. Marinate 6 to 12 hours in the refrigerator, stirring occasionally and keeping the mixture tightly covered. Follow directions on pages 79 to 82 for smoking, drying and storing. Makes 1/4 pound jerky.

Korean Jerky

Sesame seeds add special flavor and texture.

1/2 teaspoon salt
1/4 teaspoon pepper
2 teaspoons sugar
1 teaspoon monosodium glutamate, if desired
1/4 cup soy sauce

1 tablespoon dry sherry, if desired
1 lb. lean meat, thinly sliced
   (3/16 to 1/4 inch thick)
2 tablespoons sesame seeds

In a small bowl, combine all ingredients except meat and sesame seeds. Stir to mix well. Place meat 3 or 4 layers deep in a glass, stoneware, plastic or stainless steel container, spooning soy sauce mixture over each layer. Cover tightly. Marinate 6 to 12 hours in the refrigerator, stirring occasionally and keeping the mixture tightly covered. Before drying, sprinkle each meat slice with sesame seeds. Follow directions on pages 79 to 82 for smoking, drying and storing. Makes 1/4 pound jerky.

CONVERSION TO METRIC MEASURE

ENGLISH		METRIC	FAHRENHEIT (F)	CELCIUS (C)
1/4 teaspoon	=	1.25 milliliters	175°	80°
1/2 teaspoon	=	2.5 milliliters	200°	95°
3/4 teaspoon	=	3.75 milliliters	225°	105°
1 teaspoon	=	5 milliliters	250°	120°
1 tablespoon	=	15 milliliters	275°	135°
1 fluid ounce	=	30 milliliters	300°	150°
1/4 cup	=	0.06 liter	325°	165°
1/2 cup	=	0.12 liter	350°	175°
3/4 cup	=	0.18 liter	375°	190°
1 cup	=	0.24 liter	400°	205°
1 pint	=	0.48 liter	425°	220°
1 quart	=	0.95 liter	450°	230°
1 ounce weight	=	28 grams	475°	245°
1 pound	=	0.45 kilograms	500°	260°

Index